Broccoli
and Bloody-Mindedness

Antonia Lister-Kaye

Broccoli and Bloody-Mindedness

Matador
9 Priory Business Park,
Wistow Road, Kibworth Beauchamp,
Leicestershire. LE8 0RX
Tel: 0116 279 2299
Email: books@troubador.co.uk
Web: www.troubador.co.uk/matador
Twitter: @matadorbooks

ISBN 978 1785893 766

British Library Cataloguing in Publication Data.
A catalogue record for this book is available from the British Library.

Printed and bound in the UK by TJ International, Padstow, Cornwall
Typeset in 11pt Aldine401 BT by Troubador Publishing Ltd, Leicester, UK

Matador is an imprint of Troubador Publishing Ltd

For Sarah, Frankie, Matthew,
Markus, Lily and George

Contents

Contents

Foreword

I first met Antonia on an industrial archaeology field course in Shropshire in 1973, where we became friends and have remained so ever since. After Antonia wrote *Camilla,* a fictionalised version of her early childhood, I realised what an engaging and amusing author she was. I also wanted to read more of her story, so, when she began writing this memoir, I was keen to read each chapter and to encourage her to continue.

I appreciated the importance of this story in showing how her determination, intelligence and sense of humour helped overcome obstacles, arising partly from her own disability, but also from people's attitudes and ignorance, and even cruelty.

As a consultant teacher-trainer in special needs and disability I know how, in schools and colleges, policy and practice has greatly changed in the last three or four decades. Now support is given to provide access to every possible aspect of learning and assessment. As Antonia tells us, she was too tired to type for the time given in her final degree exams and thus failed: an amanuensis would now be provided in such a case. Schools now cater for a huge range of pupils and appreciate the abilities of those who may need help to be able to fully take part in all aspects of school life. Hopefully legislation and education have changed society's attitudes and behaviour too. However the very lack of such help for Antonia strengthened her resolve to be independent and resourceful. This too reminds us that challenge is important and personal choice is vital.

This historical perspective should however not detract from your enjoyment and delight in reading a very good story which will hold your attention at all times.

Dr Elizabeth Cowne

Prologue

Finally, the silent prodding and poking were done. I'd kept my eyes open for most of it, to help stem my embarrassment, judiciously gazing at the dark oak panels covering the walls beside me or above his thinning, white-flecked hair to the high windows still carrying the war-time blast tape that no-one had bothered to peel off. It was 1949 and I was eighteen.

Without a word the doctor moved across to his heavy mahogany desk. I watched his back as he bent to write in his folder, his white coat as starched as his manner. I tried to relax, to close my nostrils to the smell of disinfectant seeping in from the tiled corridor. Finally he turned, took three strides to stand over me and, blank-faced, delivered his final verdict.

"Yes, Miss Price, it is just as I thought. These tests confirm my original diagnosis. You are suffering from a form of cerebral palsy...the athetoid variety, which means there is reduced muscular control of the upper limbs. In your case, the lower limbs are less affected, which is indeed fortunate."

His address finished, he turned towards the door. I was left lying naked under a dingy hospital blanket on the hard leatherette couch, my agitated arms flailing like windmills in a tornado. I managed to waylay him, to ask him why this had happened to me. He replied testily, "Birth trauma, lack of oxygen. I think you said your birth was medically unattended. You are a fortunate young lady to have got away with relatively little congenital injury."

Fortunate? He had used this word twice. A sudden swathe of anger overcame me. I kicked out with one of my "fortunately" not so afflicted legs, nearly catching him in his delicate region. He hurried towards the door, but I had not yet finished with him as there was something else I had to know.

"Will I be able to marry and have normal children?" He hesitated, but replied, "Yes, Miss Price...the condition is not hereditary, but..." And his voice trailed off. He stepped quickly out of the room, snapping the door shut.

CHAPTER 1

Wales: Land Of My Father

As I have become older my attachment to Wales has grown, or perhaps it is more the idea of Wales as the country where I was born and spent my first few years. At the merest hint of a Welsh accent tears often well up in my eyes. Even the sound of a Welsh male voice choir on the radio can move me to a far greater extent than a much more exciting emotional experience. These recent responses have encouraged me to try to concentrate more intensely on remembering the earliest years, the time which without doubt was the happiest of my childhood. It is said that the first five years are the most crucial, so perhaps they played a big part in enabling me to survive the rest of a fairly difficult life with a certain resilience – or "bloody-mindedness"!

Shortly after my birth we moved to rural West Wales, to live near Carmarthen in a large old country house called "Ish Coed" which is Welsh for "Under the Wood". Dad was stationed at the local barracks, which meant he spent more time at home than at other times in his career as a regular army officer.

I adored him and he was a devoted father. In those days this was fairly unusual in our kind of stiff-upper-lip background. Much later, I noticed, after retiring from the army when he became a small farmer rearing pigs, he always had a particular feeling for those small runtish piglets which struggled for life, and too often lost it.

But most of my time in the mid-1930s was spent with Netta, my nanny, a dark-haired bosomy girl from the valleys. I remember how she would often tie rags in my dead straight hair because of my longing for curls, based on the pictures of little girls in the picture books. Netta, I imagine, really felt a lot for me, as I remember her with so much affection, as the most constant presence around in those earliest years, although of course the images are quite blurred. It was Netta who, though not very well schooled herself, first gave me my lifelong love of books, I reckon, as I still have vivid images of *The Famous Jimmy* and *Babar the Elephant* and, of course, *Peter Rabbit* while sitting on her lap in the kitchen. Perhaps she enjoyed these timeless tales as much as I did. Later, she taught me my letters and how to count.

My earliest memory is of playing catch with a large red rubber ball in the garden with Dad, Netta and Mrs Williams, the housekeeper. Perhaps it was my birthday. I know I felt very happy, even though I dropped the ball most of the time.

I was not at all conscious of being "different" during these very early years, I suppose. I assumed that everyday life presented the same sort of difficulties for all small children, though there were not many others around with whom to compare myself. I spent more time with puppies, and they had a rather simpler lifestyle.

Though Netta was almost always there for me, by far my most exhilarating hours were spent with Dad at weekends. He was very fond of old bits of Welsh cottage furniture which he and my mother would pick up as bargains at small town auctions. There was an old oak corner cupboard I remember helping him clean, which my daughter still has. While he used a sharp knife to scrape off old lining paper, I worked with a penny. Dad had a great repertoire of First World War songs which he would belt out at the top of his loud and raucous voice.

He also had a penchant for popular songs of the day. I

just loved to sing along with him in tuneless unison when he roared out the words of *Bye, Bye, Blackbird* and *Ol' Man River*, which were great favourites, particularly at bedtime. During the night, it was Dad, not Mum, who got up and, cradling me in his arms, comforted me with Welsh songs and lullabies, perhaps remembered from his own childhood. "Nos da, Toni bach," he always said, before he closed my bedroom door.

But on other occasions, there were the almost sadistic rhymes remembered from his childhood, of which I can only remember one, which went something like this:

> *Toni Price is no good,*
> *Chop her up for firewood.*
> *If she kicks, pull her tail,*
> *Send her off to Cardiff jail.*

What would be made of such savage doggerel now in these days of political correctness?

I hardly remember my mother, and what memories I have are nothing to do with much interaction between us as mother and child. No cuddles, kisses, or even kind words – nothing really. But she was a very sociable woman with a huge number of friends who would drop in at all hours. She and Dad often went out to posh parties and I remember her all dressed up, like a fairy princess, giving me a cursory goodnight kiss before floating off on my dad's arm.

Having all my mother's friends and acquaintances milling around meant I learned to interact with adults from a very early age. And then, after bedtime, I would creep out to sit on the stairs and observe all the comings and goings involved in the frequent dinner parties thrown by my gregarious mother. I think this habit led to my becoming addicted to people-watching, peering through metaphorical banisters, and inventing scenarios for many of those in my field of vision.

My mother's real passion, apart from her friends, was animals: horses, dogs, goats and hens were all around, and once there was even a pet ferret. There were three dogs: Sloppy Sue, a brown and white spaniel; the favourite, Boo, a Sealyham, a small white dog with long tangly hair; and Patsy, a notably bad-tempered Airedale who was an early rescue case. She bit me when I tried to share her dinner with her!

There were continual litters of puppies; Mum loved puppies and, of course, I shared this with her. An early snapshot shows me absolutely naked in a play-pen, with about six small terrier pups. I expect this was how I was managed on Netta's day off. It was not only the dogs which Mum was devoted to. I remember her crying over a hen which had to be killed because it had an injury, and then refusing to eat her.

As Netta and I ate our meals separately in the nursery or kitchen, and spent most of our days together, I was not aware of the relationship between Dad and my mother except for the occasional loud argument about my mother's spending habits. Dad, unlike most army officers at that time, had no private income; not much cash for his young wife's indulgences.

Later, there were more frequent disagreements so I was more aware of the disparities between the two of them. The age difference between them – Dad was sixteen years her senior – may have meant that my mother regarded Dad as something of a father figure, her own father having been killed in 1916.

There was one difference between them which was to have catastrophic consequences. My mother had been reared as a Christian Scientist, my grandmother having joined this cult after the loss of her husband. She had sent both her girls to a Christian Science school called Claremont, which I was to go to some years later. Christian Scientists do not consult doctors, on the assumption that God heals disease if it is approached by "right thinking".

My mother had taken on board the idea that doctors were to be avoided while, I suspect, jettisoning any serious commitment to the "right thinking" supposed to replace medical attention. The initial result of this was that, when expecting me, she refused any medical help. Had she done so, it is a moot point as to the difference this might have made to my life. It might have been suggested, for example, that she should limit her horse riding to gentle trots instead of cross-country gallops during pregnancy, though these might not have been altogether incidental.

★

My arrival just seven months after marriage was, I am sure, a serious mistake. In those days knowledge of contraception was limited and I can hardly suppose my grandmother contributed anything to my mother's understanding of it, with her "lie back and think of England" attitude. My mother Helen was only twenty when I was born, her life experience consisting of boarding school and a domestic science course in Tunbridge Wells. My dad was her first boyfriend, though apparently she had had many ardent admirers.

And then there was my arrival which was, as I gathered from various sources over the years, too soon, too quick and without any medical help.

★

On a November Sunday morning, my parents, who were stationed at Cardiff Barracks, were attending the usual weekly lunchtime cocktail party when my mother complained of stomach pains. My dad knew this meant something as she rarely mentioned any discomfort, so he took her back to their quarters and laid her on the bed. She was barely seven months pregnant so, at first, he didn't think it was the baby, but later he did try to phone the doctor as her pains were getting sharper and more regular. The doctor was out playing golf.

Poor Dad, but just then the doorbell rang, and there was Mrs Gus Edwards, the quartermaster's wife. She was not a nurse but had five children of her own and was a kind and practical woman. A great talker but also a great doer, she kept an eye on the young army wives and was particularly fond of my mother.

As soon as she saw my mother she knew the birth was imminent. She bustled about and, after trying to phone a maternity nurse she knew, without success, she instructed Dad to boil up as much hot water as possible. She set about putting my mother on her back with her knees up and suddenly I slipped out, just like a baby seal. The cord was cut just as the belated doctor strode in.

My mother was bleeding badly, and Mrs Gus had no idea if I was dead or alive. Doctor Will apparently gave me a smack and shouted to my poor waiting father that the child was a live girl but that mother and child should go to hospital at once. Even in her debilitated state my mother protested, shouting that she was not going anywhere. Doctor Will was nonplussed but concentrated hard on stitching her up.

My father said he had a friend who was a farmer who would lend them a chicken incubator. Would this do for me? The doctor hesitated before saying he had delivered the odd small premature baby before into a chicken incubator and, provided Dad agreed to employ a good maternity nurse, he wouldn't insist on hospital.

Dad nicknamed me Carnera after the heavyweight boxing champion of the time, as I weighed just three pounds – very small for those days. I was told that, though my dad would rush up to see me as soon as he got home from work, perhaps to ensure I was still breathing, my mother, who became quite ill after the birth, did not want to hold me for a few weeks, so of course there was no question of breastfeeding.

Truefood formula kept me going, plus the good nurse, who was just known as Nurse while looking after me for the first few months. A short time after I was strong enough to emerge from my chicken home, Dad was posted to Carmarthen where we were to spend the next few years.

*

What sort of families merged to produce me? In these days, when interracial partnerships are commonplace, an Anglo-Welsh marriage would, in itself, be very small beer. But when you mixed class, which in those days could be counted as a heady element in the English mating game, differences in background were bound to play a role in the making of a new family.

Granny Baines, my maternal grandmother, who was to play a big part in the Yorkshire years of my childhood, came from a northern country gentry background: deeply provincial, conspicuously anti-intellectual and scored by ingrained snobbery. She was a First World War widow who lost her country home and had to settle for small city life in York, though she never stopped yearning for former times: glorious countryside, horses, compliant country-reared servants, and dancing at hunt balls. Her girlhood and young womanhood was spent enjoying that wonderful eternal summer of Edwardian England, before the blinds came down, before she lost her beloved husband, Cecil.

She had been brought up in a substantial country house in Derbyshire. She never went to school and was taught, but not really educated, by French governesses, which was why she never appeared to know anything much, not even French. I seem to remember, during those York years, *The Times* came and went unread each day, but *The Daily Graphic* was definitely scanned! In 1908 she had married the son of a neighbouring landowner and a year later had a son, Oswald, who, sadly died of scarlet fever at eighteen months. In 1911 my mother Helen was born and soon after she had a second daughter, Rotha. But Granny Kathleen never got over the death of Oswald, her beloved first-born.

There never seemed to be much of a true bond between her and either of her daughters, though she doubtless did her best for them. Much later, I connected this lack of deep maternal feeling in my mother's attitude to my sister and me with this inability of my grandmother to move on from the loss of Oswald. Granny was a sad woman. An air of melancholy hung round her and tears often welled up in her tired, pale blue eyes. Perhaps today she would be considered a depressive. And one of the factors in her life which caused her real anguish was her elder daughter's marriage to my father, whom she referred to as "that common little Welshman", a category he shared with Lloyd George, the previous Prime Minister, though Dad was certainly not "little".

Dad's family background was very different and it is easy to see Granny's objection to him as her son-in-law. Not only was his family in trade, he was Welsh. The English, until recently and perhaps even now sometimes, regarded the Welsh as inferior; true, they could sing, act and write poems, and even produced clever (but devious) politicians, but they were untrustworthy, slimy and ingratiating, and to be avoided except on the rugby field. "Taffy was a Welshman, Taffy was a thief," sums it up nicely.

Dad came from Builth, a small town in mid Wales. His father had been a corn merchant, his grandfather a bank manager. His mother was the daughter of a local farmer. True, he had attended a public school but not an English school – a Welsh one, Llandovery. Now, had he come from a less bourgeois background and gone to a good English public school, he would probably have been more acceptable. That is how it was and perhaps still is in some quarters.

His mother Annie was a great character. Her family called her Boney (after Napoleon Bonaparte), as she was strict and always knew what was best, but was seen to be kind and fair. Widowed early with eight children, she needed to be in charge of the ship. She herself had done well at school, with the best mark in the country in School Certificate (O-level) for Botany.

The story went that she begged her father to let her train as a teacher, but he refused her. "What would the neighbours say, Annie? They would say I hadn't got enough money to keep you." It is telling that all five of her daughters became teachers! Her sons didn't do badly either: the eldest, Uncle Tom, trained as a doctor, Dad made the army his career and Uncle Alan went to Oxford and then into the colonial police.

This meant we children were class mongrels and, because of the vindictive feelings too often expressed between Granny and Dad, we were constantly reminded of this. In these days of interracial partnerships this social split may sound inconsequential, but to me it mattered as a question of basic identity.

*

The news that the Welch Regiment was to be posted to India gave rise to many conflicting emotions. Dad was probably pleased at the idea of having a more active military role – the possibility of fighting someone again at last after his experience in the First World War.

My mother was excited at the prospect of the non-stop social life associated with being a colonial wife, servants to clear up after her and, above all, the horsey sports such as polo-playing and pig-sticking she would be able to enjoy. The question was – what about the children? – me and the new baby who had just arrived. She did not want her new life to be spoiled by having to cope with motherhood. The answer lay with Granny, who had instantly fallen in love with her new grandchild, Veronica, a chubby child with blue eyes and winning ways. Apparently, she was only too keen to take her but not nearly so eager to give house room to the much more challenging (bloody-minded) elder sister.

But soon enough it was decided that both of us should stay with her, plus Netta of course. Much later, Dad admitted the whole thing had been a bad mistake and that he should have put his foot down and insisted the family be kept together, but then Helen usually got her own way. I can remember how she would cuddle up to him, pull his rather large ears and say, "Oh, Taffy, please. Please, Taffy!" This was to result in a dramatic life change.

Antonia with her mother

Antonia with her father and childhood pet, Sloppy Sue

CHAPTER 2

Orphans in the Attic (York)

And so, when I was just five, we were taken to live in the north, in York, with our maternal grandmother and her mother, my great-grandmother. With Netta, my new sister and I inhabited the bleak attic of this yellow-bricked Victorian terraced house, insulated from the rest of the household by bare wooden stairs, consisting of a vast scrubbed wood landing, day and night nurseries, and two box rooms lit by gas lamps. The night nursery where we slept with Netta, and then Nanny, who snored, was a desolate place, with no heating at all and a small north-facing window. The day nursery was more cheerful and had a small gas fire, but the landing was the real playing space. Here, we had an enormous old rocking horse called Dobbin, and we could race around and play Cowboys and Indians. This great space represented a freedom not available anywhere else in that antiquated household, where, for the most part, children should be neither seen nor heard. This sort of apartheid regime was out of date even in those days, but then Granny and Great-Granny had both been born in Victorian times.

Cook and Dorothy, the two live-in servants, lived in a dingy back room with iron bedsteads and little else, on the first floor. I was sometimes allowed downstairs for an hour in the evening to play genteel games with the two old ladies. Draughts, Spillikins and, of course, Snakes and Ladders were set out on a card table. Sometimes Granny played the piano:

tunes like *In a Monastery Garden, The Blue Danube* and lots of nursery rhymes. I loved thumping around the floor (I called it dancing) in time to the music, feeling like a ballerina but probably looking more like a baby hippo.

My beloved Netta remained with us for a few weeks, but it was evident that she didn't take to the cold climate and more formal conduct she met with in the north; her rough village ways did not please our grandmother. I can remember Granny later saying to my mother, "No wonder Toni has no manners, brought up by that awful little Welsh peasant girl." And possibly Netta had not realised how much work the new baby would make. Anyway, I had been her baby for a long time and it was probably hard for her to divide her affections. On her half day off she took me to Marks & Spencer's on the tram to buy a special toy as her leaving present. Of course I chose the biggest, fluffiest teddy on offer. He cost three shillings, a huge sum in those days. He was my companion and bedfellow for many years. And so Netta went and another nanny came.

I think we hated each other on sight. This nanny was a trained, brusque Yorkshire person who was always known simply as Nanny. She wore a white uniform dress and had red hair. From the start she obviously regarded herself as Veronica's nurse; I was just a demanding extra, the grumpy older sister who had to hold on to the side of the pram handle, as Nanny walked too fast; I was a drag in every sense. I remember Nanny telling another nanny as she proudly pushed this baby in the huge high pram, "I am Miss Veronica's nanny, not Miss Toni's..." and, once, I heard her say to her particular friend Maisie, in a low tone, "Cook told me her mother swore at her more than once... Miss Toni is a right wicked one, just a little troublemaker, and a right little liar, and you should see her tormenting her poor little sister." I would slink back against the wall. No love lost between me and that household, even though there were aspects of it which fascinated me.

★

Granny always seemed sad. I sensed this almost immediately after I came to live in York. Later I learned that her husband, Cecil, had been killed in the First World War at the battle of Gallipoli in 1916. A few months after this, an epidemic of scarlet fever swept through the village of Higham where they lived and Oswald, her first-born, caught it and died aged seventeen months.

Many years later I went to Higham and found Oswald's small grave in the churchyard. It seemed that Granny had never recovered from this double loss which probably accounted for her melancholy. Very rarely, one glimpsed the lively girl she had been, the one who had enjoyed riding to hounds and dancing at hunt balls in those Edwardian days, before the horror of war had brought a new and awful sense of reality to every social class.

A sepia photo of Cecil in uniform hung above her desk. He was tall, bearded and fair with a long Viking-type face. At first I confused him with Jesus because of the reverential tone Granny used when speaking of him – also her endless talk of "suffering", one of her favourite themes. How poor Cecil had suffered in the war; how she had suffered through almost every turn of fate; presumably her latest "suffering" was to put up with me.

Granny carried herself well and was quite slim with a face which, though wrinkled and bewhiskered then, had obviously once been pretty. She wore an anxious and often puzzled expression, rarely laughed and sighed continually. I missed hearing everyday laughter as much as I missed colour. Granny wore beige, the sort of colour which now is identified as property-developers' carpet beige, an anti-colour really. She favoured beige coats and skirts over beige blouses and jumpers. Even her petticoats and bloomers were beige. I suppose she thought of it as a safe shade. Her sitting room and bedroom were both done out in the same shades of beige, reminiscent of variegated vomit.

Great-Granny, who was immensely old, was surprisingly erect. Her hair, still abundant, was pinned up under a black lace kerchief. She had a very dignified presence, though sadly she was very deaf which made communication difficult, even with the aid of a black speaking tube which we had to yell down. She wore long, black garments, as was the custom for old women in those days. She took snuff, inhaling it from the back of her mottled hand.

She had a racy sense of humour. I remember her telling a great story about her knickers falling off at York races and how she thought everyone knew when the crowd yelled, "They're off!" She often repeated that, in her opinion, kissing a man without a moustache was like eating beef without mustard!

Her drawing room, called this to distinguish it from Granny's sitting room, was very different, being a riot of colour. The walls were painted a deep turquoise which set off the elegant black and gold French furniture. There was a huge mirror above the red marble mantelpiece, in a deep gold ornamental frame with moulded cherubs at the corners, and a set of charming watercolours, mostly seascapes. The flowered chintz chair covers glowed in shades of magenta, orange, green and purple. Plump pink cushions with ruched edging completed the fin-de-siècle sense of elegant excess.

Occasionally, when the old people were not around, I would creep into this Aladdin's cave and bounce around on those deliciously squashy cushions while taking in the glorious kaleidoscope of colour, so different from Granny's boring room next door.

The hall, on looking back, was furnished with items which might have escaped from a museum of colonial history. On the wall by the doorway hung an array of native Australian boomerangs. I tried one out in the back garden but it failed to return as the books said it should. These had been acquired by Charles Lister-Kaye, my great-grandfather, who, after a wayward youth, had been sent to Australia where he had spent ten years "maturing".

On another wall was a fearsome-looking wooden object called a knobkerrie, a choice aborigine weapon. This was a heavy club with a round head covered in walnut-sized lumps. It intrigued me; I often wondered how many people it had felled. In bad moments I had wicked musings about using it to bash my baby sister, Granny and Nanny. I would spare Great-Granny because she was funny and never made me feel as if she wished I wasn't there.

On the wall at the bottom of the stairs hung a collection of brightly burnished swords wielded in various wars and skirmishes. Granny said they had been used in the Crimea, in various parts of Africa and in India. Some were still sharp. I knew because I cut my finger on a naked blade once when investigating these beautiful, well-crafted killing objects.

★

But there was a life outside the house: school, at another house ten minutes' walk away where I shared a governess, Miss Moss, known as Mossie, with three other children. These were twins, Pam and Anne, and Sheila who eventually became my best friend for a time. The twins were the daughters of the York coroner and they lived in the posh modern house where we had lessons. Sheila's father was the head doctor of York Mental Hospital. I often envied her her parents who were Scottish, particularly her mother, who was pretty like my mother, but also very loving. Sheila got a lot of cuddles. I remember thinking that I would like some. We spent a lot of time playing in the vast grounds of the Mental Hospital, often listening to fragments of strange talk, like the strange-looking man who asked everyone to wrap him up in a Marmite sandwich!

It was now that I really became aware of my difference which showed up in classroom activities, although my school friends never made me feel bad about it. While I could read before I started lessons, writing was very difficult and I could see the way my hands and arms worked was not the same as the other children. I then realised my walking was a bit odd, too.

Mossie was kind but demanded high standards of learning and behaviour. She and I struggled with my writing, which was easier when I was standing up. It was a long, long time before I was allowed to use a pen like the others. When I got hold of a dip-in pen, the ink would spread everywhere: over books, desks, clothes and hair, and of course my hands would be covered in blue. I loved arithmetic and always came top of the oral tests, and reading was sheer heaven. And I soon graduated from primers to children's story books, like *Grimms' Fairy Tales* and, later, the stories of Rudyard Kipling, which I loved partly because my parents lived in India. Later I discovered the place which became my Mecca, the York Public Library in the town centre.

But there was the walk to school and back. It wasn't very far, but meeting the kids from the local school who lived on the Water Lane housing estate became a ghastly ordeal. They would laugh at me and taunt me in such a way that when I saw them approach I would hurry into a nearby shop or scuttle down a back alley. Raucous yells of "You nasty little freak!" and "Kids like you belong in the funny house up th'road!" and other such choice phrases made me almost wish I had never been born. This sort of humiliation was a penance which was to continue for years, not only with kids but with adults, too. Quite an old man once said: "What planet do you come from, miss?" I never told anyone about this abuse. I just sobbed alone, mostly in the loo.

I often wished for a more definite and distinctive problem, like a missing limb, because I think some people stared in a really rude way or gave me sidelong glances, depending on who they were, because of their uncertainty and curiosity as to what was wrong with me. I had the right body parts, and even quite an attractive face, but it was the way the whole thing operated which obviously puzzled and intrigued them: a wobble here, a tremor there and my peculiar gait. All these quirky movements, in addition to facial muscles which would grimace horribly under pressure, must have made for an intriguing spectacle for those who enjoyed human freak shows, free at that.

These daily humiliations meant I had to toughen up and stand up for myself if I was going to have a proper place in the world as a whole human being. I came to realise that, although I may have been seen as defective in some ways, I was in fact perhaps rather more gifted in other ways than most of my tormentors! Put this way, I undoubtedly sound arrogant. Perhaps I was, but to me it was a question of redressing the balance.

It wasn't only from on the street that I had to endure insulting comments. It was at home, as well. Granny arranged tea parties and invited some nice little girls, mostly her friends' grandchildren. My place at the table would be covered with black oilcloth and I would have to wear a horrible pinafore. The little girls who came to tea may have been all sugar and spice in the presence of grown-ups, but as soon as backs were turned they would leave me in no doubt as to what they thought.

They would start by whispering behind their hands; they would gather round me and chant horrible little ditties, tapping their heads meaningfully. "Dotty Totty" was one of their favourite names given to me. I wasn't slow in reacting to insults and would lash out at my tormentors with surprising vigour. (My thoughts sometimes turned to that vicious

17

weapon downstairs!) They would shriek and Nanny would rush to protect these poor little victims who would be given Walnut Whips while I was sent to bed.

Granny's carefully made kneecaps certainly did not improve my image. With her horsey background, she remembered they used to tie thick cloth kneecaps on their old nags' knees to prevent injury from falling down, and so she reasoned she could equip me with similar protection from my numerous tumbles.

She proudly presented me with these kettle holder-like objects with attached tapes to tie behind my legs. I took one look and burst into tears, saying, "I'm not an old horse! I'm not wearing those bloody things!" (Bloody was a bad word then.) As if it wasn't hard enough on the walks to school and back, I could only too well imagine the additional taunts these grotesque objects would provoke. I wore them when playing in the garden but tore the beastly things off as soon as I turned the corner going to school. After a moment's thought, I hurled them high in the air and they landed in the lower branches of a roadside tree. I hoped the birds would make use of them. I forget what I told Granny about their disappearance, but she didn't try to replace them.

★

For many months I missed my dad desperately. He hardly ever wrote, though Mum wrote to Granny from time to time. Occasionally these short letters would be shared with me, but they were not particularly interesting – about parties, bridge games and polo ponies – and above all the excitements of pig-sticking, a sport at which she excelled. She obviously thought she led an enchanted life. There was hardly ever any reference to us, her children, or perhaps these were in the letters Granny did not care to read out. (Years later I learnt from Dad that she had had a torrid affair with a beautiful young lieutenant, though of course he had forgiven her.)

Though I was very concerned about not hearing anything much from Dad, I used to wonder what was said that Granny kept to herself. But it was more than curiosity that impelled me to go foraging in Granny's desk in order to read these letters. I had sharp ears then; I had heard a peculiarly upsetting remark made by Nanny to Cook on the stairs. Cook was grumbling about some minor wickedness of mine and Nanny said, "Who knows, she might not be with us for long. Mrs Baines can't take much more of her behaviour...she was saying the other day." What was behind this frightening remark? Of course, I had to know.

I waited for Granny to go shopping, and as soon as I was sure she was on her way into York and not just popping out to the post office round the corner, and Nanny was out walking with the princess, I stole into the sitting room, opened the old oak desk and had a good rummage, kneeling on the chair to give me a wider reach. Desperate to find those letters from India, I left no document unturned.

Piles of papers covered with columns of figures slipped through my fingers; those fingers were far better controlled than usual though they hurt under pressure, so intent was I, and knowing how important it was that I should cover my traces. I found no personal letters though I opened all the drawers and spilled out the contents of the pigeonholes.

I was really frustrated and was about to slam the desk shut when I dragged out of the back of a little drawer a cloth bag which clinked. I pulled open the strings and peered inside and there was a cache of small, sparkling coins. Gosh, I thought, these must be real golden sovereigns. Dazzled by their shine, I knew what they were because Mossie had shown us one in class when we were learning about the Victorians. There must have been about ten of them.

I thought for a few seconds, and then slipped just one into my overall pocket. Granny had a poor head for figures so I reckoned she might not miss just one. In any case, though I knew it was wrong to steal, I felt she owed me something. This excitingly wicked act made me forget about finding the letters and overcame the anxiety caused by that overheard chance remark. I was now concentrating on the present.

I knew the sovereign was "hot stuff", to be traded in as soon as possible. I had just begun to use the buses on my own, so, telling Nanny I was just going to see Anne, I caught the bus to town and made for Stonegate, an old street full of jewellers and antique shops. I chose a rather seedy-looking place, reckoning there would be less chance of being questioned about the coin's provenance there. I was, after all, a rather strange-looking seven-year-old child, an unlikely source of trade. I went boldly in.

The shopkeeper, a stout old man in a greasy jacket with eyes like hard gooseberries, nodded at me. "So what can I do for you, lass?" he asked, while I bent down to get my purse out of my knicker pocket, the ultimate place of safety. I struggled to open the small purse, but he couldn't bear to watch me so he leaned over the counter and with a flick of his wrist the coin lay in his palm. "And where did you get this? I hope you came by it lawfully." Of course he had to ask, but seemed satisfied when I told him it was a birthday present from a rich uncle.

"I'll give you ten shillings, a good price," he said, which I instinctively knew was a ridiculous offer. "That's not nearly enough. I want three pounds, please," I said. Pretending to be really shocked, Old Gooseberry Eyes responded, "What a hope! Tell you what, I'll make it one pound and that's the end of it." "No, it isn't. My uncle told me it was really valuable. I will take it to that shop opposite if you keep on trying to cheat me, just because I am a little girl." "A cheeky little girl, I'd say, too," he said.

After a bit more haggling, which I really enjoyed, I walked out with two pounds, very pleased with myself without a twinge of conscience. Granny owed it to me. I bought an enormous ice-cream cornet and the rest went into an old tobacco tin which I buried in my little patch of garden. My frugal nature stopped me spending more and anyway how could I explain any new acquisitions? I labelled it Runaway Money in case things grew desperate.

*

My use of the buses had enabled me to discover the public library. I soon made a friend of Miss Thorpe who was in charge of the Children's Library. She would put aside interesting new books and point out good old ones. Hours were spent in a corner enjoying living in other worlds and other times. Encouraged by Miss Thorpe, I was soon enjoying classical stuff like *The Water Babies* and *The Three Musketeers* and, of course, *Alice in Wonderland*, though I was haunted by the picture of Alice distorted by a giraffe-like neck in her over-growing period. Pictures of distorted people still upset me.

I also spent hours in a really friendly bookshop called Storey's, curled up in an obscure corner, reading books I could never buy. The occasional assistant would just hop over me. Edwin Storey, the owner, never seemed to mind as long as I was careful in returning the books to their place. I had to be very careful with the paper covers, not to tear them, but I willed my jiggly hands into obedience, though it hurt a bit. Books, no matter to whom they belonged, had become sacred even then.

In the school holidays I became a sort of fixture in the library. I used to disappear from the house after breakfast not to reappear until lunchtime and then, after my compulsory rest, hoppity-skip back again. Sometimes I would stray into the Newspaper Room where I would pretend to read *The Times* but actually acquaint myself with some of the readers, mostly elderly men. Occasionally inappropriate invitations to visit the local sweetshop were given me. Often tempted, I declined; though never actually warned about stranger danger, I thought it better to stay on familiar ground.

But real people, as well as those in books, fascinated me from a very early age. I wanted to extend my knowledge of them far beyond the very predictable types met in Granny's social circle, so the old men in the library were the start of my quest. Talking with them mostly consisted of banal comments, but there was one elderly man with whom I had proper conversations.

Hector was tall and stooping and had small, twinkly blue eyes with red rims. He had a posh accent which was why he monopolised *The Times* and *The Daily Telegraph*. We had serious talk about important matters, like the possibility of another war. He would open our talk by asking, "And so, what do you think about the state of the world? ..I don't much trust that Hitler chap, though our man Chamberlain seems to. Do you?" Of course I hadn't much idea but was flattered to be addressed in this way. Another reason I liked Hector was that, although he was always keen to listen, he didn't ask intrusive questions in the manner of most grown-ups. My second window into others' lives was a surprising one. Nanny, of the starched white coat and superior air, had a large, boisterous local family on the other side of York, in New Earswick. Every so often she would take us to see them. I loved these outings.

Most of the family worked in Rowntree's chocolate factory, just down their road, and would load us up with chocolate titbits as soon as we arrived. But it was their whole way of being which I liked. We mostly went to Olive's house – she was Nanny's eldest sister. Everyone crowded into the small back room which was lovely and warm, centred round the kitchen stove; it was half the size of Granny's sitting room or even our nursery, but full of bits of furniture and bric-a-brac.

There were lots of chairs, all covered in different materials, nothing matching, and in the corner sat a dining table covered with various thick, tasselled cloths. In the window there was a pair of Staffordshire china dogs, large, white and benevolent, sort of household god-dogs... But the pride of the room was invested in the black upright piano whose top was covered in small china and brass objects, many inscribed "a present from Scarborough" where the family went on their holidays and days out. All this against a vivid floral wallpaper patterned with huge yellow and purple roses which had not had the grace to fade as it had only been hung a couple of years before.

The dissonance of design in no way reflected the ethos of this small, cramped living space. Olive was generously built and, with her throaty voice and gusty laugh, was a commanding presence. She always wore an overall, which was just that. Sleeveless, shapeless and made of cheap cotton, it was tied round her middle. Most working class women wore such garments when at home, keeping proper clothes for going out and for best.

I loved Olive, not only for the titbits with which she constantly fed me, but for her kindness and, of course, because she allowed me free range to bang about on the out-of-tune piano, whereas at home I was never allowed to touch Granny's beautiful baby grand. But I loved Olive most of all because she would gather me up, plonk me on her knee and hug me tightly to her. "Come here, me darling, let's give you a cuddle," she would say. Nobody else showed me such affection since Dad had left, and Olive wasn't even family. For me, there was warmth and acceptance here, which I never enjoyed at home.

It was Olive who gave me unconditional love, but Nanny's younger sister, Dorothy, a thin, red-faced woman, gave me an awareness of the inequalities of class. She didn't only work at the chocolate factory, she was an ardent trade union member, a bossy type called a shop steward. This meant she was forever going to meetings and talking what her sisters called "guff", which, I suppose, meant union politics. She had very thick, mobile eyebrows; when she got excited they disappeared into her hair.

Though I didn't understand anything much of the talk, I watched her, fascinated. There was a ferocity about her, the way she expressed her ideas, which I had never encountered before, in the quiet Welsh countryside or in the genteel circles of my grandmother. More than once, she would turn to me to tell me that it was all very well for folks like my grandmother who had never gone without. "People like her don't know nowt. They read about the dole, but they never have to live on it. Imagine your granny living on ten shillings a week, her, with her big house and maids, and I bet she never did a day's work in her life! So, where does her money come from? From the sweated labour of people like us... From Rowntree's and the like, though they are better than most... But what about our brethren, the coal miners, busting their lungs so grand folk like Mrs Baines can live in luxury?" Olive, seeing that Dorothy's speechifying was really taking off, in trade union style, bid her "Lay off the kid – she has nowt to do with it, and she has her own load to carry."

But I had got the message, which was reinforced at home with Granny's use of terms like "nice people, but not out of the top drawer" and "he's not quite a white man" when describing apparently respectable people whom she had met at a bridge party or out shopping. Further down the social scale there were those she called "the lower orders", people like Dorothy of course, or worse still, "the CBs" which stood for Common Brutes! People she felt on a par with were known as "GQs" which meant Good Quality. I think such terms were fairly usual among those who, though not quite gentry, were definitely not "trade", a sort of intermediate class whose social insecurity found comfort in these offensive labels. Some years later, Nancy Mitford was to write a popular book on the use of "U" and "Non-U" which Granny would have understood well. Of course the remnants of this linguistic snobbery are still with us. Except on railway stations, pubs or on the street, most middle-class people would probably not use the perfectly respectable word "toilet", in favour of the old-fashioned "lavatory".

★

If Granny's mindset gave me an acute awareness of class, those Sunday afternoons in that small council house in New Earswick helped me understand its irrelevance to friendship, which has meant I have always had a rich mixture of friends. Being disabled, hence a member of a minority, has no doubt played a part too. Sometimes I have found more acceptance among Granny's so-called "lower orders" than elsewhere, in spite of my posh accent, made more so by elocution lessons to correct a speech defect, which though slight, was another little trouble.

The days in Granny's attic passed as I tugged hard at the household strings to gain a significant life outside, where I spent more and more time. Of course there were my lessons which I loved, but then after lessons, at weekends, and in the holidays, there was York. The library was the beginning, but I soon mastered many of the bus routes and so by the time I was eight I knew the city better than most. I gazed in wonder at the splendid rose window in the Minster, explored many mediaeval churches, hopped along the Roman walls, visited museums and treated myself to a shilling seat at a matinée at the theatre once, when in funds. Funnily enough, I did not do films; that discovery was made later. Most of my excursions were, of necessity, free.

★

At last, in spring 1939, news came that our parents were coming back. I was quite looking forward to seeing my father, but he had been away so long in terms of a young child's life that I don't remember feeling very excited. Perhaps it was because I had consciously set out on my own road to survival and independence and felt anxious as to how my parents' return would affect it.

But when they actually arrived I flew into Dad's arms, refusing to be prised from them until he laid me gently down so that he could eat his lunch. My mother and I exchanged a cool greeting, though I remember noticing how thin and worn she looked as if burnt up by the Indian sun. We spent the next few months in a rented house, not far from Granny's, but not far enough, I heard Dad say quite often. Granny visited frequently as she missed her little angel, Veronica. It was then that I first became aware of the intense feeling between Dad and his mother-in-law: a dislike which, after my mother's death, was to turn into fierce hatred.

War was approaching. The family clustered round the wireless set powered by big, evil-smelling batteries, listening anxiously to bad tidings delivered by newsreaders in impeccable Oxford accents. Gas masks, extraordinary contraptions, were issued in neat cardboard boxes that were worn over the shoulder. We kids thought them a great joke, particularly the Mickey Mouse ones issued to small children.

★

Shortly after the Declaration of War in September, Dad's new posting came through on which he was to train gunners in Northern Ireland. My mother was very excited as County Down was great riding country and she looked forward to joining a local hunt with all its social ramifications. I was to go to proper school for the first time. My feelings about this new departure were mixed; being sociable I relished the idea of all the company, while not knowing for sure what reaction my problems would evoke, but deep down I reckoned I could probably give as good as I got. As to the approach of war, though I cannot say I remember the actual flow of events, I was aware of a growing air of tension among the grown-ups.

Perhaps more important than stirring events to me, was the tortoise we found in our small garden. He appeared one morning, with a shell split on one side. I was thrilled and begged to be allowed to keep Tinker Tortoise, as I named him. He became part of the family for several years, sharing our years in Northern Ireland and later returning with us to York and then Cardiff, a well-travelled tortoise. I loved watching his small, scaly head slowly emerge as his tiny, alert eyes spied a luscious lettuce leaf in the offing. He was really mine.

I was sorry to leave York, a place I knew and loved, but pleased to get away from Granny who was my least favourite person. I couldn't wait for the move: the big adventure.

CHAPTER 3

Northern Ireland

I was hugely excited at the thought of going over the water, even though it was only the Irish Sea. Having Dad back and going to foreign parts was a double whammy. Mum, Veronica and Nanny did not really figure in this scenario, although it was to be the last time we would spend together as a family.

We were first sent to Banbridge, a pretty little market town in County Down, where we were quartered in a neat Victorian terraced house on a high ridge on the town's outskirts. As always the house was furnished; living with others' tastes was part of army life. But, as my mother detested the inevitable net curtains, the first thing she did after moving in was to rush round, tearing them down and opening all the windows wide. She was a fresh-air fiend, a country girl with a love of wide-open spaces.

I liked living in this modest house, all the more after I discovered the boy next door. Donald MacAfee was eight, too. He was an odd-looking boy, scrawny with a strangely elongated head, but then I was no Shirley Temple look-alike. He lived with his elderly mother and an incredibly ancient grandmother. His father had gone to Canada and, looking at Mrs MacAfee, I was not surprised, but then my good-looking mother set a high standard. But Donald's mother was a kind woman and always plied us with homemade cake and lemonade, and gave me more kisses than I was used to. Donald and I soon became great friends and played fascinating doctors and nurses games. We learned a lot from each other!

I went to Banbridge Academy. Having never been to mainstream school, this was a challenge. I was thrilled but frightened too. Just supposing the children mocked me, like the street children in York? But they didn't. I soon made friends and enjoyed swaggering around in my new uniform. The black blazer with a pink crest on the pocket and matching gymslip with its braided girdle and white shirt with pink tie remained smart for the first day or two, but soon were crumpled and food stained, giving rise to much grumbling at home, as I was still made to wear horrible drab overalls for easy maintenance.

I liked everything about school, even the dinners – mostly cabbage and potatoes – but I loved Miss McNeil, my teacher. Miss McNeil liked me too; she made me feel clever and found time to sit and help me with my tortured handwriting. We experimented with different positions and ways of holding the pen. I still found it easier to write standing up, which must have seemed weird but nobody laughed. Miss McNeil told me not to worry a bit about the inkblots and stains, as what I wrote was more important than how I wrote it. Mum and Nanny did not agree! That was all they cared about at home – the mess; no-one ever wanted to read what I had written with some pride and great physical effort.

Mum, too, was happy in this land of horses; she soon discovered the riding stables down the road which were owned by a handsome Irishman called Russell McFarlane. Soon she was riding a very fine horse: a huge hunter called Jarvis Bay. She became quite besotted with him, just as, according to Dad, Russell was with her. She went to the stables most days to help him exercise the horses. Every so often during the season she would go hunting with the County Down Harriers, looking very smart in her hunting gear: cream breeches, black jacket, white shirt and a tie fastened by a jewelled pin, with an elegant black bowler hat perched on her head. I suppose most men in the hunt must have admired this young army wife who had suddenly appeared in their midst, though possibly their lady wives were not so thrilled. For years after her untimely death, those exquisitely narrow hunting boots lay around our junk room. No-one could fit into them and so they were known as the Cinderella boots; I used to feel they harboured something of her spirit.

Pride in my mother's looks was tarnished by envy and, of course, deep resentment that, as has already been emphasised, she didn't have time for me or my sister. When at home, she always seemed to be preparing for a party, or getting ready to go out to one. I thought she looked like a princess when she came to say goodnight all got up in party clothes, but I really yearned for a more ordinary mum, though one not quite as plain as dear Mrs MacAfee. I dreamed of a nice plump mum whose lap I could sit on as she told me how much she loved me, while she kissed the top of my head.

After parties at our house I remember getting up early to eat the leftovers and drain the glasses, and making my little sister come with me. As to drinks, I preferred sweet sherry and advocaat, but the blobs of trifle were really the best. Luckily, the next day was generally Sunday. Nanny never guessed; she must have thought I was having one of my extra clumsy days!

Then there were the Sunday morning cocktail parties in the officers' mess. My mother had some very elegant dresses for these events, but the one I really remember was a sleek black silk number, cut in such a way that revealed her slight curves to good advantage. With this she wore a perky little hat with a most seductive veil and a pair of high-heeled shoes made from the skin of a cobra – the cobra she had shot the previous year in her Indian garden, evidence of yet another of her sporting interests...

★

Dad's working hours were long but he was at home most weekends. He played exercise games with me. Having been a good all-round athlete he knew the value of regular physical exercise and that any sort of controlled movement would be good for my wayward limbs, though no comments were ever made about my difficulties. At this time he did not seem to have much time for the three-year-old Veronica. Though she still looked like a podgy cherub, her behaviour often fell below angelic standards. I remember how pleased I felt when Dad smacked her for putting her fingers into our dog's eyes. Nanny was furious and told everyone how she could see the colonel's finger-marks on the poor little mite's bottom. The cook, the batman Marks and the maid Ruth all sided with Nanny in voting Dad a cruel man, though I can't remember my mother having any view. She was probably out enjoying the horses and, possibly, Russell.

Being very Yorkshire, Nanny never liked living in Ireland, far away from her roots, or very probably working for my mother. While sitting on the stairs I used to hear her saying to Brenda, the housemaid, "It wasn't like this when I worked for Mrs Baines in York. The colonel's wife is such a mucky woman. She expects me to clear up after her as well as the kids." No love was lost between her and my dad either, particularly after he attacked her little treasure.

★

Just before Nanny left to work in the munitions factory back in York, I had the Rude Encounter. Sandy was the chaplain's batman and lived in next door. He was a lanky, pale-faced, red-haired youth. I had noticed his small, sly eyes gliding over me, but I was used to being an object of interest so it just seemed a normal reaction. One sunny morning he shouted: "Hey, I got some Liquorice Allsorts from the NAAFI…! Come over here and I'll give you some." Of course I loved Liquorice Allsorts (sweets were doled out in small rations to wartime kids), so I immediately galumphed round to Reverend Davis's kitchen. "Here, come and sit on me lap and read me the paper. You know I never learnt nowt at school. ..Not like you, clever sticks."

The wily youth guessed I was greedy for sweets but, even more importantly, he knew I just loved showing off my reading. So I plonked myself down on his bony knees and started to read a story from the local paper. I soon became aware of his cold, creepy fingers crawling up my small, fat thigh, under my cotton skirt, towards my knicker leg. Of course I knew it was rude, but I did so want those tantalising goodies; then I felt him pulling at my knicker elastic, getting near forbidden zones. What a nasty man; our batman, Marks, was certainly not like this. "Stop it! Stop that!" I yelled and, gabbling the last few words of the story, I sprang off his knee with astonishing agility and lunged for that box of luscious sweets on the mantelpiece. I just managed to grab them before he jumped up and, catching his foot, fell over Trix, the family corgi. After falling flat on his face, on the hearth rug, he shouted a very bad word – the worst I had ever heard. I can still hear his nasty Brummie voice swearing at me, "Fucking hell! What a fucking little crip you are!" as I rushed back home clutching my goodies. Though I had in a sense won, I was really upset and, after stashing the box away under my bed, cried into Nanny's flat chest, though of course I couldn't possibly explain what had happened. In those days children didn't tell; they were unlikely to be believed, and I, the consummate little liar, certainly would not have been. Sandy and I saw to it that we never crossed paths again. But it worried me. I couldn't get the scenario of those fingers, wandering up my leg, out of my head. And, even now, the whole wretched episode is as vivid as if it was yesterday. A minor trauma, perhaps; not really a life-changing experience.

★

A few months later we had to leave that cosy town as Dad was posted to Armagh, a pocket-sized city dignified by two immense cathedrals, Anglican and Catholic. The older Anglican one dominated the city as it was built on the hill around which Armagh had grown. Our new billet was quite a grand house just opposite the cathedral. It was called Abbey House and had a large, fruitful garden and a yard with stables where my mother kept hens, though of course she would have liked a horse or two. These hens all had names but they were not great egg layers as Mum had been cheated – they all died off one by one from some fell disease, but we ate them anyway. Meat was scarce.

I joined Armagh Girls' High School and wore a new uniform: a green and black striped blazer this time. This school was very different from Banbridge Academy. It was all-girls and the teaching was much more formal, the discipline stricter. It was too easy to get sent out of class for talking and I spent too much time on the wrong side of the classroom door. Thanks to Miss McNeil my writing had become more legible and I managed to get good marks though I was the youngest in the class. I made some good girl friends, though I did miss Donald and our educational games.

My mother found another horse to ride, Dad was often away visiting various barracks and Nanny was preparing to leave. I was overjoyed but my poor little sister was miserable. A replacement was found: Mary, a fat, jolly Irish girl who giggled a lot, particularly when Marks our batman spoke to her. She was kind and funny: not at all like Nanny, more like my Welsh Netta. Yes, for me, Mary was a turn-up for the books, but my sister cried and even refused to eat anything much for days after Nanny went. Mary taught me and my tribe of school friends games from her very recent childhood and made bonfires with us at the bottom of the garden. She was round and dark with a laughing face, flirty brown eyes and a boisterous manner. She suited Mum as her playful ways meant Mum, who preferred her own pastimes, did not have to waste much time bothering herself with us.

But sometimes she took us for walks with the dogs, and when I lagged behind she would shout, "Come on, you bloody little imbecile!" These hurtful words echo down the years, just like the Rude Encounter with Sandy. I hear them even now and see her pretty face red and creased with fury. I could have forgiven her much sooner had she not used the sort of language which was even more abusive than the "street" lingo which had been hurled at me. It was about this time I became aware of tensions between Mum and Dad, mostly over money. Dad was close with cash while Mum, when not riding, loved to go shopping.

I remember him giving her money to settle a bill, only for her to ask him later if he liked her new hat, a bewitching concoction of feathers and veiling. "How did you pay for that bit of tat?!" he shouted. "With the dough I gave you to settle old Wilkins, I suppose. Helen, you are hopeless! Why do you do this to me?" She responded in a cajoling tone, "Oh, Taffy, it's so pretty and I have to have something new to wear next Sunday at the Regimental Tea Party... After all, I am the Colonel's lady." I can't remember how this row developed, but the shouting got louder; there was even a flow of naughty words. It all ended, until the next time, with the slamming of doors and Dad going off to the Officers' Mess.

I do recall telling Mum she could get a thing called a divorce if she didn't like living with Dad any more. I, of course, would stay with him! In many ways, it seems as though my mother never really grew up and Dad continued to be her father figure. Another time, when I was sitting on Dad's knee feeling loved and comfortable, Mum came in yelling, "Get off, Toni! I want to sit on Taffy's knee!" Was she jealous…? Was that one reason I never felt loved by her? I forget the upshot of this particular incident.

I don't think she appreciated my precocious ways either. Aged eight and a half, I thought I might start on my autobiography (it has taken me a few years!) and asked her how to spell "intellectual", indicating the lie of my interests. She was most put out and, far from helping me, proceeded to berate me, in scathing tones, saying, "Gosh, Toni, are you going to be one of those? You will be joining the ghastly Bloomsbury set next!" Many years later, I discovered that she had got her Higher School Certificate, equivalent to A-levels, and had actually written some good stuff in her school magazine. But now she reflected the philistinism so prevalent in many middle-class circles; artists and the like were regarded as effeminate, lacking morals and definitely somehow un-English. Of course this spurred me on. I became an even more obsessional reader – on the lavatory, under the bedclothes, and even walking along the street, until I almost fell down a drain. I haunted libraries and bookshops as always. If I could not join Mother's dreaded Bloomsbury Set, I imagined I was heading towards my promised land, somewhere known as Bohemia where artists and poets congregated.

★

Then I met Charlie Hirsch, the elderly uncle of one of Dad's young officers, who came with his nephew to dinner at our house one evening. He had been the head of a prestigious grammar school somewhere in Northern Ireland, but was now

retired and widowed. I knew as soon as we started talking that
here was a real, live intellectual. We were in the garden on a
fine summer evening. I was supposed to be on my way to bed,
but my mother was so glad this old man had found someone
to talk to, as she had misgivings about inviting him, that I was
allowed to stay up, as a social asset, but not for dinner.

It was a very strange meeting of minds: a kind of love at
first sight, completely innocent, though it would surely have
lifted a few eyebrows today. Known in the family as Toni's
Old Man, nobody thought of it as anything more than a rather
idiosyncratic friendship. We would meet in the Shamrock tea
rooms after school, near the green, and make our refreshment
last until closing time. We talked about grown-up things like
Winston Churchill becoming the new Prime Minister, and
the awful way Hitler had bamboozled silly old Chamberlain
at Munich. I took to reading the headlines in *The Times* in the
school library, so as to keep up my end of the talk. Charlie
was a bit like the old man I used to chat with in York Public
Library, but much more interesting. At home we just listened
to the six o'clock news, which was accepted as God's own
word. Sometimes Charlie would encourage me to play truant
so that, as film buffs, we could enjoy the latest Hollywood
offerings at matinee showings. "Come on, let's go and see
Frank Sinatra!" I was all agog as I loved the cinema, but I felt
bound to say, "What about school? You used to be a teacher,
Charlie." He chuckled, saying, "Oh, never mind. I'll fix Miss
Reid. ..Known her for years."

Charlie was a small, spare man, quite dark, almost bald,
with a big nose, quite unlike most of the men I met: Dad's
fellow officers were large, hairy chaps. I liked Charlie's lovely
mellow voice with his precise pronunciation. He was always
well turned out and wore very fancy socks. But it was his
encyclopaedic mind which really turned me on. I think he
must have been an outstanding teacher as he talked so clearly

and listened so intently. He made me feel intelligent, not just a nerdy show-off as the family made me feel. I was particularly drawn to his Jewishness. Perhaps this was an alliance of outsiders, as, in those days, even after the war started, but before we knew about concentration camps, a low-level anti-Semitism was rife in all classes. Dad's fellow officer, Charlie's nephew Alex, was subjected to some nasty comments and Dad had to intervene sometimes, though he himself was not above referring to "Yids". But to me Jews seemed exotic and I prized my friend for his origins as well as his mind and his fancy socks.

*

Suddenly we were told we had to cross the sea again as we were to be stationed in York. There were many farewell parties from the host of friends that my mother had made during those Irish years: a much-loved lady, this child-wife.

The memory of life in Ireland remains with me as the best years of my childhood, after my Welsh infancy, in spite of my mother's shortcomings and, of course, the Rude Encounter. My first school days there confirmed me as a social being, able to make friends despite my difficulties. Being with Dad was always a plus and, thanks to that brief period of family togetherness, I have some idea of who my mother was, though I don't think we would ever have felt much real love for each other, with her intolerance of my problems which gave rise to real cruelty at times: the savage name-calling, the impatience with my ineptitude, and her insensitivity when, for example, she sewed up my blazer pockets because I used to screw up my hands in them to still my arms from their incessant flailing.

In late middle age, I was able to forgive her in a way, realising she had never really grown up and her own parenting had been quite inadequate and lacking in warmth. Had she had a loving dad, like mine, I expect she would not have been so immature. But the joy of going to school, living in a sort of foreign country and, of course, being with Dad, tended to outweigh at the time the problem of living with Mum.

CHAPTER 4

Death and Dispersal

And so we returned to the mainland, to another house in York, a modest suburban semi this time. It had another set of lace curtains for my mother to tear down, except she didn't. She seemed to have left her high spirits behind in the land of horses. She looked thin and fragile, and was always tired.

At first my dad put her change of appearance and lacklustre mood down to her return to England, and to Nanny having gone. "More work and less play," Dad said. But when Mum's voice changed over the weeks to become hoarse like that of an old smoker, he knew something must be seriously wrong. At last he managed to make her see the army doctor. (Mum didn't *do* doctors, having been brought up by Christian Scientists who regarded them as unnecessary, as God heals; but then I don't think Mum *did* God either.) I used to hear Dad shouting at her, "You will, Helen! You will!"

The army doctor, Captain Barney Sewell, was a personal friend, always one for a good laugh, but after examining my mother I saw his face as he went out. He looked grim. He had told Dad that she must go at once to the hospital, where another doctor explained that she had advanced TB and should be sent to a sanatorium in North Wales. When Dad told me, I was shocked more than sorry, though I certainly didn't realise the gravity of the situation. In those days the old rule of "not in front of the children" still prevailed, and Dad was very silent during these few days before Mum was taken away in a big army ambulance.

One of the few joint decisions made between Dad and his mother-in-law was that she should take us to visit our mother during the Christmas holidays, as her condition was apparently worsening. Poor Mum. Had she lived another couple of years, she would have been treated with streptomycin, a new drug at the time which cured TB and, though already being used in military hospitals, was not yet available to civilians, although perhaps it would already have been too late.

One freezing December morning, just before Christmas 1943, Granny, my sister and I set out from York Station to travel to a tiny village in North Wales called Llandyrnog, famed for the purity of its air, which was why the King Edward VII Sanatorium had been built there. We huddled on the platform waiting for the train to come from Edinburgh. It was cold and dark but I really loved railway engines, with all their noise, blackness and power. So, when the Midlothian Queen came rumbling in, I was so excited that I forgot all about my mother and just jumped up and down in glee, and had to be told off by Granny for my unseemly behaviour.

On boarding, we saw that the whole train was flooded with soldiers. They crowded the compartments and lined the corridors, jostling and pushing each other, going home for Christmas. We found a small corner by the toilet and sat down on our suitcases. Granny looked exhausted before we had even started, but the age of chivalry was not dead among these Tommies and before long we were offered a couple of seats in a nearby compartment. Granny immediately fell asleep while we fraternised with the lovely soldier boys who plied us with sweets, crisps and fizzy lemonade. Best of all, the lads in the corridor began celebrating by singing some very rude ditties. I particularly liked the one that went: "Roll me over in the clover, roll me over, lay me down and do it again!" I wasn't quite sure what it meant but I knew it was interestingly rude! Granny woke briefly and told us to put our hands over our ears.

We travelled all day, changing at Crewe, and got to Denbigh late in the evening. Here we were met by a very ancient Welshman driving an equally ancient Morris. Mr Evans drove us to the Red Lion pub in Llandyrnog, where Mrs Jones gave us a lovely supper of real eggs and bacon, and homemade scones. She knew the reason why we were there and saw to it that we were as comfortable as possible. "Poor lambs," she kept on saying, stroking our hair in an infuriating way.

In the morning we walked up the hill to the sanatorium. TB is very infectious so we were not allowed to go near our mother but had to stand outside, below the balcony where she was lying in a hospital bed. She smiled weakly and threw us kisses but was almost unable to speak, only managing a hoarse whisper. Her face looked grey and gaunt, and her eyes were enormous. She wore a cherry-red dressing gown which seemed out of place in this pitiable scene. I told her how much I hated school, while ignoring Granny who was shaking her grey locks at me while trying not to cry; everything was miserable, and it was absolutely freezing. I thought I would try to cheer things up so I decided to recite to Mum a couple of poems I had learned, *Tiger, tiger, burning bright* and *Little lamb, who made thee?* She looked quite pleased and this made me sad that I had so seldom managed to make her smile before. My little sister did not really understand how things were and after the first few minutes started grizzling about the cold and asking to go back. Granny, with tear-filled eyes, was almost lost for words, but did manage to send greetings from some of Mum's many friends, and told her how God was there for her if only she would listen, and could still make her better. Mum sighed.

I kept wishing Dad had been there instead of stupid old Granny. At the last moment I felt a lump in my throat. Before I became another weeping wreck, I managed to shout up to her: "I'm sorry, Mum!" She smiled at me again. Then it was all over. In her cherry-red dressing gown, she waved from her bed on the balcony. We slowly walked down the hill, silently, not knowing if we would ever see her again.

She died a few months later and I have never quite known how I felt about it. She had lived her short life with tremendous zest, although she never shared much of it with us children. But she had more friends than most: people, horses, dogs and goats.

★

My real concern was that I was to be dispatched to a boarding school, also miles away, in Berkshire. My sister was to go back to Granny, which made them even closer as Veronica went to day school in York; she only saw Dad and me in the holidays, and the army sent him to Portsmouth. Our small family was scattered all over the country. We spent most of the holidays in the old Victorian barracks in Brecon, where we were looked after by a series of dreary army widows, never the same one twice. Somehow, they never seemed to want to come back.

The commanding officer's house overlooked the barracks square where the raw recruits did endless square-bashing. The air was rent by the bellowing voice of the Regimental Sergeant Major, a monstrous man with a huge lung capacity. I can still hear those strident commands: "One, two! One, two! About turn!", "Stand at ease!" The compensations of this army life were few, but the best was that I was sometimes allowed to stand on the town hall steps in my new red coat with Dad when he was taking the salute on a Sunday. This ritual march past was quite a sight and many townspeople turned out to watch it. There was the band with the magnificent drum major, followed by various officers and sometimes a white goat called Taffy who was the regimental mascot. After them came column after column of training recruits with blazing gold buttons on immaculate uniforms – all turned to look at my dad and me! The fact that Dad wanted me, his odd-looking daughter, there with him in the public eye, gave my ten-year-old self an enormous boost.

★

The small boarding school I was dispatched to was called Kane End, a gracious Queen Anne house in Berkshire. For me, the house was the best thing about the place. Miss Clutton, the headmistress, was an acquaintance of my mother's. This personal connection meant nothing, as I felt that she and I disliked each other on sight. She reminded me of a small ginger pig with her short formless torso, tiny suspicious eyes and dyed orange hair.

I was miserable even before I became Miss Clutton's bête noire. Most lessons were enjoyable because I nearly always came top of the class, but of course this probably contributed to my feeling that nobody liked me and I was constantly bullied. My strange movements and lopsided stance made me an obvious target. The other children imitated me and laughed at me because of the way I walked, ate and even cleaned my teeth. I stopped doing my teeth after this and desperately tried to use my knife and fork like other people and eat "nicely". But it was all a terrible strain. I made numerous plans to run away but was stopped by the question of where to?

Only my English teacher, Miss Williams, really valued me, I felt, and tried to understand why I behaved so badly. I knew instinctively that she also disliked Miss Clutton which gave me a little comfort. She encouraged me to write poems and so I did, although they were doggerel really and some were rather rude, in a scatological way. The other kids liked the rude ones, but when one of the dirtiest ditties got out and landed in the hands of Miss Clutton, I was in real trouble. She told me amongst other things that I was a weak character and easily led, on account of my disability. A few days later the handbag episode occurred. Some visitors were sitting on the terrace with the Ginger Pig. As they started to leave their chairs, she said, "I think you'd better take your bags with you. Toni is about, and that child is not to be trusted." I was shocked. A liar I might be, but I was not a thief – since the sovereign episode, anyway.

This led to my last and worst exploit. A narrow ledge ran round the top of the house which could be easily reached by the junk-room window, one of the few not to have bars across it. I often thought what fun it would be to slide down the sloping roof onto this ledge, circle the school and even perhaps spring across to the old oak tree which stood at one corner. Bored and lonely one Saturday evening, I tried the junk-room door and to my surprise it opened. So I hopped over to the window, opened it wide, got up onto the sill by climbing on a chair and then slid down the tiles in no time. It was perilous and of course I knew my muscles might not hold out, but the excitement overcame fear and reason. I was standing on this two-foot wide ledge, fifty feet above the ground, when I spied Miss Clutton entertaining some posh visitors in the garden. I just longed to shout out, "Hello, Ginger Pig!" but, though a little disorientated, I was not quite mad enough to act on this impulse.

I stumbled round the corner, holding on to the roof tiles with one hand, and wondered who would miss me if I were to slip. Only Dad, I expected. I would be in the papers, only sadly I would not be there to read them. As I went round the second corner I began to tire. I had had enough. After all, there might just be some sort of life after Kane End and those dreary barracks house holidays.

I spotted another bar-less window, which I took to belong to a second junk-room. Up I clambered, holding onto some useful iron pegs. On reaching the window I looked and saw, not a lot of old boxes, but a neat, small bedroom. "Golly!" I thought, "It must belong to one of the teachers," and, after getting through the window, I scurried towards the door and into the passage, realising that this part of the top floor was staff territory. It could only be reached by a staircase leading out of the kitchens.

At last I found the way down, most intent on getting to the main schoolhouse, and was congratulating myself on a mission accomplished when I heard my name being called. It was Mrs Jones the cook, a red-faced, loud-voiced woman, and, although I tried squashing myself into an alcove, I knew the game was up. Apparently I had been seen by the gardener who told the cook. Neither of these people had any reason to protect me as I had been caught nicking chocolate biscuits from the kitchen the day before and raspberries from the orchard a couple of weeks before that.

Once again, the Ginger Pig and I confronted each other in her over-stuffed little sitting room. This time I was not mute when she went into her predictable spiel about the terrible danger and irresponsibility of my behaviour, and I let her have the full barrage of my anger and misery, crying and screaming, throwing books and papers around and even knocking over a small table. I suppose she was frightened, as she called the cook and the gardener as reinforcements. I was shocked at my own behaviour, but at the same time felt quite euphoric at being able to express all this fury and frustration – and even managing to scare the Ginger Pig. "I hate you, you horrid old woman! If my dad knew how you treated me, he would take me away at once! I hate you!" And, with that, I kicked her hard on her shin. It was only too clear that she had no idea how to deal with this wild child. Dad was completely incommunicado and so they couldn't even inform him. They dragged me into a small bedroom and locked the door where I cried myself to sleep. It had been a long day. I was left there for hours, though a terrified-looking maid opened the door quickly and dumped a tray with some nasty-looking vegetable stew on a nearby chair. It was a long night.

After this I was in line for instant expulsion. But Miss Williams, who still liked me, and came to see me, imprisoned in that cheerless little room, persuaded the Ginger Pig to take me to see a child psychologist she knew, who practised in nearby Reading. I liked Miss Gurney on sight; she was a small, compact woman with very short hair and smart trousers, unusual in 1943. I knew as soon as I started talking to her that here was a grown-up who would show real involvement in me and my problems. She seemed deeply interested in what I had to say and talked to me as if I were an intelligent, worthwhile person. She asked me gently about how I had felt when Mum died. I thought for a minute and said, "I was a bit shocked, though I was glad we went to see her at the sanatorium. If she could speak, I just think she may have said she was sorry she had called me nasty names like "bloody little imbecile"; after all, I didn't ask to have wiggly arms and shuffly feet. She did smile at me, but I suppose she really did like dogs better than us kids because she didn't much like my sister either…not like Granny, who calls Veronica her cherub and tells everybody I am her trial and tribulation. That is very unfair because Veronica does bad things too." Thus I encapsulated my feelings about family life, and felt no need to elaborate further. Miss Gurney looked sad but made no comment. I didn't like talking about the family and was glad when we moved on to less personal topics like the war. She gave me some very difficult puzzles to think out and then let me play in the huge sandpit, which was equipped with lots of figures, houses, trees and animals. I enjoyed inventing some extravagant scenes, such as big brown bears eating little ginger pigs!

Miss Gurney also told me the facts of life, which was just

as well; who else could have undertaken this delicate task? I expect my grandmother had a faint idea about these things (a lie back and think of England stance), and my father would have been totally at a loss. More importantly she gave me a sense of having a place in the world and encouraged me to be proud of my decent intellect, making it plain that people who mattered would see beyond the difficult body and appreciate the positive qualities on offer. Among these she commented on my strength of character, the very thing Miss Clutton had tried to deny me. Seeing her became a watershed, the most important encounter with an adult I had ever had.

Many years later I found the report she had sent to my father; essentially she said that, although I had a very high IQ, this was frequently undercut by unfortunate emotional traits such as lack of self-control, a strong exhibitionist streak and a marked need for instant gratification. The impact of these negative aspects, which I still own as part of me, she felt could be lessened by maturity and careful handling. She advised my father to send me to a particular school which specialised in dealing with gifted, difficult girls. The report ended by saying she thought I would be quite capable of getting a scholarship to an Oxford College.

And so, ironically out of Miss Clutton's desperation, came these fruitful meetings with a sensitive, insightful woman, which gave me a way of putting my physical shortcomings into some kind of perspective, although of course this did not mean there were not continuous challenges ahead, in one way or another. Adolescence is an uneasy time for most, but for those of us who are "different", it obviously presents huge problems connected with body image and emerging sexuality.

My developmental difficulties were compounded by my grandmother's refusal to buy me a bra until I was a very well-developed sixteen-year-old, which led to many rude remarks from school friends with their uplifting bust bodices, as bras were called then. I remember trying to squeeze myself into my mother's delicate little handkerchief-like underwear which I found in a trunk in the box room. She had had hardly any breasts at all (I saw her in the bath once) so this futile attempt made matters worse. At last I asked Granny if I could go to Marks and Spencer to buy this urgently needed piece of underwear. She looked surprised, but after months of nagging gave in. She was a Victorian and bust bodices did not replace corsets until she was middle-aged so, although at the time this threatened to be one more nail in the coffin of our relationship, it was really a matter of the generation gap.

Dad did not send me to that special school for difficult gifted girls. Though he showed more understanding of my physical problems than most, I discovered later that he had deep-seated male prejudice which ran counter to my ambitions; he was not really enthusiastic about university education for women. Better by far to marry an officer in the services where you would be properly looked after, as he put it later, referring to my sister Veronica. (But would the average officer want to flaunt a spastic girl on his arm? A curious piece of eye candy!) Dad was a Victorian too, but more importantly, my mother had asked him to send me to Claremont, her old school which was ostensibly for the daughters of Christian Scientists.

Anyway, leaving the Ginger Pig's enclosure under a big black cloud might not have made it easy for me to go to any other school, so it was just as well Claremont had been my mother's alma mater. Another new start meant a posh pink and brown uniform to be purchased from Peter Jones, and a leather-bound bible with matching volume of *Science and Health with Key to the Scriptures* by Mary Baker Eddy, the American woman who had founded Christian Science in the late nineteenth century. My grandmother regarded herself as a Christian Scientist, though she went to York Minster on alternate Sundays. (Dad explained this as a two-way insurance policy.) She told me that if I read certain set passages from *Science and Health* each day it would protect me from illness. I don't suppose it was even opened before I started school. I never remember considering God a possibility, never mind believing in any extra-terrestrial healer, meaning I would never have to see a mere physical doctor.

The uniform was much more interesting, and I loved the strawberry pink blazer with the school badge on the pocket. The pink and brown tie worn with a white blouse seemed very smart but was to provide me with daily difficulty for years. The brown pleated tunics were simple to put on, but the braided girdles were also a problem for me to tie, though eventually I managed them. Being helped was mostly not an acceptable option; I hated being treated like a baby or even an incompetent, though I undoubtedly was when it came to tying my tie and to many other practical matters. In those days we wore voluminous knickers whose elasticated legs came almost down to the knees; our school uniform ones were dark brown with pockets in them and were worn with white "linings".

For the first three years, going to Claremont meant returning to Wales. The school had been evacuated from Surrey, which was too close to London bombing, to a small town near the Brecon Beacons called Llandrindod Wells, a few miles from Dad's birthplace, Builth. At the time this did not really impinge on me, though it did mean that various new cousins and aunts would be around to take me out for the odd Saturday tea. I remember thinking it strange that they all had marked Welsh accents whereas Dad didn't. His had been discarded as part of the Sandhurst process, I later supposed. As it was, poor Dad was certainly not in Granny's top drawer, and had he sounded like most of his relatives in Wales, he would without doubt have slid down to the bottom one!

So there I was, clad in my brown serge gym tunic over a white flannel blouse with neat pink and brown tie, pink blazer with school badge, the torch of learning, emblazoned on the pocket, standing at York Station waiting for the Scottish Express to take me south to yet another new life.

CHAPTER 5

Claremont

Nowadays Claremont would be described as a faith school since it was founded for the daughters of Christian Scientists, members of that strange denomination set up in nineteenth-century America. Their principal belief is that God casts out sickness, in the same way as more orthodox Christians believe he deals with sin, thus they see no reason to consult doctors or take pills. As mentioned, Granny attended their services sometimes though she did not avoid doctors, but my mother neither continued with Christian Science nor consulted doctors, which as already suggested was probably the cause of her untimely death.

Until a few weeks before I started there, I knew nothing about the world of Christian Science. My grandmother had suddenly thrust a couple of leather-bound books into my hands: one was a bible and the other, *Science and Health with a Key to the Scriptures* by Mary Baker Eddy. I was supposed to read a bit of both every day, as laid down in a little paper booklet called *The Lesson*. Presumably this was meant to keep the doctor away as well as the devil!

Their beliefs might seem peculiar, but I was treated with more kindness at this unorthodox school than I had known since the Welsh years. Being the first child of an old girl, motherless and somewhat "odd", was a combination which attracted a lot of warmth from teachers who were mostly spinsters, casualties of the First World War death toll. At first

51

I was really quite spoiled, being given marks I did not truly deserve: an A for Housecraft, which I hated, and an A for Science when all I did was to drop test tubes, spill chemicals around and generally create havoc.

But I really earned other good exam results in English, History and Geography, and always came first in the school's general knowledge competitions. I spent hours in the library, and had read most of the interesting books during my first year. I was, of course, the ultimate geek, but though I was teased it did not really amount to bullying. I soon realised the best way to cope with this was to play the buffoon and make people laugh with me instead of at me. I got up to the most idiotic pranks, like climbing clumsily on top of a classroom cupboard just before posh visitors were about to come round with the headmistress.

After the initial honeymoon period, my innate wickedness really began to surface; I was soon spending time outside the classroom door, as usual, but continued my disruption by sticking twigs through the keyhole or coming crashing back in, having not quite shut the door after stomping through it. And then I was back to writing rude rhymes which the class then chanted to our frumpy old form mistress, Miss Bates, known as Batty By! For this I was sent to the ancient head, who gave me a mild telling off, and said she knew I read some very grown-up books but it would be better if I kept my advanced knowledge to myself! I certainly enjoyed books which were marked "VI Form Only" but they were hardly responsible for my continuing childish perversity: inventing horrid little rhymes.

My "conversion" to Christian Science received a definite set-back when the house-keeper, a dreadful old trout known as Ma T, declared two butter dishes which had been broken the night before were found whole the next morning, mended through prayer! "And do you know, little girls, this just shows us Father-Mother God watches over every small detail in our lives. What a splendid demonstration of love and care – to think that God should have known how upset I was about my precious butter dishes!" Admittedly, there was very little perceptible illness around: very few days spent off lessons through sickness and the only epidemic was chickenpox started by me, which was caught by only a handful of others. Perhaps they were fellow closet sceptics, or had failed to do "right thinking".

*

After the war the school moved from Wales back to Esher, in Surrey, to a magnificent mansion built by Capability Brown for Clive of India in the late eighteenth century, and afterwards lived in by Charlotte, daughter of the Prince Regent; it was subsequently often visited by the young Victoria before she became queen. I loved this grand house with its royal ghosts, which reignited my love of history originally developed during my years in York. It was quite dilapidated and the bathrooms all had mysterious French basins called bidets which were abruptly removed. Regarded as symbolising European decadence, perhaps!

School life became fuller in every way: more pupils, more space, and more staff offering many more options and, to my delight, a much larger library with many more books. Even though the décor was very shabby, this meant that some of the wall coverings dated, almost unbelievably, from the Regency period. Our IV form classroom had a blue silken tapestry with a pattern of Chinese dragons, very tatty, but authentic. It was in this room that Princess Charlotte had died in childbirth about 1820. The room next door, our library, would have been filled with anxious ministers, privy councillors avid for news of the royal birth, and hoping desperately for the birth of a son. What a sad scenario.

On a mount near the school was a very derelict eighteenth-century folly; although in a dangerous state it was not out of bounds, though it certainly would be in these days of health and safety. We would climb up the broken staircase and jump on the floors until the rotten planks gave way, and generally tempt providence. Once when I was stomping around, the floor collapsed around me and I found myself sitting astride a joist, only just avoiding falling through a whole storey. The best use made of the folly was as a venue for midnight feasts. We would steal out of our dorm and whisk down the fire-escape, having collected together some odd bits of grub: chocolate powder, tins of sweetened condensed milk, peanut butter, scones stolen from the pantry and, if we were lucky, wedges of stodgy cake. We thought it scrumptious fare, but then these were austere times when anything sweet and sticky was found to be delicious.

Another wicked delight, strictly forbidden, was getting through a barbed wire fence into the wider grounds of the estate: a wonderful mass of neglected woodland with a lake which had a magical island reached by a dangerously decayed wooden bridge. All very romantic, though we, as pubescent schoolgirls living in an all-female environment, were beset by fantasies of men lurking in the bushes. Whether these were of wicked rapists or romantic boyfriends I suppose depended on temperament. The Camellia House, a shattered but still elegant glass structure abounding with wild camellias, was, for me, the most wondrous wreck and never ceased to touch me deeply. It was in a little hollow enclosed by massive beech trees and tangled undergrowth: an unexpected discovery; a real romantic ruin. I loved these forbidden excursions into the interior, as I suppose I have always enjoyed leaping over boundaries of one sort or another.

I think my disability was easier to cope with at Claremont than it would have been at any other school, because of the

odd beliefs embraced by Christian Scientists. I was expected
to take part in all sports, tennis, hockey and netball, though of
course I was very bad at all of them. I liked gym, particularly
scrambling over the horse, and clambering clumsily up the
wall bars. Those early exercise games with Dad had given me
a taste for these work-outs. Tennis was difficult and I soon
graduated from the tennis court to the umpire's chair, after
the games teacher reckoned that my loud voice and quick eye
could be put to good use and so my flailing arms were saved
for the swimming pool where there was more equality; I loved
the water and was keen on jumping off the high diving board
with the maximum splash.

Acting was an early passion; I loved taking part in the school
play, being something of a drama queen. I was always found
a part, generally as an oldie. Lady Bracknell in *The Importance
of Being Earnest* and Shylock were my favourite roles, though
I also put my heart and soul into playing monsters of various
kinds. I was quite good in these character parts and would
have wild dreams of making it to the West End theatreland – if
only! I was interested in politics too, and stood as the Liberal
candidate in the mock election. It always seemed important
to make a statement about who I was, so as not to risk being
dismissed as "a poor brave thing". I suppose this, too, has been
a life-long tendency. I was an inveterate show-off. My older
self recognised this tendency as compensation. Also, when on
stage I ceased to be bothered by those tiresome involuntary
movements; I was being somebody else, somebody "normal".
Did I really appear less different or was it all in the mind?

Of course even here I was hurt sometimes. In school
photos, those taken for publicity, care was taken that I should
be out of the range of the camera. And the domestic staff
tended to want to make me feel "special", calling me "a little
ray of sunshine". Too often I would be greeted by Leslie, the
under-housekeeper, with the words: "And how is my lovely

Toni today? Everybody loves dear old Toni, don't they?" Like Hell, they do, I thought. Too many such people rushed to straighten my tie or do up a trailing shoe-lace, but then this was a syndrome I have always experienced. Now I am an old lady, I receive a helping hand with grace and gratitude, but as a child and young woman I could not bear being patronised. To be normal was my aim and any attitude or act that reminded me I wasn't was deeply resented and often brushed brusquely off.

As already mentioned I was not really bullied; my physical differences were never laughed at though they couldn't have gone unnoticed. I was known as Buggins the Barbarian in junior school, which said more about my behaviour than anything else. Rooted in the same complex as my love of acting, showing off became a lifelong survival technique, in childhood days often a cover for bad behaviour.

★

Dad did not write often, though his rare letters were always funny and I would sit on the lavatory cackling with laughter, as if I was touched in the head in more than one way! Dad could have been described as semi-literate as I never saw him read a book, but he knew how to turn a phrase all right. One day in the middle of the summer term when I was 15, I got a letter which was certainly not at all funny. He wrote about his recent marriage to some woman I had never even met. She was called Hilary and they were to come up to London for the weekend so that I could meet her. I was shocked. How could Dad, the only person in the world who had ever given me unconditional love, do this to me? I saw it as the great betrayal, particularly as I had not been allowed to vet this bloody woman, though I suppose he knew my rejection of anyone on sight was almost inevitable.

We met in the Great Western Hotel, Hilary and I, and predictably neither of us was favourably impressed. She was tall and tweedy with lots of wrinkles, grey hair and eyes as cold and grey as the Atlantic. She looked me up and down and said, "So this is Toni... How do you do? I have met your sister and I know your grandmother well because I lived in York, so now I have met the family." So she knew Granny, who must have given me a stunning reference! I looked her up and down and knew, at once, Dad was marrying her because she was "posh" and not short of a bob or two. Very cynical, for one of tender years, but I knew Dad, just retired, was desperate to buy a small-holding where he could keep a few pigs and a cow, but, alas, he had very little capital. Also, I intuited that this woman, with her entitled air of the wealthy, just wouldn't do – not that any woman would, but Haughty Hilary, as I had already dubbed her, was the last female on earth that Dad should have alighted upon.

Poor Dad. As I had guessed, this union too was fated; it only lasted a year, after which Hilary packed her bags and left, taking with her most of the money in the small farm they had bought together. Dad was left with enormous financial problems, but that belongs elsewhere in this story. I had little to do with this break-up, though we had had a few run-ins. In the holidays I would sit upstairs writing Hymns of Hate to Hilary! So of course I threw my school hat in the air when I heard it was all over, little thinking of the implications it might have for Dad and his ideas about my role in his future.

★

School had become home to me over the years. I loved to study and liked most of my teachers and many of my mates. I never had a real best friend; there were times when this irked me but I hardly ever lacked company. Perhaps this pattern re-echoed down the years. No good at marriage or live-in lovers, though nearly always a handful of cherished women friends and never really short of off-site lovers!

During the last few years there was Coops. She was the deputy head who taught French and had been at Oxford with the head, Miss McAfee. She was tall and could have been elegant had she carried her height better. She had greying-black curly hair and very blue eyes which mirrored her kind and concerned character. She was very well read and keen to share her literary enthusiasms. Above all she had that brand of upper-middle class charm which, blended with her very real interest in others, her interests and her knowledge of the world, made her a great mentor to me. I came to love her as I am sure she loved me. I suppose on one level it was a schoolgirl pash, but given my lack of family care, Coop's lack of husband or children and the shared intellectual passions it was much more than that. Our friendship lasted for about 30 years, until dementia overcame her.

Anyway, Coops was a really great mother figure to me, except she was nearly six foot and rangy, far from the plump, comfortable prototype mum I had idealised. But she showed me love and fed my mind. She introduced me to such writers as Saki, Katherine Mansfield and Max Beerbohm (how I loved *Zuleika Dobson*!), not the kind of literature to appear on exam syllabuses, and probably not in the rather limited school library. She liked my company which made me feel honoured, I think. I remember she took me shopping with her up to London to help her choose a new winter coat. We went to several big posh stores like Harvey Nichols and ended up with a hazy blue number, which I remember thinking matched her eyes, so I suppose I was not entirely unaware of her physical presence.

Strangely, in view of my behaviour, I also got on very well

with the head, Miss McAfee, also an Oxford graduate, who had, as a young Maths teacher, taught my mother in the early days of the school. It was not a close relationship like the one with Coops, but I felt she saw that my awfulness was not the whole child, that I had a few compensating qualities. I was sent to her on a regular basis in the early days so we were well acquainted. But it was one of her last messages I still remember well: "Toni, you must never drink; you are quite bad enough without it!"

★

Work was a great consolation for physical shortcomings. Naturally I preferred the arts to the sciences as, apart from inclination, as writing exams was impossible, I had been given a really modern portable typewriter on which it would have been difficult to express the complexities of geometrical theorems or scientific formulae. In any case, Botany was the only science on offer, but as it meant slicing up delicate specimens, as well as drawing them, it proved beyond me, though I attempted it as an O-Level and failed, of course. I was so frustrated by my futile efforts to cut up a seed pod that I lost my temper, threw the bits up in the air and shouted, "Why the bloody hell are they so small?!" Fortunately, I only disturbed the under matron, my invigilator. My favourite subjects were History, English, French, Latin and, somewhat surprisingly, Religious Knowledge.

There were just three of us A-Level students, Dilla, Sheena, and me, but then, in those days, Claremont had few academic pretensions, concentrating more on being the only English school for the daughters of Christian Scientists. This also meant that staff were recruited from a narrow field, preference being given to those of the faith. But for us three, at the top, there were obvious advantages. Our English teacher,

Mrs Jewett, was inspirational in her love of language and her huge literary knowledge which she shared so enthusiastically that, apart from covering the syllabus, we were exposed to a number of writers both living and dead, from Chaucer to TS Eliot.

But my one-to-one History lessons were very different with Miss Johnson, a new graduate whose sole teaching method consisted of transferring notes from her file into mine. I don't remember any significant discussion at all. Luckily my passion for the subject was not diminished by this boring experience, though it might well have done for it. Miss Greene, with whom I studied Religious Knowledge, was an enthusiastic scholar of her subject and her lessons were meticulously presented. I remember much of what I learned from her; as a life-long agnostic I surprise myself and others sometimes by coming out with the odd biblical quote.

For many weeks there had been no word from Dad, which was unusual as he regularly wrote funny letters, mostly about the farm animals which we both loved: how the pigs had got out and grunted their way into the vicar's kitchen, for example. Out of the blue, a letter came from my Aunt Doris to say that Hilary had left Dad and, what was much worse, she was demanding he pay her back the money she had put into the farm. This meant that poor Dad was so broke he could not afford more school fees or anything much else. This of course meant I had to leave Claremont before I acquired the Higher School Certificate, which I knew I needed as the all-important passport to a proper life.

I never knew how much Claremont meant to me until I left it. My mother's last wish that I should go there was undoubtedly the best contribution she made to my life. My difficulties were largely ignored and being expected to just do my best and get on with it, in the gym, on the games field and on the stage of course, meant the effect of my difference was minimised. So, during the tender and sometimes fraught adolescent years, I was protected from unwanted medical attentions, for the most part the sloppy, sentimental attitudes of do-gooders, and of course the buffetings of the wider world.

A serious moment, 1945

CHAPTER 6

Cold Comfort Farm

The next year, 1950, was to be the most testing of times. From living in a gracious mansion, full of well-meaning people, with lots of social stimuli, albeit all female, marked by expansion of intellectual horizons, I found myself dumped into a damp, derelict old farmhouse in a dreary little Monmouthshire village with a bad-tempered, stressed-out old father who was faced with paying a huge mortgage and running his farm single-handed. I had to face attitudes to disability which I had been sheltered from, such as the village riff-raff shouting, "Here comes Useless Eustace!" as I wobbled my bicycle down the main street, and even old men sitting outside the Mason's Arms sometimes tapping their foreheads meaningfully as I passed by.

Of course, even during my protected time at Claremont, I had been acutely conscious of my physical shortcomings throughout my teenage years, particularly regarding boys; not that there were many around, but even the idea of them, I suppose. When girls giggled self-consciously about the possibility of boyfriends, I felt like a complete outsider, a non-competitor in the sexual stakes. I rarely made any attempt to posh myself up or even to make myself look half-decent. Clothes were a matter of covering or warmth and, other than second-hand school uniform items, I generally relied on hand-me-downs from aunts and cousins. I have particular memories of striving to do up the buttons of a really ghastly red polka-dotted dress, stretched to bursting point over my ample curves. This had been given to me by my Aunt Doris as a reward for some little service or other.

My difficulties were rarely spoken of, certainly not in the family, though once my Aunt Elsie mentioned "Toni's little problem", saying it was just as well I had it or I would be far too strong! This really was a case of putting the cart before the horse. Not much insight was ever shown by most of the family, but I was sometimes aware of Dad's silent sensitivity and occasional sympathy. Strangers who dared to tread where family did not, had their come-uppance. A kindly shop assistant once asked, in pitying tones, "Was it the air-raids, luv?" I screamed, "Mind your own bloody business!" rushing hell for leather out of the place, never to enter it again.

Alongside this extreme sensitivity, there was a desperate need to know. Because of the way I had been brought up no diagnosis had even been sought. Now at least I felt free to go and find out why I was the way I was. After seeing the local GP an appointment was made to see a neurologist at the Cardiff Royal Infirmary. Dad was not privy to this plan. The result of this expedition was difficult to absorb – I was depressed for weeks. What made it worse was the lack of anyone to share my distress with or even to share anything at all with.

In retirement Dad was very self-contained, being content with the company of his old bull terrier Bully, given to him by a policeman unable to control the dog, though by now he had mellowed, which was more than I could say about Dad. His moods and frequent rages were not easy to live with, but it was the intense loneliness, the absolute lack of congenial company, which got me down. I tried even joining the Young Farmers' Club until one member tried it on in a telephone box after I had missed the last bus home. In despair I went along to the Women's Institute, but making quince jam, complicated crochet patterns and talk about bowel operations was less than fascinating.

Dad and I had very few common interests. He had been an excellent all-round sportsman in his day, but had been left an armchair version of his former self, though his passion for the farm meant that he had to work hard, all hours: Daisy, the cow, calving at dawn; Bruce, the boar, injuring his vital equipment on the barbed wire fence trying to get at Bluebell, in the small hours; his midnight fear that he hadn't locked the henhouse. Poor Dad was nearly 60 and had not got the physical resources to make it pay nor the money to employ a good farm hand. So there we were, both struggling, but unable to appreciate each other's problems. I suppose I must have been aware of our being hard up before he sent me back to the village shop with the bananas I had just bought, saying, "Take them back at once! Who do you think we are – Rothschild?", though I think I attributed this incident more to stinginess and his dislike of fruit!

The old house was filthy, not just dirty. Mouse droppings often covered the kitchen floor, in spite of Bully's frantic attempts to catch the vermin. Food was kept in an old meat safe in the dairy with its leaking roof. It was often a bit off in summer though we generally ate it just the same. The sole means of heating was a vast old stove in that odious kitchen where we were forced to huddle during winter in unsympathetic proximity. I was supposed to do something towards keeping the dirt down, but I didn't bother much; I was damned if I was going to waste any spare energy on domestic tasks. Besides, dirt did not really concern me, as it did the occasional visitor. As Dad had been looked after all his adult life by army factotums, he mostly just put up with it. Sometimes, however, he would rant and roar, though he was powerless, faced by my refusal to wield a broom, well backed up by my physical short-comings. "Well, go on, sweep that mess up, you lazy lump!" he would shout, after a load of mouse droppings had been found at the bottom of a kitchen cupboard.

"No, I won't! I can't get down there," I would lie, and felt like adding, "Do it yourself." And so the dirt piled up, until it stank so badly that the old man was driven to ask a local woman to help out for a couple of hours a week. This I counted as a victory, though it was really a Pyrrhic victory as I had to pay Mrs Hannam out of the meagre allowance Dad gave me.

Lying on my army surplus iron bed with its lumpy horsehair mattress, covered by coarse government-issue blankets, did not bring me any comfort. The window frame was so warped that the wisteria which clad the front of the house had grown through the gap, pursued its way over the ceiling and was now climbing down the opposite wall. Even though it was late October I was cold, though the blankets felt heavy enough to cover a whole regiment.

Of course, no kind counsel came my way. Dad, terrified of female emotion, took trouble to avoid me, eating his bully beef sandwiches in the barn. Our Land Girl, Lil, not much given to talk at any time, just went on silently forking the manure. Poor Lil – Dad thought her a few pence short of a shilling, but she was cheap, just like the beds and blankets, and the best he could afford. She enjoyed working with muck and was not frightened of the huge pigs which were being fattened up for market. She was funny-looking too; Dad reckoned she was half-caste. I would have liked to have made friends with her but she rarely said a word to me.

After days of weltering in self-pity, that part of my brain which worked well sprang into action, and my natural toughness re-asserted itself. I knew I was not going to do what was expected of me: stay on the farm to look after Dad. No, no, no! I jumped out of bed, rushed to the heap of old newspapers in the corner and yanked out a crumpled copy of *The New Statesman*, which I bought occasionally when in funds, as much to enrage my true blue dad as anything else.

I turned to the back page where I remembered I had seen, among many miscellaneous ads for mind-improvers of one sort or another, one for an Oxford-based correspondence college offering courses in various A-level subjects. Eureka!

To think was to act, so I immediately started slamming around, eventually managing to hoist the heavy old typewriter onto the kitchen table, knocking aside all Dad's impedimenta: the pig castrators, the useless mousetrap, the chicken leg rings, and the bottle opener. I thumped out a letter to Wolsey Hall asking them to send me an A-Level prospectus by return post. Fate was with me; I found a used but unmarked stamp in the rubbish pile. I lolloped off to the village post office, yodelling all round the village green with hope in my heart.

I couldn't stop myself from telling Dad about it – Dad, who had always made it clear that, in his opinion, university education was wasted on women; it gave them ideas above their station. (Perhaps this was really a reflection on the fact that he had not had one!) Dad laughed, but sounded a little nervous, saying, "Ho, ho! I expect it will all be over by Christmas, Toots, mind my words. So you are planning to leave your poor old dad on his own-yo, are you? I will be putting on my best bib and tucker to go visiting that nice old widow up the road." I replied: "Yes, try again, Dad. There must be lots of lovely widows out there who'd find you irresistible, you know, the House and Garden types – they'd find you a right challenge. You'd better get that old suit out of moth balls, because, Dad, I'm never staying here." Dad, looking grumpy and sad, retreated to the barn, muttering to himself.

★

The next few months passed very quickly. The college tutors were good and, I think, recognised a dedicated student. My history tutor, Miss Jackson, even asked me to spend a weekend with her in Oxford. But of course Dad did not agree to the idea, going on about women intellectuals with strange habits. I was very upset and threw my plate of mutton stew at him. At this stage I really hated him. He seemed intent on frustrating my every attempt to get a life. He even refused me kerosene to fuel my small oil heater so that I could study in my bedroom, away from the smelly squalor of the kitchen. In desperation I used to take my books down Well Lane to Mrs Morgan's cottage and sit in the corner of her tidy living room with its lovely, warm coal fire. But Dad, with his MI5 spy system, soon discovered this manoeuvre and effectively stopped it, by saying I was taking advantage of this poor old pensioner.

Spring came at last to our bleak hilltop and with it the realisation that I had to apply for a university place. The procedure was not centralised then, as it has been for many years now. I knew Oxford was out of reach, in spite of the advice of that child psychologist all those years ago, and I had decided to try to put as many miles as possible between the farm and wherever I was going to spend the next few years; no coming back for weekends to chase errant pigs round the village green. Durham University was my first choice but I also applied to Manchester, Leeds and Liverpool. As it was, these red brick civic universities, as they were known, did not want the bother of a disabled student with writing difficulties, so there was no real choice. I had really set my heart on Durham anyway, so when the letter came asking me to attend two interviews there I was highly delighted.

"Dad, aren't you going to congratulate me?" I said flippantly, knowing he was quite upset about my news. "You are not there yet, you old bluestocking," he replied.

A few years back, when my mother was still alive, the family had visited Durham on the way to see an aunt. This small, beautiful cathedral city had impressed me: so much concentrated history, in fierce contrast to the squalor and meanness of the surrounding mining communities and their opencast working, and the utterly ruined countryside. It was, of course, this coalfield which had, over the last few centuries, produced huge profits not only for the local nobility but also for the Church. The Bishop of Durham had been for centuries the wealthiest churchman in the land.

I became a whirlwind of excitement and anxiety, desperately trying to collect enough cash for the journey to this distant place, but also to buy some decent clobber. Dad grudgingly came across with a fiver, and my grandmother gave me another. I used to trail around in bits of old school uniform and some of my dead mother's garments, so the idea of going to Cardiff to buy a new outfit was in itself quite a novelty. I went with Mrs Morgan from down Well Lane. She reckoned you would get most for your money from the British Home Stores. So I bought a grey flannel skirt with all round pleats – not the best choice since I was quite plump – and a warm, dark-blue duffle-coat, as it was bound to be colder in the north, and a pair of black lace-up shoes.

A purple and orange flannel blouse, another of Aunt Doris's donations, was a possibility but, on second thoughts, like the polka spotted dress a bit on the tight side and I reckoned it might be a hazard if the buttons flew off. So I opted for my old school beige pullover, which was unstained though it had threadbare patches, and utilitarian, but at least it was warm and clean. While in Cardiff I decided to invest the last of the money not earmarked for the train fare in a good haircut. My hair was about the only thing I liked about my appearance: it was dark blonde, fair mouse, perhaps, but not the colour of our kitchen mice, thick and lustrous (I liked that word). Mrs Morgan and I went to the Cadena café for a sardine sandwich and then on to a real pub (I had never visited one before) for a port and lemon. "Don't tell your father; I wouldn't like him to think I was leading you astray. He would never trust me again." Part of me, well hidden, was dying to be led astray, but not by dear Mrs Morgan!

The day came. Dad, grumbling away, actually took me down to Chepstow station. I had to change trains several times and arrived, immediately falling in love with Durham all over again. I knew I was destined to come here, not just because it was the only university to offer me a place. I found the recommended B&B with its comfortable Geordie landlady and, after eating fish and chips out of a newspaper sitting on a couch bed, fell asleep over a book.

The next day I walked down a narrow cobbled street which passed below the great cathedral, along a shabby terrace of eighteenth-century houses looking for the History School. This was housed in Number 22. It looked rather rickety and in need of more than just a coat of paint. On stepping inside I was surprised by the dirty windows, unswept floorboards and general air of decay; too close to home for comfort perhaps.

But all this was irrelevant after I met Professor Hughes. He was a big, shambling bear of a man with a broad, florid, north-country face and an accent to match. He gave me a proper smile and his friendly manner made me warm to him. I answered his questions fluently and had read everything asked of me, which included *War and Peace* and a couple of books by Trollope and, of course, a few by Dickens. I guessed quite early on in the interview I would be offered a place, as he seemed so interested in what I had to say. After an hour or so, patting me gently on the shoulder, he said he hoped he would see me in October. I learned later that he had a disabled son who had been given a place at Manchester University to read medicine so perhaps there was an element of quid pro quo in the situation.

I now had to face the second interview with the principal of St Aidan's College, which meant catching a bus to Shincliffe, a small village a few miles out. The bus was full of black-faced miners going home after their shift. This short journey put me in touch with the other Durham, the industrial under-belly on which the elegant super-structure of the city had depended for centuries.

The principal, Miss Scott, with her grey "shingle" haircut, erect stature and eager manner, seemed to me to be the epitome of an Oxbridge female academic of a certain age. Before we actually met, as I approached the front door I heard through the open window the strains of what I thought was Bach being played with great energy. The book-lined study where I was interviewed was dominated by a fine grand piano, but was a very comfortable room. I sank gratefully into a well-sprung sofa feeling surprisingly at ease. After a very short time I knew Miss Scott represented the type of woman I would like to become.

She seemed to inhabit a world where physical shortcomings such as mine were not seen as having much consequence. She wore a black academic gown over a brown tweed coat and skirt with starched white linen blouse. No perceptible make-up; at this time most women wore bright lipstick. She had a beaky nose and darting brown eyes that probably missed very little. As our talk progressed her hugely intelligent face lit up; I felt she really liked me and appreciated my intellectual curiosity. The clock ticked on until I realised I had been there for almost two hours. Our talk ranged over many things outside the obvious subjects of politics, religion and society, and was based mainly on books read. At length she offered me a cup of tea which I of course refused, not wishing to spoil a perfect afternoon by putting myself through the teatime trial. While showing me out, she said, "Well, Miss Price, I will be delighted to welcome you here in October, so good luck with those A levels."

After the short bus trip back to the city, I lolloped up the hill to the station to catch the Bristol train. My heart sang as I got out my *Life of Gladstone*; though the journey took hours not many pages were turned. I was preoccupied with thoughts of being within sight of making a life for myself. Of course there was the

A-level hurdle, but encouraged by this venture to the north I felt confident that this time my wayward muscles would not let me down and I would escape the horror of life with Father.

Thanks to Coops I had arranged to sit the exams at Claremont in June, and approached them in a very positive frame of mind. I had worked so hard – there being so little diversion was perhaps an asset. I almost knew, provided my arms held up, success was a strong probability. Failure would be unthinkable; I didn't dare entertain the idea. To cut it short, I took the papers, my arms behaved, and I got good enough results to be awarded a state scholarship. This was a tremendous boost to my confidence as well as my pocket. It meant not only fees and all boarding costs would be met, but also that I would have about £50 left over for books and holidays. The Age of Austerity? And what of Dad? I could not expect much immediate positive feedback I suppose, but some 40 years later he did tell my daughter, Frankie, that I was the most bloody-minded person he had ever known!

Cold Comfort Farm

CHAPTER 7

Durham University

My impatience to start my new life in the north was set against tremendous anxiety about how my fellow students might react to my disability, to my wayward body with its curious coping mechanisms. I suppose the thought of living among all those men terrified me. (Students were mostly men in those days.) For me the male sex came from another planet. The few men that I had known were mostly either family friends or middle-aged professionals. Of course I had the usual adolescence pin-ups, like Frank Sinatra and Gary Cooper, but that was where I wanted them, pinned to the wall, unable to stare back. Sex was barely on my agenda; at this stage I could not afford it a place. I thought if I ever fancied anyone it would certainly not be reciprocated. I had read several novels in which girls who had even slight disabilities tended to be ignored or used as rough paper.

*

These musings were far from my mind as I plunged down into the depths of a coal mine. I had chosen the only really exciting option offered by the Freshers' Conference. I was so excited about it I did not realise, until afterwards, that I was the only girl among a dozen men taking part in this adventure. Here I was, wearing a steel helmet, much too big for me, and an ultra-waterproof jacket, careering at great speed in a very rusty,

Durham University

dilapidated old cage, down into the depths of the earth. After a terrifying few minutes the cage suddenly lurched, shuddered and stopped, the doors clanged open and we stepped out into a tiny space, aware of the sound of water dripping everywhere and the pungent smell of extreme damp. A friendly older miner warned us to keep our heads down before leading us along one of the maze of corridors which were cramped and low; they appeared to have been made for dwarves. Most Geordies in those bad old days were on the short side, but it was a hampering crawl for anyone, so narrow that in some places we had to shuffle sideways. No wonder child labour had been used in former times. Our clean yellow jackets were soon blackened and the sharp-edged walls frequently pricked our backs and sides. My huge helmet kept tipping over my face, which made navigation even more hazardous. We turned a bend to see three miners all doubled up, hacking at the rough coalface with small axes, wearing nothing but helmets, blackened shorts and gumboots, black sweat dripping off their bare skin. It was unbelievable.

This was 1951. These men might have stepped out of an old illustrated history book I had as a child. The shock of the old has stayed with me down the years and I guess it had a profound and immediate impact on my emergent political views, the practical equivalent of listening to that old trade unionist, Dorothy, ranting about workers' rights, years ago in that small family kitchen in York.

★

A challenge of a very different kind loomed that evening – the Freshers' Ball in the Great Hall of Durham Castle. Back in college I was aware of frenzied girls dashing around in face masks and curlers, the pungent smell of Odo-Ro-No, and squeals of delighted panic. Part of me felt that I wanted to stay at home with my good book, Tess of the D'Urbervilles, but another part of me, which did not want to be excluded from this student ritual, proved stronger. And so I went to the ball, dear reader.

I had actually bought a party dress from C&A. It was made of cheap, highly-coloured, paisley-patterned material and had a high neckline with a matching bolero. It was already fraying at the seams. I sighed and decided it didn't matter as it would probably only have one outing anyway.

I arrived aware of the general air of excitement and anticipation but sharing none of it. I felt only dread. I sat next to a black girl who smiled and said her name was Mavis. She came from Trinidad and was studying theology. We exchanged a few words; she seemed nervous too and kept tapping the floor with her feet. The men were mostly lounging by the bar, but a few were walking around, pretending they weren't inspecting the merchandise. Most of the girls to my unsophisticated eye appeared to resemble Hollywood starlets. I glared at them, aware that all the most attractive were now on the dance floor.

My arms became even more uncontrollable than usual; it was as if they were intent on doing their own little dance. I tried sitting on my hands until they became quite cramped. I felt sick. As the band played a particularly seductive number, most of the remnants were quickly being mopped up and soon there were only Mavis and me left. We smiled weakly at each other as a bulky older man approached us, hesitated for a moment and then chose Mavis, of course. There I was, alone, a small island of intense misery, the ultimate wallflower.

Suddenly, there he was, my knight in a shiny suit. Bouncing up to me, he looked me over and finally said, "Can you dance?" I hesitated and, taking this as a yes, this small russet-faced man whisked me onto the dance floor. A slow waltz was being played which I could just about manage. He introduced himself as Michael and said he was training to be a clergyman at St Chad's College; obviously already interested in good works! We circled the floor and, although I trod on his feet many times in my nurse's lace-ups, I felt quite good. He had an attractive voice, which I remember thinking would sound well from a church pulpit. "Where do you hail from?" he asked me. "I'm from South Wales, where we have a small pig farm. Where do you come from?" He told me his father was a country vicar in Devonshire. "So we are both country bumpkins," he said. After this exchange and a few rounds of the dance floor, I was beginning to warm to this small chap with his melodious voice. Perhaps he felt the same, as he was holding me quite close and I could feel his breath in my hair. I was even thinking it might be possible that he might ask me for a cup of coffee in the Students' Union sometime and that I might even accept. Suddenly, the tune changed and we were flung into what seemed to be a very fast quickstep; it was beyond me. I grabbed onto him while begging him to let me sit down, but, entranced by the dance, he ignored my desperation, whirling me round even faster. "Stop! Please stop!" I cried. And then, as we turned, came the great crash. I fell heavily, displaying, I was quite sure, large suspendered thighs as my dress flew up around my ears, but, worse than this, I had dragged the poor man down on top of me! The band played on while the dancers delicately circled us; our catastrophe was viewed by all. The bruising on my body was slight but my fragile self-confidence was utterly shattered. Michael extricated himself at speed and slunk away, not even glancing back to see I was all right; not such a caring cleric in the making after all. A kind couple helped me to my feet and I fled out of that torture chamber, picked up my old duffle coat and caught the last bus. No more dancing in Durham.

★

Though men were out of the picture, my three years in Durham were not lacking in social activities. I had a handful of bright women buddies and my weekends were full of visits to coffee bars, tea rooms and to the flea pit cinema where they showed marvellous foreign films like *Bicycle Thieves*, *Open City* and *Panique*. Much time was spent in poring over maps of Europe, planning hitch-hiking adventures for the summer vacation with my chosen travelling friends, Margaret and Joyce. Margaret was a third year Sociology student, good-looking, kind and engaged to a chap at home in Wolverhampton, and Joyce was studying German, and very keen on travel but, like me, had limited resources. She was the closest friend I made in Durham. These continental excursions were to be among the most joyful holidays in my life though they were physically very challenging and forbidden (fruitlessly) by Dad. As Joyce was studying German she was spending a year in Bonn, so that was our starting point, our goal being northern Bavaria where some distant cousins of mine lived. We whizzed down the Rhine in a Mercedes with a rich old man, who was greatly taken with Margaret, the pretty one. He wanted to take her for a drink, but we explained that he had to take us all or none. He changed the topic. We imagined he might have been an arms dealer; he spoke English very well but, of course, we did not mention the war. A flying start but the pace was not kept up. Subsequent lifts, after we left the Autobahn, included a refrigerated butcher's van, a coal lorry, and a steamroller. We slept mostly in YWCAs but were sometimes reduced to convents, hay barns and, once, a Home for Fallen Women! On Margaret's birthday, we treated ourselves to cakes in a posh café where we ate wonderful pastries, the sort we never saw at home, which puzzled us. After all, we were supposed to have won the war! The clientele was mostly older men with good-looking young women, their secretary birds, we guessed.

We meandered through the Black Forest and some

industrial towns, being rapidly rebuilt, eventually reaching Nuremberg where we spent the night in Hitler's ex-bunker, remade into a very scruffy youth hostel, before reaching Aunt Clara's estate, where they lived in a modest but charming manor house. To the east lay a broad strip of ploughed land marking the border between East and West, years before the Wall was built.

We were amused that my cousins' farm labourers wore blue smocks and touched their forelocks to us as we passed them on the long drive up to the house. But, while appearing deferential, some of them had apparently informed on Clara and Joachim during the war for listening to the BBC, which had meant both had been imprisoned for many months. Clara and Joachim seemed delighted to meet us, and were very kind to three weary travellers. We had a good rest before returning through Holland and France. I became addicted to this cheap and unpredictable mode of travel over the next few years, though I found it increasingly hard to carry a rucksack on my back. But my liking for adventure usually prevailed over aches and pains. The answer lay in taking the minimum: eventually, a pair of pants and a toothbrush!

★

I mostly managed to avoid the Students' Union because it was full of men eyeing up women. I was even too shy to talk to my fellow male History students; true, they were not a very enticing lot, mostly short and spotty. My attitude was reinforced when, one morning, a crowd of them passed me in the street, and yelled "Snob!" in concert, very loudly. I suppose this was because I always sat at the back, never mingling with them, and, possibly, on account of my posh southern accent. Of course part of me yearned for a suitable boyfriend. But, as no-one ever propositioned me, I had no idea how to arrange the goods in the window, and, as I assumed I was probably doomed to life-long celibacy, I hoped to find solace elsewhere. After all, I had been taught by many unmarried women at Claremont who appeared to live full and involved lives.

Most of the lectures we had in our grubby old History school seemed uninspired, as if they had been given countless times before. But Durham had a generous tutorial system, based on the Oxbridge system, which compensated for this lack. Our weekly essays were scrutinised by a member of staff who saw us in twos, generally in their own studies. Apart from being a sound academic practice, it was so interesting to see how and where they lived – from the disgusting, cigarette-stub beer-bottle-strewn room of young Fred James, to the elegant Georgian manor house of the professor.

The beautiful mediaeval library was my Mecca – though of course men used this too, but they tended or at least pretended to be concentrating on study. I was given access to a very special book collection, as yet uncatalogued, which was known as Bishop Cosin's Library. I was working on a dissertation on eighteenth century political pamphlets, of which there were many in this enchanted place. I revelled in the smell and feel of these antiquated volumes. Some were very tattered, needing a tender touch, so I had to ensure my shaky hands were under as much control as possible. I spent hours in here collecting pieces of poetry and prose from the late eighteenth century. It was a rich intellectual experience which I remember hoping, at the time, would be the prelude to many more. I became so entranced by this place that coming across a mouldy copy of *"Pigs' meat: or, lessons for the swinish multitude"*, published in 1792, was probably as thrilling to me as being kissed by a member of the Durham boat crew!

At this time, I had no doubt that my only ambition was to become an historian. As time went by, I came to love Durham even more, spending hours wandering around the cathedral and its precincts, marvelling at the intricacy of the mediaeval stonework, and the sheer beauty of the stained glass windows, just as ten years or so before I had loved discovering mediaeval church architecture in York. Sometimes I would take the bus to Newcastle, 15 miles away, along the road fringed by hideous open cast mines, and such urban degradation I had never seen, even in South Wales. I liked the contrast. Newcastle, with its docks, old warehouses, grandiose Victorian architecture, and sheer size, even then, before it had been restored, later in the century, was a fine nineteenth-century city, a huge contrast to mediaeval Durham.

★

I had staunch support from our college principal, Scotty, as she was known; she seemed to give me the regard I had almost always felt I lacked. Her short, sharp manner matched her short cropped hairstyle, but under the brusque bearing there was warmth and understanding, particularly for those students that she liked, although many saw her as something of a dragon. She would upbraid those who were seen to hold hands with boyfriends along the driveway and students had to put their beds in the corridor when entertaining men friends on Sundays! Although this rule did not worry me personally, I could see that it was daft. Scotty may today have been assumed to be a closet lesbian, but I expect she was just an old-time lady don.

She presided over high table dinners with all the dignity of a Victorian bishop and often entertained senior members of the university and cathedral, and even the Bishop of Durham himself. It was her custom to ask a student to join her and the visitor, which was supposed to be an honour. To my astonishment she asked me several times and I found I really enjoyed conversing with the Great and the Good. True, I did once spill a little gravy over the French professor's trousers, but nobody seemed to notice as the talk was so lively and argumentative.

My third year was spent in the Diocesan Mission House. As this was a few doors away from the History School, it meant great savings in energy and time. My room there was like a large cupboard, with a small window. I did not have any clothes worth hanging up but had huge piles of books which I was continually stumbling over, until I got some planks with a few bricks, and with the aid of friends I got a bookcase together.

The meals here were very meagre, consisting of greenish vegetable stew and pink blancmange called "shape". Too often, we three students who lived there, still hungry, would go up the road to buy delicious fish and chips which we ate in a nearby graveyard. Our fellow lodgers were mostly ex-missionaries from far-flung fields, like Outer Mongolia, New Guinea and Central Africa. Miss Morton-Smith was my favourite. She looked limp and colourless but her memories of living among head-hunters in Borneo were wonderfully vivid. I guessed that her spare little body was the reason she did not end up in a cooking pot, though she apparently brought many of these lifelong cannibals inhabiting New Guinea to Jesus, giving her much comfort in her old age.

But my real relationship in this godly household was with Margaret Harrison, a deaconess. She was a tall, imposing woman in her late forties, with sharp Viking features, a high complexion and glittering blue eyes. She possessed a certain charm but was ferocious when aroused. She and I had many talks in her sparse sitting-room, mostly about religion and politics. We became quite close, but when she began to pick stray hairs off my jumper and to push her bony, serge-clad thigh against mine, I realised that she may have wanted us to become even closer. We still talked, but I was careful where I sat and discouraged physical attentions. I really liked Deaconess

Margaret but within limits. I suppose this was the only pass I experienced during my three years in Durham!

And so time passed; the final exams loomed: the climax of the university experience. As mentioned, in those days they did not "do" the disabled; perhaps this was because the disabled were not encouraged to think about university, it being easier to direct them into basket making or Remploy factories. Of course, this meant that universities had put no thought into making alternative provision for taking exams, let alone aid like easy access for the disabled, now mandatory.

And so I found myself in a tiny office with a junior typist as invigilator. I had been given some extra time to complete the papers, but some days this meant that I was expected to type for nearly eight hours on days with two papers. No medical opinion was sought about my weak shoulders and arm muscles, and so this was cruelly unrealistic. Perhaps I should have asked for an amanuensis but, never having used one before, I just struggled to get enough of the answers down. On the third day of this ordeal I was suddenly covered with cold sweat as I looked at the paper on "Roman Frontier Studies". I knew I could have answered all the questions but, faced with another day of extreme physical difficulty, my poor over-used body exploded in revolt; my shrieking back, neck and arm muscles went into huge spasm. My shoulders felt out of joint and the pain in my upper body was such that I could barely undo my typewriter. I burst into tears and, before the poor invigilator reacted, I was stumbling down the street into the mission house to get my purse and then on to the railway station. I had to get out. Body over mind.

★

I sought sanctuary in York with my grandmother. She knew nothing of academic life but of course she could see I was in deep trouble. She called her doctor who prescribed me barbiturates to help me sleep. My grief was great; so, all my endeavours over the years had come to this. Dreams of having an academic career seemed shattered. Walking by the River Ouse, I paused and looked into the deep water. The urge to jump was huge, but I didn't.

That evening Scotty rang me to tell me that the History School had decided to award me an Aegrotat degree; this was a special degree given to students who had worked hard but had failed to complete Finals because of physical illness or mental breakdown. I was grateful and glad I had not gone for that last plunge. I felt able to return to collect my parchment scroll from the shaky hands of the ancient Chancellor, GM Trevelyan.

★

That Aegrotat did not give me access to any higher degree study. I was disappointed to realise that there would be no more reclusive hours spent in places like Bishop Cosin's Library. After a few weeks' rest, once I had recovered from this absolute disaster, I looked around for some modest post-graduate course and, because I had always had an interest in social questions, and particularly in social differences, I found myself in Edinburgh studying for a Diploma in Social Studies. At the time I thought this was very much second best, but as it turned out it might well have been a surprisingly good move.

CHAPTER 8

Edinburgh

I was completely overwhelmed by the size and diversity of both the city and the University of Edinburgh. The elegance of the Georgian New Town with its perfect squares and terraces and the grandeur of the views from Princes Street were breath-taking. I had never been in a large city before, except Cardiff which seemed very provincial by comparison.

But I was soon to discover a bleaker side of Edinburgh: the so-called Old Town around the Grassmarket and the poverty-stricken ports of Leith and Portobello. Here, thousands lived in looming tenement buildings which were separated by evil-smelling alleys. As I was later to learn in the course of my studies, too many children in these and other slum areas of the city lived on diets of bread, jam and tea. The Social Studies department of the university was housed in a dingy basement in the Old Quad near the city centre. Although this was one of the older parts of the university, being underground perhaps reflected its status as a newly developed suspect discipline in this ancient seat of learning. Miss Doris Brown, the Head of Department, with her broad Yorkshire accent and her tightly permed hair, looked and sounded more like a northern businesswoman than an academic; not at all like our lady dons in Durham with their flowing black gowns and modulated voices.

After a couple of false starts I found a large room in one of those elegant terraced houses in the heart of the New Town.

The rent was affordable due to the unworldliness of the old landlady, Mrs Isobel McKay, a widow who had spent most of her life in the Argentine. She already had one lodger, her niece Annette, the indulged daughter of a rich Scottish farming family. The attraction between us two lodgers was certainly not instantaneous. Annette took a keen interest in her appearance; to me she looked like a Vogue model when dressed to go out, with her expensive rig-outs and her perfectly made-up face. And there was me, hobbling around in my clod-hopping lace-ups, in my dear old Aunt Doris's cast-off tweed suit, with my innocent soap-and-water complexion and draggle-tailed, mousey hair! For days we circled round each other, merely passing the odd mealtime comment.

Sitting round the breakfast table one Sunday morning, Isobel, on rising from her chair, let out a gargantuan fart, and as it was a quiet Sunday morning the noise seemed to reverberate around the room for several seconds. I caught Annette's eye and she immediately started to splutter into her table napkin. In a trice we were both giggling away like a couple of ten-year-olds and this soon developed into loud, hysterical laughter. Poor old Isobel stalked out. She was rather deaf but she certainly knew she was in some way the object of our mirth.

Thus our differences were sunk in this wild surge of unkind laughter; it seemed as though we had found some common ground. A few days after this incident, Annette came out with a challenging remark which was to have a powerful effect on my lifestyle. Annette did not "do" diplomacy at this stage, though she later got a job in the Foreign Office. As we were preparing to sit down to a meal she said, "Toni, why do you go round looking like a Grassmarket tramp? You could at least have a decent haircut!"

This was the catalyst; off I went to her hairdresser and, not content with half measures, I returned with a neat, strawberry-coloured bob. Annette was so impressed that she persuaded me to go for a complete makeover. She had a huge wardrobe full of clothes which she had hardly worn, being a wealthy impulse buyer. That evening she came into my room with an armful of colourful garments which I looked at with astonishment. "Come on, try some of these. It's either you or the jumble sale." Luckily we were about the same size. I chose a very chic A-line blue woollen dress which showed off my hitherto unappreciated 22-inch waist. This was for best; tight jumpers and full skirts were chosen for everyday and then she marched me off to buy a decent bra. We went to a posh underwear shop and for the first time I got a bra which fitted me. Shoes were a problem as Annette's feet were much smaller than mine, but the church jumble sale produced a lovely pair of red courts, with small manageable heels.

As I pirouetted in front of a full length mirror in a tight red sweater, a black circular skirt and those seductive red shoes, I realised I not only had quite a decent figure but shapely legs, up to the knees anyway, and ankles that were better than most. Annette looked on with approval at this roller coaster refurbishment. She said, "Gosh, Toni, I could bear to be seen with you now. Why don't we go to the student hop on Saturday?" The fiasco of the Freshers' Ball in Durham was still with me, so I replied, nervously, "No, I'm not up to that…I'd be a liability." Annette alternately nagged and flattered, and so I eventually said I would go with her.

After a critical glance at the general effect, she dug out a couple of gauzy scarves. When these were wound round my neck, my slightly lopsided stance was no longer so obvious. "There, Toni, you look almost human!" Annette's remark was accepted in good part. After all, it was she who had enabled me to look "almost human". The absolute finishing touch was a long, elegant, amber cigarette holder I found in a local antiques shop. This dashing article had a crucial role – it enabled me to transform my involuntary arm movements into what I hoped passed for extravagant Parisian gestures. My first attempt at applying make-up made me look like a circus clown. It was truly a hit-and-miss affair – mostly miss! At last I found a solution: I piled up books on the dressing table so that I could rest my arm and start painting. My largely unread course textbooks had found a use after all.

And what about my studies? I didn't really have that much time to attend lectures or even read very much, which probably contributed to my ultimately failing my diploma, though I did pass some of the papers. But, in any case, too much of my book money had been spent on new underwear, haircuts and make-up. I did go to the odd lecture but somehow found it hard to concentrate on the dull detail of social administration and felt little in common with most of my earnest fellow students. My mind was on much more important matters, like what was I going to wear to the dance on Saturday night. It seemed that my intellect was taking a sabbatical.

Annette and I preened ourselves in front of the mirror in the ladies' of the students' union. She looked good, no question about it, and she knew it, but I was quite apprehensive about my image. My eyes stared back at me, huge and anxious, but on the other hand I guessed they were my best asset, when properly used. I practised what I thought was a seductive smile, while Annette skilfully applied more mascara. She gave me a look-over, saying, "Toni, you know something? You look almost OK! You might even grab a Fresher!"

We stepped into the arena and sat down by the door. I was awash with gauze scarves and brandished my cigarette holder in what I thought was a sophisticated fashion. Annette had gone off to see a friend and so I was left on my own; the old frightened feelings began to return. Suddenly a short but decent-looking chap stood over me. He sat down and introduced himself. He was a geography student from Croydon and his name was Bill.

Since the humiliating episode at the Durham Freshers' Ball I hadn't, of course, done dancing, but decided it was time to have another go with another small, unpretentious chap.

We got up and shambled round the room, constantly stepping on each other's toes, quite reminiscent of that former occasion, but my balance had definitely improved, and of course, my confidence. We laughed a lot. Bill said, "Do you think we should patent this as the Toe Dance?" I liked this; it led on to a lot of jokey chat.

We stayed together all evening though I had at first expected he would rush off after the first dance. What's more, he asked to see me home, and outside the front door we brushed lips. "Would you like to go to the pictures sometime?" Bill asked, shuffling nervously from one foot to the other. I was really surprised, in spite of us having spent a pleasant trauma-free evening dancing. "Yes, I would like that," I replied, trying not to sound over-enthusiastic. He promised to phone, scratching the number on the back of his hand. I went in feeling pleased that my first social outing had been a success, and ended with an invitation. Progress on the man front had been made. I liked Bill and thought he quite liked me, but I was disappointed that there was none of that instant passion I had read about in women's magazines and romantic novels.

We saw each other about once a week and as it grew colder we spent more time in my bed-sitting room. My ancient landlady cast us nervous looks as I let Bill in and we passed through the hall. Perhaps she thought we were about to turn her flat into a place of ill-repute. It immediately became obvious that Bill knew no more about women than I did about men. We gradually remedied this lack of experience but it was more like a mutual tutorial than a passionate awakening. The workings of the male genitalia fascinated me: the way you stroked that thing which immediately responded with a life of its own. I found it quite alarming, at first. It was so large and weird. But I laughed and said: "Bill, it's just like a mechanical toy. Do you have to wind it up?" He laughed of course. "Toni, are you serious?" I replied: "The only one I ever saw was when I was eight. What about you?" He just laughed so I presumed he was just as innocent as me but was not going to own up to it. I was secretly amazed by the sheer size of it, and wondered how it would ever gain access. He was not rewarded with such a dramatic response from me, but though we were both fascinated we never progressed beyond the handling stage as we did not want to take any risks. It wasn't difficult, as we were not driven by anything beyond intense curiosity, though I didn't feel at all used; we were really each other's rough paper. The truth was that neither found each other attractive enough to rouse much feeling beyond curiosity, but it was a very useful test-drive for us both.

After this important learning curve, I realised I wanted to expand my exploration of the male by perhaps moving into more exotic areas, with possibly meeting a man who really turned me on. I had heard of the Polish Club. Any girl frequenting it was said to gain an instant "reputation", so potent was the Eastern European charm, the desperation of the Free Polish Forces and of course the vodka. No, I did not feel quite ready for a "reputation".

Cosmop was a small university club where Commonwealth students could meet the natives. Apart from various cultural events, they held regular dances in a derelict church hall in a poor outlying district of the city.

Annette did not fancy trekking out there and certainly did not share my interest, and she was quite puzzled by my eagerness. I had never even spoken to a black man though there had been a few at Durham, mostly theology students; but I did like the idea of meeting another sort of "different". I boarded a tram, wearing a very fetching, scarlet nylon lace dress, daringly low-cut, buoyed up by my new uplift bra, partially covered by my shabby old duffle coat. The place was certainly dreary, with peeling green paintwork and a very musty smell, but as the door to the dance hall opened, the blasting of the small energetic band, in calypso style, lifted the whole atmosphere and the odours of male sweat, aftershave and enthusiasm soon obliterated that of damp and decay.

And the men! I took a deep breath as I looked round. At first glance they appeared absolutely gorgeous in comparison with the home-grown students at the university: all acne, dandruff and ginger jackets. Black shiny hunks of humanity, some dressed in robes of many colours and others in neat, clean suits as perfect replicas of old-fashioned English gentlemen, gladdened my gaze. Leaning on the bar with the usual cigarette holder in motion, I sipped my white wine, served in an extra-large glass as requested. I continued to survey the scene, when suddenly a pair of resting eyes met mine. They were huge and honey-coloured and belonged to a light brown man, standing near the band. I couldn't see much of him because of the crush but we smiled faintly at each other and then looked away. Gosh, I thought, it really was "a pair of smiling eyes across a crowded room" this time.

A small ink-black man stepped neatly up to me and asked me to dance. He smelt of ancient curries and he told me his name was Abdul. He pressed his stubby little body much too close to me in an objectionable manner. I cast him off quickly while continuing to try to catch a further glimpse of those honey-coloured eyes. I sat down on a wobbly chair and suddenly the man was there beside me. For a moment we gazed at each other full on. He was quite short and stocky with a light brown skin, but he did have the most arresting expression – a huge embracing smile. After getting us both some more wine, he sat down next to me and we talked easily about many things.

His name was Roger and he came from Mauritius but

had recently been studying at the Sorbonne in Paris. French was his first language which meant he spoke English with an enchanting accent. Roger was a real mongrel. Mauritius had been colonised by the French and the British; it had harboured waves of emigrants for a couple of centuries. He could trace many strands in his heritage; his father was Indo-Chinese and his mother French Mauritian. He seemed to have acquired the most attractive facets of all these different cultures. We talked for hours and it was obvious that we found each other very entertaining as well as physically attractive. Having never met a man who turned me on, meeting this gorgeous man was a truly exhilarating experience.

We did get up to dance the last waltz in such a way that further meetings seemed likely. We met each day that week and by the end of it I threw caution to the winds and found myself in his bed. It had taken me long enough to discover the joy of sex and, now that I had, I was going to go for it! Roger was a great lover, true; I only had the inexperienced fumbling of Bill as a comparison. But he was clever and cultured. We would talk far into the night about existentialism, the new philosophical movement attributed to Sartre, then de Beauvoir and "The Second Sex", the wellspring of post-war feminism, Camus and of course Proust, though I never did finish his great novel. He took my physical shortcomings in his stride. He wanted to help me manage things which were difficult for me, insisting on carrying everything, sometimes doing my shoe-laces up, and even helping me lift a glass to drink when I was flagging. In those days, when "different" was inevitably a sight for stares, we must as a "double-different" have made a few heads turn. It was an amazing time, those months spent with this beautiful, cultivated, kind man from the so-called Undeveloped World. I knew Roger had set the bar high, and that I might never manage to find this combination of Body and Soul again.

And I don't think I ever did. I knew I was "bright and bubbly", in today's lingo, but Roger, as he cradled me in his arms, told me I was beautiful! "Je t'adore, Antoinette. Je t'adore, tu es ma belle femme." I can still hear those gentle French accented tones.

Sad as we were about his departure and the end of our affair, we had always known of its inevitability. We wrote for a year or more and I kept those flimsy airmails for years and still think of him with great fondness, and wonder that it had taken a sophisticated man from the Third World to unlock my passions.

★

With a somewhat oddly classified degree in History and a failed diploma in Social Studies, quite apart from my odd body, I was not exactly first choice in the job market. Incidentally, before I left I had the cheek to ask Miss Brown for a reference. She looked at me with horror, saying, in biting tones: "Miss Price, I accepted you, against my better judgement, in spite of you having a handicap which meant you could never have got a job on the front line, in the belief that you might find work in the back somewhere. You have shown almost no interest in the course, attended only 50% of your lectures, missing vital tutorials, and not surprisingly you have ended up by failing half the exams, and you have the gross impudence to ask me for a reference! Miss Price, your impertinence beggars belief." Oh well, I had actually done a lot of learning that year, though of a sort that I could hardly ask Miss Brown to appreciate. I was remarkably unbothered; completely unrepentant, I reckoned my luck was in and that something would turn up.

In those days it wasn't necessary to have a postgraduate teaching diploma, so in theory I was qualified to get a teaching post. I answered a few lacklustre advertisements in *The Times*

Education Supplement, mostly from small private schools in dead-end places, and then fate intervened.

I looked at the yellow envelope just delivered by the telegraph boy and prayed that old Dad had not had a stroke. After tearing it open I gazed in astonishment at the message:

> *Claremont School desperate for history teacher. Please come now.*
> *Coops*

I did not have to think about this call for my services for a moment and was on the next train to London. Thus Miss Gilson's sad mistake had become my blessed opportunity. This unfortunate woman who had been teaching history at Claremont had suddenly become pregnant with no possible marriage in sight; in those days this situation was still one of the worst that could happen to a girl as abortions were not yet legal.

I had, in a narrow sense, wasted my year in Edinburgh, but as I said, I cannot remember feeling a twinge of guilt about it. More importantly, I had grown from a shuffling, self-conscious, head-down being, overwhelmed by anxiety that her cerebral palsy would deny her any kind of fulfilling social life – in other words, she would never get a proper boyfriend – into a not unattractive girl who was on the way to becoming "a proper person". And I had been called "beautiful"!

If I had won that converted first class degree, I might very well have opted for a closeted life in research which could have meant a cut-off existence – well, out of the way of much of the fun and fulfilment I was able to enjoy as things turned out... I had seemingly metamorphosed from a rather unpromising chrysalis into, if not an exotic butterfly, then quite an acceptable moth!

CHAPTER 9

London Life and Loves

I enjoyed teaching – my flamboyant presentation of historical characters and scenes perhaps compensated in part for a lack of more serious teaching skills and diligence! It certainly gave the frustrated actor in me an outing. After all, this job had been thrown at me and, though I had been very glad to get it, I suppose I was still busy playing out my delayed adolescence. On looking back I reckon I got away with minimal effort and little dedication, being the first old Claremont girl to go back and teach at the school that I had attended as a pupil only a few years before. Of course this had its disadvantages too. One or two of the teachers who had taught me tended to treat me as a sort of superannuated schoolgirl. This attitude meant that I was told not to wear sparkly earrings when teaching, as they might distract the girls. When I lived in the school for the first term it was suggested that perhaps the photo of a light brown man should be put away when I had the sixth formers to tea! (This light brown man was of course Roger.) One term living in staff quarters over the room of dear Coops was quite enough. The poor dear woman would moan endlessly: "Dear Toni, yet again I had to wash up your dirty dishes and I know you love that gramophone thing you acquired recently, but why do you have to play that hideous music at such a volume? Really, how is it that you are still such a barbarian?" I didn't mind, because my love of Coops was unconditional, as hers was of me; so perhaps I even turned the noise down and did my washing up, but co-existence was never going to be easy.

So after that first term I found a room in a boarding house in nearby Claygate, kept by an eccentric Irish lady, Mrs O'Flynn. The other boarders were all ancient males, mostly sad relics of the war. One, Arthur, a widower of at least 55, developed a crush on me. He once kissed my hand and I remember blenching with disgust, and yet I allowed him to take me to the Folies Bergère, where we sat in the most expensive seats. I suppose really I was quite fond of him, regarding him as a sort of temporary uncle but knowing that this was not really the role he was after.

The house was very dark, as it was surrounded by huge fir trees; this bleakness was reflected inside by the monumental pieces of dark stained furniture, the worn brown lino and faded wallpaper. My room was painted a ghastly shade of green, the same colour as the soup we were served all too often. After a few months I left and found a flat at the top of a house, just two minutes from the railway station. I came to love this little eyrie which was to be my base for the next two years. I felt it was the first real home I had lived in for many years, perhaps since that time in Northern Ireland when we were a real family so many years ago. I remember sitting on the floor of my small sitting room one Sunday afternoon, by my big Black Box gramophone, playing a record of Harry Belafonte singing some magical calypsos and conscious of being in love with life, yet knowing this was a fleeting feeling, a moment to be savoured and preserved.

My small flat consisted of two attic rooms, one with a screened-off kitchenette which had a sink and a Baby Belling cooker. There was a single-bar electric fire in the sitting room and, as was usual in those days, no heating in the bedroom. I was allowed to have a bath once a week, on Sundays, which seemed quite sufficient: a luxury after life on the farm where I never had one in a year! There was a splendid view of the railway line which I loved: a constant reminder of my liberation from the very constrained life I could have been leading in rural disconnect, "looking after" Dad. The bed was very narrow and there was only one soft armchair; friends were expected to be out by 10.30, so neither parties nor night stopovers were practical. Male visitors were often subjected to intense scrutiny by Joan and Glyn, my landlords.

They were an unusual but kindly couple. Glyn was Welsh and god-fearing – his father had been Bishop of Llandaff. He was a small, square man with a crisp sense of humour, but his wife, Joan, ruled the roost. She was almost six foot tall with a commanding presence and had been a senior officer in the ATS (women's army) during the war. I liked Joan and Glyn but I think they were quite relieved when I left to get married, as their random inspections inevitably revealed piles of dirty crockery in the sink, unswept floors and general mess. I washed up twice a week and swept the floors far less often, but then domesticity never had been my thing. I was allowed to receive calls on their phone, but there were rather a lot of them and some from men with a variety of strange foreign accents, calling late which sometimes caused comment. Looking back, I can appreciate how tolerant they were as I was far from an ideal lodger and, having had many lodgers of my own since, I would definitely have given me the boot!

On the whole, I valued my women friends more; they tended to be of a higher calibre than the men I attracted. It is obvious that a lot of men will not go for a disabled girl even if she be ever so bright and bubbly; it would hardly add to their street cred and so I knew that, short of meeting that singular fellow whose priorities were different to most, I had to put up with the best I could get. I returned temporarily to the international student set which I had discovered when joining Cosmop in Edinburgh. At the Royal Commonwealth Club I met the handsome Dev Bannerjee, a rich man's son from

Calcutta, a student of aeroplane design who wore beautiful silk shirts. I think I fell "in love" with him and also with what he stood for – the cream of the emergent world. Dev was not only well-dressed and enchanting to the eye, but clever and well-mannered as well. Our courtship, if it could be called that, was slow and sedate and never came near to being consummated. I think the fact that my father was a colonel and had served in India almost made up for my physical shortcomings, but ultimately not, as he dumped me for his boss's daughter after six months. I thought I was devastated and drowned my sorrows in half a bottle of cherry brandy, which made me sick. Anyway, after a few days I realised that it had all been a bit of a mirage, since for all the superficial attraction we were utterly unsuited, and in any case, I was not looking for a long-term commitment as much as a jolly time. Yes, I suppose at heart I was a good time girl during those years. Perhaps I have always been something of one!

One Saturday in 1955 my friend Jackie suggested we go to the Slade Art School as it was supposed to have very lively Saturday hops. It turned out to have all you would expect from a throng of crazy art students.

Suddenly I was seized by an older man. He was quite slight, with a fuzzy mop of fair hair. After a minute he said, "You don't dance, do you? Perhaps you would like to come and look at the stars with me on the roof?" Luckily, I had the sense to decline the invitation, saying, "No, I'm sorry but I don't do astronomy either." This, I learned later in the evening, was Lucian Freud, on his way to becoming the best-known British painter of his time, and who also had a reputation as a great womaniser, substantiated by the fathering of at least eleven illegitimate children over his lifetime. "What a pity," he said, before brushing me off with a brief kiss, and then hurrying off to search for a better bet. What a claim to fame, turning down Lucian Freud! But better by far than the might-have-been consequences of star-gazing with him on the roof!

My next liaison was by far the most profitable. Anthony Cortez-Leigh was the stockbroker to whom I had entrusted the small inheritance I had been left, by an almost unknown great-aunt, on account of my "little difficulty". Anthony was large and fiftyish, presentable on account of his beautifully trimmed Velazquez-type beard and Savile Row suits, the fact that he ran a hugely successful investment agency and knew the right people. He was also very well read, cultured in a way which was rare in a city gent, even then, speaking French and Spanish, and, I was to discover, a fantastic cook and a sensitive lover. He had a wife, lost to drink somewhere on the Dorking line, but he spent the weekdays in a small flat in Jermyn Street, opposite the Turkish Baths, in the heart of the West End, a smart address. As a very provincial young thing just emerging from student-hood, I had approached his posh, marble-halled offices with great apprehension, clutching my precious cheque, received from Aunt Susan's executors. After a very short time he had doubled my few hundred pounds, taught me something about how money could make money and had taken me out to lunch at the Carlton, a very smart club for the Great and the Good (all men of course, except in the Guest Room). We talked a lot about books: Tolstoy, Proust, Camus and Thomas Mann, as well as many English writers, went to galleries, and a few avant-garde films like *Les Enfants du Paradis*. I never regarded him as an exclusive lover; he knew this and didn't seem to mind, after all he was only part-time, never available at weekends. Neither did my "little difficulty" seem to worry him; I think the feel of young flesh more than compensated for this. I suppose he represented the cultured parent figure I would have liked to have had. The marvellous meals he cooked for me were important too as they were symbolic of what my mother had never given me – hands-on physical care. He called me Little Bee, because I was always busy, buzzing around and occasionally stinging.

We continued to meet at intervals for about a year and then, after I got into a serious involvement, and later married, we continued to correspond and do business until he died suddenly, much too early, in 1960. I missed him, certainly not just as a money-maker. This friendship had given me a great deal more than a few extra pounds – it made me feel "interesting", another step away from being the substandard physical freak of my childhood, or even the shy, singular-looking girl I had become during my Durham days. I sometimes wondered how I managed to reconcile my burgeoning capitalist self with my long-term left-wing tendencies, but looking around I saw all those champagne socialists, and reckoned being a fizzy white wine one did not amount to outrageous hypocrisy, although in later years I have found it more difficult.

★

These lotus years continued until I began to realise that at 25 it was time to take a more serious view of relationships. In those days you were on the shelf if you were not married by 30. Of course, I had little idea of what marriage was all about with my fractured childhood and my "live now, bother later" attitude, but I had seen the desperate look of girls in their late twenties, who were scared of looming spinsterhood, and I didn't intend to join them. So I changed tactics, cutting down on hops and starting to go to serious weekend courses advertised on the back page of the New Statesman. I chose the subjects with care, with a view to picking the ones most attractive to men and least attractive to women. For example, "Economic trends in post-colonial South East Asia". These courses were usually held in delightful old houses in deep countryside, and the food was usually good and the cost low.

At Beatrice Webb House in Surrey I met Freddy, a very intellectual economist with a handful of degrees from universities in England, America and Europe. He was a large bear-like man with a good bass voice and a dignified presence. Freddy lived in a communal household in south London. His very progressive landlady, Nora, lent us a spare double bed at weekends. She was probably the only landlady in England at that time that would be so accommodating! Freddy and I got on well and I even risked taking him to the school dance, where the sixth formers all gave him the seal of approval. We attended many left-wing meetings, read some of the same books and went to concerts, the opera and ballet. Freddy was a really emotional music lover. When the heroine Mimi died in La Boheme he cried, and coming from a military family I thought this behaviour quite awful. I poked him, whispering, "Do shut up, you old cry-baby." Of course he was a continental – his father had been a Czech baron and his mother a German actress – but soon I had more important reservations about him.

I discovered that he did have some rather eccentric interests which I did not share. He belonged to a nudist club which he went to on Sundays in the summer. I went with him once but resolutely kept on all my clothes. The nudists were pleasant enough people but boringly addicted to their cult. The evening that I went, they had a fancy-dress party; while they got all dolled up, I thought what fun it would be to go as a nudist! But Freddy's interest in modern witchcraft – he actually belonged to a coven in St Albans – caused me more of a problem. I teased him sometimes, which didn't go down well as for him it was a kind of religion. Most of the time I tried not to think about it, because I was really fond of "my old bear".

I actually took him to stay with my grandmother in York but she didn't really approve of him, apparently because he didn't wear pyjamas and left the top of his shaving cream off in the bathroom, but I think it was more about suspecting he had Jewish origins. She actually said to me, "Toni, he must be Jewish if his family had to flee to Switzerland in the war, and he has a German accent. He is rather dark and I wonder why he doesn't wear pyjamas. Do Jews not wear them? I have nothing against Jewish people really, especially how they suffered in those dreadful camps, but the idea of having one in the family is a very different matter altogether; that would not do at all." I groaned, saying, "Who I decide to marry has nothing to do with you, Granny, you know. If I decide to get together with a head-hunting cannibal from Borneo, you couldn't stop me." Our relationship had not really improved with the years.

Freddy and I went out together for some time, although Granny's fears were groundless as I really knew he wouldn't do as a husband. Firstly, there were his eccentric interests, but basically I thought he was quite boring. He could sound pedantic and was somewhat lacking in humour, but my relationship with him did prove that I could attract a fairly suitable man, someone who the family might not embrace with enthusiasm, but at least they would not be saying, "Poor old Toni, I suppose she had to settle for that ghastly man as no-one else would look at her." A strange dichotomy this: although I had always felt the need to shock the family, at the same time, when it came to looking for a husband, I wanted one who would not completely outrage their innate conservatism, and of course to prove I didn't have to settle for just anyone.

After Freddy and I parted, I went on my first real holiday, as all my other adventures abroad had been as a hitchhiker, which means I was more concerned about the journey than the arrival. This fortnight in Florence had also been advertised on the back of the New Statesman. It cost £25 which included all train fares and bed and board. Our hosts were Eric, a handsome, slightly sinister-looking Yugoslav, and his beautiful but worn Italian wife, Violetta. Her family's ancient crumbling villa was to be our exotic home for the next fortnight. We ate the most delicious Italian food, the like of which we had never tasted before, at a table in the garden under a canopy of vines and roses. For us, coming from a grey and still stringent country, this was like a peep into paradise. The villa was in Fiesole on a wooded hillside overlooking Florence.

Florence was the first continental city I had really ever explored. I spent hours in the galleries looking at the pictures I had only known as postcard reproductions. I was entranced by the ancient buildings, though they were very battered, slowly recovering from war damage. I liked my travelling companions and spent most of my time with a girl called Shirley who, because she was quite a pale character and followed me around, became known as "Antonia's ghost". The men were mostly inarticulate scientists but they became quite animated at meal times after drinking several glasses of Chianti. I had a bet with myself that I would kiss all five of them, and I did! Quite a feat in those inhibited times!

I continued in my teaching job, though, had I not been some sort of emblem of the school's short history, I might not have survived. Susan and I sat at one end of the long staffroom table, chatting and giggling whilst we were supposedly marking exercise books. Susan was a really hopeless Latin teacher and eventually got the sack. She was much more interested in writing short stories for women's weeklies and, having little amorous experience of her own, she made use of mine as copy, I knew. She would listen all agog while I recounted the previous evening's adventures in South Kensington or Earls Court, or wherever else I was hanging out at the time. "Yes, and after meeting these two chaps in The Troubadour, where did you go?" I teased her: "Oh, Sue, that would be telling you, wouldn't it?" While I let out little titbits, we giggled irrepressibly, even after being told crossly that others were trying to work.

After Freddy, I returned to "good time girl" mode, which included taking up with some very delightful Ghanaian students, together with my new friend Pam who worked in John Lewis's and shared my taste in men. We were invited to some very exotic events, including a posh diplomatic garden party where we were introduced to Ghana's first President, Kwame Nkrumah, a very polished person who tried to charm me into taking a teaching job in Ghana. Pam and I had a lot of fun over the next few months, going to endless dances with gorgeously robed young men, the intellectual cream of this newly independent African state. There was the odd fling or two but nothing at all serious.

Tshume was studying Japanese and later became his country's first Ambassador to Japan. He was very bright and breathtakingly beautiful in his rainbow robes. He worked hard but played hard too, as he was the lead drummer in a small West African student band. I actually loved tripping around in time to the loud, rumbustious music they played. I appreciated my "different" friends, not just because they belonged to another minority but, ever since knowing Roger, I found black skin more appealing than white, both sexually and aesthetically, and of course I was still playing out my need to shock the father figure, old Dad, on a temporary basis anyway. This was to be the last of my wild times for many a long day. Tshume and his fellow students eventually returned to West Africa while I went back to serious husband hunting.

I met Hugo at a graduate dance at Chelsea Town Hall. He was on leave from his work as a land surveyor in Northern Nigeria and, as he was almost 30, was being pressured by his family to use this three-month period to look for a suitable wife. He was quite plump, fair-haired though balding and wore heavy horn-rimmed glasses. Though he lacked the instant physical appeal I had so recently experienced, he was very clever – a scientist, but literate and artistic as well as being practical; something of a Renaissance Man. He had an engaging wit and an instant charm. My disability didn't appear to faze him, and we shared many interests, as well as a similar robust sense of humour.

The first time he took me out to dinner, we went to Schmidt's in Soho, where we talked, drank and ate for about four hours. Schmidt's was known as an inexpensive eating place which produced interesting "foreign" food, rare then. Its ancient Austrian waiters complained about their bad feet, and you could sit there as long as you liked. I recall two things about this first dinner with my future husband: no man ever made me laugh so much and I had never seen anyone eat so much at one sitting! We discovered very soon that we shared a social background, as we were both born into the military – Hugo's father being a retired brigadier from the Royal Engineers, which meant that we had both experienced the fractured childhoods with frequent moves and often absent parents: the lot of most service families.

After three weeks of intensive courtship, Hugo proposed, in a car park on the A3 – the road from London to Guildford. At first, I said I would think about it, knowing well I was certainly going to accept him but not wishing to appear too eager. Luckily he repeated his offer immediately. "Well, what about it, then? Do you think you could put up with this old goat? We might rub along all right together. You laugh at my jokes and bed's good, isn't it?" I had never been proposed to before, and for all I knew might never be again! Anyway, I liked him, he was very funny, and as he said, we were sexually compatible. What's more, my difficult old dad actually found Hugo suitable, all the more so since his father was a higher-ranking army officer.

We journeyed down to The Dorretts as Hugo wanted to do

things properly, by asking the old man's permission. He took with him a large bottle of malt whisky, most gladly received. The old man said, in my hearing, "Hugo, me boy, let's say we share this good bottle between us; if you can drink half without showing it, you can have her!" I suspect that he was delighted that someone was going to make an honest woman of me, as I know he had long had inklings of my goings-on in the wicked city. Not just inklings – I knew he had read the odd telling letter taken from a drawer over the last years. In any case, I had always wanted to go to foreign parts, particularly Africa. And, what's more, it meant I wouldn't have to cook. My pragmatic attitude seems cold and calculating in retrospect, but love grew over time.

But had he not been his own man, his mother's view of things could have meant a swift end to the engagement, as she regarded me as the very worst disaster ever to have befallen her family, making this plain from the very start. The first time I went to dinner with the family in Guildford, after the engagement was announced, I was so nervous that I spilt my tomato soup all over her well-starched tablecloth. After that it was downhill all the way. Later that evening, she drew me to one side and said, "Antonia, I will always be Mrs Peake to you, not Audrey." So there would be two Mrs Peakes! She continued, "I have told Hugo he must tell all his friends in Nigeria that he is bringing out a handicapped wife. It is only right that they should be told, as this would not have been expected of him and it would be most embarrassing if he just appeared with you, as you are, without warning." Not surprisingly, I began to know my enemy; it had been years since someone had defined me by my physical condition.

A couple of weeks later she sent me to have lunch with her cousin, Catherine, a retired psychiatrist, for reasons obvious to her, though actually both food and talk were so good that I suspect the report back was disappointingly positive. Catherine was not at all like her cousin Audrey. After that, she even asked if I would meet another relative who was a City man, in order that he could check my modest portfolio of stocks and shares, the result of my relationship with dear old Anthony. That was enough; this wealth check was avoided, though I could see that it was about making the best of a bad job. Money might be a compensating factor. His mother's bitterness about his choice did not deter Hugo, though it was to lead to a deep rift between him and both his parents later. In the meantime he and I enjoyed each other in many ways and looked forward to an interesting joint future.

Wedding picture December 1957
Brigadier Peake, Mrs Peake on the left, Aunt Gyp and Dad on the right.

CHAPTER 10

Colonial Wife and Motherhood

Hugo had to return to Nigeria early in the New Year, so the ceremony had to be organized speedily; it had all the appearance of a shotgun wedding. Hugo had asked me if I would wait 18 months until his next leave, but I said I probably wouldn't. I needed the guarantee given by the small gold band just as soon as possible!

Dad got his super-efficient younger sister Gwyneth to manage the event, which was to be in a London church. I would have liked it to have been St Martin in the Fields where my parents had been married, but we settled for an ugly Victorian church in Lancaster Gate, shortly to be converted into flats. We invited about 150 guests. Many of these were ancient ex-officers who I had long forgotten or never met, from Dad's old regiment. A bewhiskered old general, Sir Charles Coleman, who only remembered me as a mewling infant in Cardiff barracks, was dug out to make the speech, which was all about Dad in his army prime, hardly mentioning my existence. But the Old Man loved it, and after all, as he said, he was paying for this great jamboree.

I wore a very modest dress, of white satin with quite a high neckline, but I had five fuchsia silk-clad bridesmaids, including my sister, Veronica, and Hugo's sister, Lynn. The ceremony was boringly traditional, but of course I enjoyed being the centre of attention and could hardly be persuaded to leave after several hours when it was obvious that our guests were becoming restless. I wasn't even remotely drunk as I got Hugo to drink most of my champagne because I did not want to draw attention to those wavering arms and wiggly hands; being all too conscious of my off-centre neck was bad enough. The food was dreadful even by the standards of those austere times: curled-up cucumber sandwiches, three or four shrimps wrapped in ancient yellow lettuce leaves, and ice-cream with ginger topping – an attempt at gourmet sophistication!

My reluctance to leave was partly because of a strong undercurrent of fear about the sort of committal I had just made. As we drove away in a hired Ford Popular, old boots dangling off its rear, with my alcohol-fuelled husband at the wheel, I shrank inwardly. We were heading for Dartmoor, an odd choice for the time of year, the end of December. It was cold, the hotel in Chagford. Both the room and the food were cold; the waiter kept telling us about the plate in his head, but the bed was comfortable; we spent most of our time in it, enjoying allowable sex at last, with the "Do Not Disturb" notice kept on the door handle most of the time.

We had our first row after a week in these purgatorial conditions. Hugo, strange chap, wanted to have a go at "setting" my hair, a procedure I found impossible. In those days wet hair was woven over plastic rollers while drying, as straight was unacceptable; curls and waves were a fashion necessity. Things did not go as planned. "Blast you! Why can't you keep still, stupid woman?!" Hugo shouted and swore as he tugged at my hair unmercifully. I yelled in pain and fury, particularly as this unlikely husbandly duty had not been my idea. He quietened down and I felt mollified as the resulting hair style looked pretty good. But I decided the price was too high, so that was the end of husband as hairdresser. But I was surprised by the strength of his reaction to what was after all a self-imposed task. During our short courtship he had never lost his temper.

★

I had been anticipating a touch of the exotic before arriving in Nigeria, but when I saw the rows of concrete bungalows with their red tin roofs in a patchwork of rough scrubland linked by a roughly tarmacked road, my heart sank. In the midst was a large bungalow with a thatched roof which was The Club – that mainstay of English expatriates in many parts of the world – where white men played, got drunk and made assignations, mostly with other chaps' wives. Not being able to drive was a huge disadvantage as the uneven terrain made walking, even for those with good legs, difficult. From the first day I felt as trapped as I had been in that Monmouthshire village years ago. Most of the wives I met at coffee parties matched the settlement; their talk was dreary and utterly banal, endless tittle-tattle, grumbles about servants and shopping, but mostly of the endless short-comings of the "natives" in general. There was not the slightest interest shown in this country, its history or the fact that it was teetering on the brink of independence. To begin with I tried to be one of the girls, but soon took to retiring to a corner to read the week-old Guardian I had brought with me! One day, I suppose a couple of wives thought they would get at me for my anti-social behaviour. Mavis and Laura, two of the older members of the community, approached me, as I was hiding behind my newspaper. Mavis, the old scraggy one, who smelt of stale gin, leant over me, saying: "Antonia, did you know Hugo kept a native woman in his servants' quarters on his last tour? We just thought you ought to be told." I knew and had accepted his previous domestic arrangements. This intrusion took me aback and made me quite angry, but I kept my temper, and replied, "Yes, I think it was a good idea, better than some other solutions, though I haven't been introduced to the lady yet." They didn't laugh, just slunk away; that was the last coffee party I ever went to. Just after that I met a delightful, educated French woman, Michelle, whose husband, Leo, worked in the commercial sector. Luckily he played a good game of chess so that pleased Hugo. This flight to the French saved my sanity during this first visit to Nigeria.

Hugo had told me all about his previous liaison. I had lent him the money for her "leaving present", a brand new Singer sewing machine, so that she could make garments in the market. We had not met, but I was aware that Fulani women are known for their beauty, though, belonging to nomadic tribes of cattle herders, they didn't do education. I thought it much better than going after another man's wife or visiting a local brothel, which was the preferred alternative of many single men there. Hugo told me that she was always given a bath in the kitchen with carbolic soap before being allowed in his bed! Yiya, the cook, saw to this and to the financial side of things: no sordid stuff like money on the mantelpiece. Though this sort of liaison would be completely unacceptable today, at the time it was not unusual and generally not criticised on moral grounds.

Yiya was a really good old man, and a passable cook, as he had worked for a fussy French family before. His wrinkled face, with cheeks deeply scored with tribal marking, was nearly always lit up with a warm smile. He had a good, almost fatherly, relationship with Hugo, feeling free to chide him on occasion. Hugo lost his temper almost on a daily basis over the most trivial matters. I was very often reduced to tears, which was painful and humiliating. Once, really upset, I ran away. I stumbled through the bush round the rocky outcrops, though God knows where I thought I was heading – just away from Hugo, I suppose. He sent Yiya to get me back. That dear man was shocked at his master's behaviour and kept shaking his head as he said, "Madam is raining, sir. You have made poor Madam to rain. It is not good of Master to hurt his Madam."

I think his words were taken to heart, as for some time my husband's temper was restrained. Though most of the time he was a loving husband, these "toddler tantrums" often made me wonder where I was going, and why I was here, in the middle of a desert, in this ghastly little place, with a man who frequently became a near monster.

There was the time when Hugo got really drunk, a one-off as he usually held his whiskies well. A wild cat had been stalking round the house and befuddled Hugo decided to shoot it. He got his gun and started to pursue the wretched animal up and down the stairs, shooting wildly as he went. I was terrified as the bullets ricocheted off the walls and screamed for him to stop. He yelled at me, "Shut up, you silly woman! It's just indoor hunting!" Luckily he soon fell over a stool and I let the poor terrified cat out, then lay on the bed quaking with shock. Talk about an accident waiting to happen! Old Yiya had heard the shots from his hut in the compound and came running to see what his errant master was up to now. It proved to be a one-off, but it made me anxious about his drinking.

After a few weeks I knew I was pregnant. I don't remember any discussion about family planning, only that Hugo no longer used condoms or French letters, as they were known in those days, and to which he referred as going for a swim in a mackintosh. The pill had not yet been invented and I had never been able to cope with the Dutch cap, the muscular contortions necessary to insert it being totally beyond me. In those pre-marital liaisons I had relied on the time-honoured and optimistic "safe period", my partner going for a splash in a mac, and luck.

I had never really thought about having children, only about how not to have them. There had been some anxious moments! Now I was a decently married woman, they were, I supposed, inevitable. Over the weeks I became attuned to the idea of motherhood, though I was hardly enthusiastic. I didn't suffer at all, no morning sickness, only an intense craving for fried tomatoes on fried bread, easily satisfied. On looking back, I think having never had a positive mother figure there was no pattern to follow. Also my physical problems, particularly my horribly inept arms, meant I simply didn't do domesticity, but on the other hand, I had no fears about childbirth, no sense of wonder, viewing the whole thing as an inevitable consequence of the married state; pragmatic, I suppose.

But my condition made it possible for me to get out of this colonial cupboard, back home where I longed to be. Nice Dr Gonzalez, the local GP, agreed with me after a short chat that, because of my spasticity, it would be wise for me to get good medical supervision in England. I threw in the fact that my mother had had two premature births, and, bingo, I was on my way out.

Of course we had married without getting to know each other at all, really, and this instant pregnancy and my consequent flight after six months had meant we had spent little time together. "Marry in haste, repent at leisure" may have been a suitable adage, but there came a time later, in spite of Hugo's relentless temper, when we developed real love and respect for each other, even though, sadly, ultimately it all ended in tears.

And so I returned home, relieved to leave the ghastly ghetto, somewhat ambivalent about leaving Hugo, who appeared to take it in his stride. Arrangements had been made for me to have the baby in Guildford, staying with Hugo's parents, the only other option being Dad's dirty old farm, 30 miles from the nearest hospital. I was of course already too aware of my mother-in-law's feelings about me, which were made very apparent when she refused me the use of her first name! (Her expression in our wedding photos was a graphic indication of things to come!) On arriving I stayed a week in Guildford before moving in with a friend in Hampstead – quite long enough; to say I did not feel welcome is an under-statement. I lost no time in finding a small flat, part of a new development in Ham, near Richmond. But of course, the baby being due in the autumn, I had to move back to that dreadful woman's house after a short time.

The next month or two were to be among the most trying times of my life. Giving birth was the easy bit; co-existing with Mrs Peake was the challenge I could have done without. I had supposed that, as the product of a posh Home Counties family, she would keep her deep dislike under wraps or at least bite her lip, but no. We were having a most civilised talk about modern art one day, when she suddenly burst out with a shocking comment, but one she had obviously been nursing for some time: "Personally, I have always thought that all disabled women should be sterilised," she said. I was stunned. As this venomous comment sank in, I burst into tears and rushed upstairs. After that there was no hope of any meaningful relationship ever developing between us. Nothing could obliterate the impact of her words, made a week before my child was due. That said, when she was almost 90, we met; she looked at me and said: "It was a long time ago, Antonia." I felt obliged to smile. She was so old but it was hardly an apology.

Her husband, the brigadier, was a tall, substantial man with the most perfect false teeth. He had the air of having once been a man of consequence. Present only at meal-times, he spent hours in his study working on a large Commonwealth stamp collection. He hardly ever spoke to me and seldom to the two women. In summer he inhabited the garden and, when it rained, the potting shed. The third member of the household was Polly; she had been around for almost 30 years, having originally been hired as Hugo's nanny. She might well have qualified for help from the charity called "Distressed Gentlefolk Association" had she not chosen to live here as Mrs P's sidekick, as she was emphatically middle class, but a feeble being without the ability to form independent relationships, though she certainly let the reclusive brigadier off the hook.

In the last stages of pregnancy I grew enormous and had outgrown most of my original maternity dresses, which were sort of tents expectant mothers wore in those days, as if pregnancy was not exactly shameful but a state which needed to be decently cloaked. I frightened Mrs P with the idea that it might be twins! (No scans in those days.)

I was at the cinema when I had the first indications that the baby was ready to emerge, watching "All Quiet on the Western Front". It was such an amazing film that I stayed to watch the end, but on returning to the house was immediately bundled off to the small maternity home called Mount Alvernia, headed by the fierce-looking Sister Day who was actually very kind. She saw me all through the night during the birth. It was quite a short labour; luckily spasticity did not seem to affect it at all. After eight hours of pushing and shoving, moaning and groaning, I delivered a baby girl to the world, in perfect condition, weighing nine pounds two ounces. She was the most beautiful baby ever, with long black hair and violet eyes. The doctor came to check us and was grateful that it was a breakfast-time arrival so it did not interfere with his Saturday morning game of golf.

This was the easy bit. Learning to care for Sarah, as she was named after her 95-year-old great-great-great aunt, seemed harder work. At first I was very worried about holding her, though it helped that she was such a large and compact baby. The good Sister Day made me progress from nappy-changing to washing her on an oil cloth-covered table set up for us by the bed. Much to my relief I was told she didn't need to have a bath as I had dreaded the prospect of handling a wet seal-like creature who might very easily slip through wiggly fingers. During these ten days Mrs P visited once, just "to make sure the baby was all right," as she said.

After our return Sarah was given to Polly to look after, seeing that she had been a professional nanny. She slept in Polly's room; Polly took her out in the pram and generally played the part of an old-fashioned nurse. I was allowed to breast-feed her but had to keep to a strict time schedule: once every four hours – twenty minutes each side; I felt like a hired wet-nurse. I was not allowed to carry her up or down stairs or even wash her as I had been taught by dear Sister Day. I let myself be side-lined as Sarah's mother, for a week or two, feeling more frustrated and angry by the day but unable to protest, being outnumbered, lacking in confidence and energy.

In my misery, I turned to my doctor who had been kind and supportive. He was angry too, when told how things were. He asked Mrs P to come to see him and gave her a thorough talking-to, I gathered. As a result, the brigadier came out from his lair and announced in fine military tones, "Antonia, we took you in with the child but you have shown crass ingratitude for all the help my wife and Polly have given you. You don't know how lucky you and your baby have been," before disappearing again.

In the meantime Mrs P had written to Hugo, who was deep in the Nigerian bush, to tell him how I could not possibly care for Sarah without a trained nanny whom she would find to accompany us when we flew back. How she thought we would pay the wages for such help on a Bush Surveyor's salary, goodness knows. After I knew about this, I felt fuelled by fury and was able to launch an effective counter-attack. I asked the doctor, the good Sister Day and an old friend, all to write to my poor bemused husband to tell him I was competent to handle Sarah, and that his mother was wrong. After getting these letters, he was of course enormously relieved and promptly broke off relations with both his parents for the next few years. This filial stand-off showed me that, whatever his other short-comings, Hugo was a very loyal husband.

After this campaign we had to get out. Ruth, an older teacher from Claremont and a very close friend, rescued us. She had no time for Mrs P and rushed over from Walton in her rusty old Ford, bundled us with all impedimenta into the car and off we went, shouting La Marseillaise at the top of our voices. We stayed with her until our return to Nigeria after Christmas. During this time I managed to take Sarah to Wales to see her granddad – not an easy train journey, as apart from carrying Sarah in her basket it entailed breast-feeding in a carriage full of middle-aged businessmen. It was so hard to keep everything decently under wraps while concentrating on holding the baby securely in the right position, but knowing my priorities were not the sensibilities of these fellow travellers, I just let everything hang out. Only the ticket-collector raised any objection until a chivalrous older man told him off for harassing me. Unsurprisingly, Dad didn't really do babies any more, although it was good to see him before returning to colonial wifedom.

And so we returned to Nigeria and Hugo for a longer and much more interesting term in West Africa when I was able to understand a little of the complexities of this place and its people, of this country outside the blinkered confines of the colonial ghetto.

Hugo on holiday

CHAPTER 11

Glimpses of the Real Nigeria

This time we lived in a mud hut in the middle of bush land on a high escarpment a few miles from Jos, a small place with a rest-house for tired white people but with few resident Europeans. Hugo had a bush posting which meant living well away from a fixed colonial ghetto, which suited me and Hugo too as he had never been a club man and loved bush life. Our hut had a curious latrine, known as a thunder-box, a sitting-up bath and an unreliable electric generator. It was much cooler being on the plateau. The main feature was the huge bed Hugo had his labourers build. It had a massive concrete base with a mattress stuffed with goat's hair. Hugo had put a lot of thought into this – we had often grumbled about the meanness of the government-issue beds. Of course too, it symbolised an important focus of our life together.

This time it was much better, as even Hugo's temper seemed to reflect the more temperate climate. We made a few real friends, very different people from those colonial types in Maiduguri. Hugo took a while to become attuned to fatherhood; I never remember him doing anything as basic as changing a nappy, however he did become very attached to his enchanting little daughter in his own way.

One evening it seemed she wasn't at all well. She was very hot, with a high temperature, squirming around in her cot, crying. Our first anxious thought was that she had malaria.

Everyone out there took anti-malaria pills but there were no special baby-sized ones; I just gave her a broken-up quarter, so it was hit or miss. This time, it seemed, I may have missed. We drove 40 miles along dirt track to the mission hospital, which was housed in a series of mud huts like our own. The mission doctor took one look at her and confirmed the diagnosis: malaria. He took up a great syringe and plunged it into our small, distressed baby. Immediately she turned blue and stopped breathing. Hugo and I clung to each other, terrified, as the doctor muttered, "Oh dear, she's allergic," before giving her another huge injection. Her colour returned and her breathing became normal. But it had been an awful few minutes for us both. We had been close to losing our firstborn. Perhaps undergoing this crisis made us feel closer. She recovered very quickly, as children often do, and I tried hard to give her the right pill dose and make sure the mosquito netting was in place.

A few weeks later came the second tropical challenge; a devastating tropical storm hit the plateau. This part of the country quite often experienced violent weather during this time of year, which was sudden, spectacular and terrifying. One Sunday teatime we were reading quietly in the sitting-room with Sarah lying gurgling to herself on the rug, when the room darkened, an almighty wind began to roar and rain came smashing down. We dashed to the window; the sky was a hurtling mass of purple clouds; the wild winds were tearing the trees out by their roots, shattering everything in sight; the streaks of lightning blinded us and the thunder which followed was immense, as if the old gods had gone mad. "Bloody hell, it's a proper hurricane. Wonderful!" Hugo, the scientist, said, staring fascinated out of the window, while I held a screaming Sarah close to me and tried to pray, as agnostics sometimes do, when in extremis. A huge crash very close by made Hugo dash out of the room to find that the back wall of the hut had fallen in and was rapidly being washed away. It was only chance that we were all in the front of the house at this time. Sarah could so easily have been sleeping in her cot in the back bedroom. For the second time in her brief life she had been under threat. We were really shaken by this violent act of nature and our brush with injury or, indeed, death.

The hut was irreparable, the crushed back wall being buried deep in mud, the kitchen and bathroom simply gone, and so we were immediately rehoused. The only available place was in a newly built block of flats reserved for senior Nigerian civil servants. While appreciating having a proper bathroom with a flush lavatory, the real plus for me was the prospect of getting to live among the people of this country, particularly at this time when independence was imminent.

Our new neighbours were Hausas, the tribes who inhabited the northern provinces of this enormous country. They were Muslims, patronised and looked down upon by the more sophisticated and largely Christian southerners, the Igbos and Yorubas. In turn the northerners naturally hated them. The gentle Yiya, a Hausa, declared he would like to put an Igbo into his cooking pot every week. The British had never shown much sensitivity about tribal boundaries, which meant they continued to give the best jobs in the north to Igbos. This caused sporadic violent outbreaks, though how many Igbos ended in Hausa cooking pots is unrecorded!

Our relocated life was full of incident and variety, very different from our previous existence in Maiduguri. The Hausa wives, being Muslim, were mostly quite uneducated which suited the husbands, a traditional lot, even the ones with senior government posts. Our neighbour, a magnificent man who might have stepped out of the pages of The Sheik, that twenties best-selling novel, or stood in for Omar Sharif, was the proud owner of an equally handsome white Arab stallion and kept four illiterate wives in his servants' quarters weaving blankets all day. El Hajji Assiz was Adult Education Officer for the region. Though he spoke good English and was always immensely polite, I did not feel quite up to tackling him on this paradoxical situation! There were a few new girls' schools but they focused, for the most part, on women's skills. Yet, the village market was dominated by women traders – perhaps, at this time, basic commerce was the only outlet for bright women. As for my neighbours, it took some time to make contact with any of them. They would return a smile and then retreat quickly round a corner or into a doorway. I think most of them, the unschooled ones anyway, had never encountered a white woman at close quarters.

Then I met Juba in the market, shopping. She was an arresting figure, tall, coffee-coloured rather than black, with delicate features which suggested Fulani ancestry. She wore a long purple garment with matching headscarf. We smiled, nodded and shook hands. She didn't make me feel like a creature from outer space, as the other women did, and showed she wanted to be friendly. We sat down on the grass, while she indicated that we lived in the same building but on a different floor. I showed off my very limited Hausa while I understood most of her very eloquent non-verbal communication: facial expressions and hand signals. After a while I found myself pointing at things and naming them in English while she gave me the Hausa word. The morning became the afternoon and we were still there. Suddenly she sprang up, pointed to the stall just by us and went and bought two steaming bowls of groundnut stew with sweet potatoes to our patch. It was difficult to explain to her that I would not be able to eat on the ground, and she mistakenly thought I did not like the food. We ironed it out in the end through me demonstrating how my grotty old arm movements made it important we find a table to eat at. Yes, during this time of living with the people, I had often wondered how my physical oddness affected their take on me. (Their own disabled were often made to be beggars; as Allah said everyone had to give money to such, in extreme cases children might be purposefully maimed so that they could produce the family income.)

Before parting, Juba invited me to meet her sister and a couple of her friends at her flat. I was excited about making this breakthrough and started looking through a Hausa language textbook which had been issued to Hugo, though he had hardly looked at it. Most Europeans did not bother to learn the local lingo, assuming that if you shouted loud enough the message would be understood. But, sadly, Juba's invitation was cancelled. Her husband disapproved of her fraternising with about-to-be ex-colonial personnel, even though he himself spoke excellent English as he was an official in the Forestry department and worked alongside Europeans. But Juba and I continued to meet in the market. Her English improved faster than my Hausa.

After some weeks I managed to get a few of the younger wives together who showed some interest in learning basic English. We would meet mostly outside, though when the rains began they came, hesitatingly, to our flat. But as always the heavy shadow of male domination hung over them, showing itself in different ways, but making it difficult for us to become a coherent and worthwhile group. Outside, we were subjected to hostile stares, nasty comment and covert laughter. When we met at the flat, only half turned up, others sending lame excuses, and, once, a very large man barged in without knocking and simply picked up his young wife from the floor, shredded her notebook and ran with her down the corridor, as if he was saving her from the jaws of hell. We never saw her again. It was not a complete waste of time as a few women learnt something, but their extreme shyness, not helped by a sense of guilt, hampered even the brightest.

Our joint social life was spasmodic but this time we were

able to find a few like-minded spirits. Donald McKay, an ancient copper miner, working for himself, became a good friend. He had been in the country for twenty years, scrabbling around for minerals, eking out a livelihood, selling his stuff to the Government Mines department. He was small and wizened, and liked his whisky neat. His stories were fascinating if perhaps embellished. There had been a wife but she had long ago returned to her family in Scotland. Surprisingly, for those days, there were a few Anglo-Nigerian marriages. Our friend, Keith, actually a policeman, had a Hausa-Fulani wife who had been a teacher in Kano, a singularly beautiful and very intelligent woman, but then, as she came from the capital, this obviously made a difference. They visited us often, partly, we suspected, because not many doors were open to them in our locality though they were more easily accepted in Kano.

Towards the end of our time there we were befriended by a very ancient Hausa chief who wanted to buy our Volkswagen van. The bargain struck, he would appear almost every other day at five o'clock when Hugo arrived home, to shake our hands and have an orange juice. "I come see my good English friend, Mr Peake. He good man. The car very nice, good for business." I forget what we talked about. He spoke very bad English, but in his own way he made sure we knew he had taken us to his heart. He was very fascinated by little white Sarah and brought her a stream of small presents, sweets and small, odd-looking garments made by his wives. When I suggested he might bring one of these wives, he shook his head and indicated it was not the custom. We were touched by these short unsolicited visits, for which there was no apparent reason, other than social, and felt that we had been privileged to have got to know this venerable old man who was a much respected figure among his own people. In any case I was so glad to have had the opportunity to step beyond the usual bounds of the colonial wife, though this had been the result of that storm which might well have ended in tragedy.

When the time came to return to England, I was really sorry to leave the few genuine friends made this time round. Hugo's contract was not renewed. I never really knew why, but suspected he had offended his boss, the Surveyor-General; his temper often meant trouble at work, as well as at home. So his main concern on return was finding a new job and mine was having another baby. Sarah had recovered quickly from malaria. She had grown rapidly into a pretty little girl, full of energy and charm. Our flat in Ham Common, which Hugo had never seen, had been let. Hugo did not have any domestic skills or any intention of acquiring any. I remember him making a cup of tea but no cooking: boiling an egg was beyond him, so I needed help with Sarah, cooking and chores. We acquired a robust German au pair called Elke – a pretty nut-brown, freckled country girl with a cheeky grin – somehow squashing her into our small space. She was fun as well as being a good help. We giggled together when Hugo lost his temper. "He like my little brother," she said, rather too loudly. He must have heard as thereafter he named her "that Hun girl". We were both quite relieved when he found work. Hugo, on home soil, without a job, was not at his best.

After a few false starts he landed a post with an aerial survey company in South Africa. As I had always been very critical of the Apartheid system, then at the height of its implementation, I felt apprehensive about this, but off he went, without any political reservations, only thankful he had been offered work at last. "Never mind, old girl. I'll leave you to get on with production business." Yet another separation, the idea being that I should join him a few months after the birth of the new baby. I shed a few tears this time, knowing I would really miss him, while being quite relieved that his heavy presence and frequent outbursts would no longer dominate life in our small flat.

Pregnant again: the result of too much careless rapture in Hugo's splendid home-built bed! I suppose, too, I had believed in that Old Wives' Tale that breast-feeding acted as a form of contraception. I was quite shocked, being, as we were, in transit, between jobs and countries. This time things were not quite so straightforward; sometime after Hugo had gone I was sent to hospital for two weeks' "bed-rest" as I had very high blood pressure. Horrible ordeal, worse than prison, as I was constitutionally unable to stay in my bed and was continually being told off by a starchy, red-faced sister for cruising round the ward seeking good chat as I felt very well. This all ended in my flinging a nest of enamel basins at her feet in fury and frustration. I was of course reported to Matron, an impressive older woman with a wonderful purple veil, who explained quite tersely why I was there and the reasons for staying in bed and keeping quiet. "Mrs Peake, I'll have you know, this is not the sort of behaviour I expect on my wards. You are here to rest in your bed, not go traipsing round and upsetting my staff. Your blood pressure must be going through the roof! Go back to bed at once and stay there." After that both I and my blood pressure quietened down and I was soon released from this prison.

Our second child was born, exactly on time, at seven o'clock on Easter Bank Holiday Monday. I had a very short labour, perhaps because there had been only a few months between births. The experiences were very different. Sarah's entry into the world had been steered by the wonderful Sister Day who had made me feel very special, as if I was giving birth to a princess, while my second child emerged into an over-crowded, under-staffed ward, at a time when the night-staff were yawning their way out while the day shift came on duty, perhaps resentful they were having to work on a Bank Holiday.

I can remember tugging hard on the bedside bell, as the baby was yammering to get out and we were in crying need of instant attention. After what seemed like hours of frantic bell-pulling and eventual yelling, a worried-looking young nurse appeared at the foot of the bed with a gas and air machine in tow. It was a bit late for the pain-relieving contraption; she could see that now. "Oh, it is in a hurry! Come on, Mum, push, but not too hard." I gave it all the energy I had. I just wanted the pain to stop, and out it came like a small pink seal. I heard someone say "It's a girl", but as was the custom then, she was whisked away to the communal nursery before I had even seen her properly. Though the birth had been an easy one, I was so tired that I fell into a deep sleep.

Hours later this well wrapped bundle was thrust into my arms by a busy nurse on her way to a more urgent assignment. I opened it up carefully to find a substantial blue-eyed infant with ginger hair. She started to feed immediately, her mouth needing no gentle guidance to the breast. On her left foot she wore a yellow sock. I asked, jokingly, if she had been born with it. Apparently, as one foot was slightly turned in she had been given the sock to stop the nails from scratching the back of her other leg. I was worried about this but was told the foot would straighten itself in time. It didn't and at two she had to wear orthopaedic boots for a year.

I named her Francesca, after an amazing woman explorer about whose life I had just read. She was of course known as Frankie, which exactly suited her tomboy temperament. Soon that ginger fluff fell out and, after a short bald phase, was replaced by gorgeous white-blonde tresses, which her sister, a couple of years later, cut off, taking her behind the sofa to do the deed, leaving poor Frankie with half a head of hair! Such acts of sibling jealousy were inevitable, being born so closely together, I suppose. Though her beginnings had not been auspicious, being the least planned of our children, she very soon developed into a great character: a source of tremendous fun and laughter. Her twinkly blue eyes and wide smile, combined with her spectacular hair, attracted a lot of attention as she grew. True, she became the naughtiest of the three, but that smile and her quick tongue got her in and out of many tight corners, I suspect!

Elke and I were a good team, though at times our standards of childcare fell short; today we would probably have been locked up! One Sunday evening when Frankie just wouldn't stop screaming, after I had exchanged a rueful glance with Elke, she said, "Toni, why don't we go down the pub for half an hour...then she stop." So off we went to The Swan, which was just round the corner, and sure enough she was sound asleep when we got back!

A few months later we prepared for another foray into Africa. As already mentioned, I had reservations about our destination, though these were tempered by feelings of excitement which were as much about seeing Hugo again as experiencing life in a new country. Our passages were booked on "The Stirling Castle", reputedly the oldest ship on the Castle Line. We took Elke with us, to help on the voyage and with settling in. It was a great travel opportunity for her and she certainly made the best of it. On the first day on board she met Steve, a 40-year-old tobacco planter from what was then Rhodesia, who had been to Europe looking for a new wife as his old one had run off with the local lawyer, leaving him with two young boys. He was small and rugged with a certain piratical charm, and from first sight set out to capture Elke, with honourable intentions from the beginning. The result of this intensive courtship was that I was often left with all three children to look after, while they canoodled in a lifeboat! Help was at hand, though; a couple of nuns gave their hearts to Frankie and so she spent time in her carrycot, at their feet, grinning and gurgling, much to their delight, while I took the other three to the crèche in between meal times. Frankie was still being breastfed so she was not entirely given up to the Holy Church baby-minders.

Our cabin was small and dank with narrow bunk beds and limited washing facilities; there were four of us, and I was an ill-organised and untidy mum. I had come to rely on Elke's Germanic love of order, but, of course, she was elsewhere most of the time. Then there was the Randy Steward who would barge in without knocking at any old hour, whether I was feeding the baby, changing my clothes or just resting. He was good-looking in a cocky way and was obviously targeting me as a single woman, but I had rather too many commitments to give him a second thought, apart from being married, so when he pinched my bottom he got a swift biff on his nose with a handy shoe. It bled, so that was that. Sarah, being a very sociable child, loved being in the crèche and seemed to enjoy being with Steve's two little boys. In a small space on deck we played with a large ball. The kids laughed when I dropped it most of the time. I was quite angry about Elke's neglect and told her so, while at the same time I was aware of the scarcity of young men in Germany after the war, as she had often talked about it, and knew that she was desperate to get wed.

She was one of five girls; none of them had found husbands yet, so this was perhaps a factor in her attraction to the middle-aged but not unattractive Steve, though it would mean embracing an unknown life as a tobacco farmer's wife in a country so far from home. She was a little less absent towards the end of the voyage but left us for her new life a few weeks after we arrived. Gosh, I was glad to see the end of that journey and start our new life, even though it involved substantial political compromise.

CHAPTER 12

The South African Years

We docked at Durban and were met by Hugo after this second great gap in time since our marriage; he seemed overjoyed to see me, and me, him. He drove us up to Johannesburg in his new yellow Ford Taunus and showed us into the flat he had rented: a pleasant ground-floor apartment but, as we soon discovered, located in a fairly run-down poor white area. During our first week our milk went missing from outside the front door, and of course we were encouraged to think it must be the black caretaker, known as "the flat-boy", April, but soon found out it was our white Afrikaans neighbour, Mrs Pretorius, whose husband presided over the local rubbish dump, a job reserved for whites though clearly not well paid. Later, I found her, in my kitchen which was strewn with her dirty clothes, using our washing machine. Simply, as a white woman she had forced our black help to let her in. Such domestic anecdotes show us much about the society we were to become part of for the next few years.

Johannesburg was a large, metallic city, glittering with wealth from the gold mines on its outskirts, evident in the huge brown dumps around the poorer suburbs. Despite the expensive modernity of the city centre, it still had something of the mining camp from which it had developed. From the start I was acutely aware of the racial tension, the hatred and fear which one could almost smell emanating from the pavements. The small groups of black boys hanging around street corners, playing their penny-whistle tunes, while sounding merry enough were given many fearful glances by white passers-by. The Afrikaner police were a heavy presence, all too often in the business of street questioning and rounding up blacks generally because they could not produce the hated passes which all non-whites had to carry. These searches were particularly frequent in the potato season when white farmers were in need of free labour, as the standard punishment for having no pass was to be dumped on an outlying farm for a month or two. Most years at least one "native" body would turn up in a potato field: not exactly a country holiday for urban blacks.

I was fascinated by this City of Gold with the opulence of its luxurious department stores, the post offices and stations and other public buildings which had separate entrances for whites and "non-whites", and the poverty in the parts of the city where the Indian community lived, and the parks, reserved mostly for whites but where the races were allowed to mix, the benches were labelled "Whites Only". As a kind of epitome of this estranged society, produced by apartheid policies, I remember seeing a couple of well-dressed young white men lounging on a park bench while a very old but respectable black woman sat on the grass a few yards away!

Hugo seemed happy in his work. He gave us a very enthusiastic welcome and had prepared the flat well, though he was slightly overwhelmed by having a new baby as well as an inquisitive and demanding toddler around. I think he found the political set-up disconcerting but it didn't seem to worry him over-much, though he was not unsympathetic to my own strong feelings. The next essential was domestic help: Hugo was utterly hopeless on this front; he still never changed a nappy or got up in the night, and his large appetite was never complemented by any inclination to cook. He belonged to that last generation of husbands who just did not do domestic, and, of course, working in Africa he had always employed the locals to cook and clean. So we asked the caretaker, known as the flat-boy, if he knew of anyone who would do for us.

The very next day a handsome black woman arrived at our door. Her name was Violet; she was to be our mainstay throughout the years we spent in South Africa. Both Hugo and I were impressed by her. She replied to our questions fluently, though with an undertone of anxiety. I thought, she really needs this work. Her face shone with intelligence and we were most struck by her voice. She spoke almost accentless English, much clearer than that of the white South Africans I had met. I asked her how she came to speak like this. "Madam, I went to school and my teacher, a good man, Mr Robinson, from England, had been to Oxford University and he speaks very good English, not like South Africans speak it, and he said we must all speak like him. So we all learn proper English. Madam, I loved my lessons, but I had to leave when I was twelve because my daddy was killed in a mine accident... Bad time for our family, girls had to work...no more school." (Later we learnt that white children had free education and school books, while blacks had to pay for both.)

She wore a frayed but clean green and black dress with a matching headscarf pulled over her forehead. Her poverty showed mostly in her shoes which were down-at-heel, held together with string. No wonder; she told us she had walked all the way from her home on her tribal reserve in the Northern Transvaal. She had a three-year-old child, left behind with the grandmother. Her eyes filled with tears when she told us about how she missed her little daughter, Valerie. It was against the law for domestic workers to bring their children with them when they moved to the city to work, another indicator of the regime's inhumanity. (Later, Valerie came, illegally, and we hid her in our wardrobe when the police inspectors were around!)

And so of course Violet joined our household; she started

work the next day. She was a very competent help and our two children took to her immediately. I enjoyed her company, though admitting this publicly was probably enough to attract the attention of the police! As it was, our white South African neighbours expressed horror when I said I wouldn't think of locking up the kitchen cupboards, including even the tea and sugar. Roberta, from next door, said: "Ach, man, you've only been here five minutes. You don't know nothing about these native girls. They're all thieves, out for all they can get. The ones with a few brains, like yours, are the worst. What's more, they know a green English madam when they see one. Next, I expect you'll be lending her your best shoes to wear on her day off!"

She snorted as I replied defensively: "No, of course not, but I won't give her dog-meat like you all do. I think that's disgusting. She has the same as we do – she is human too!" Roberta, red-faced, shouted, "Make no error, Antonia, bleddy liberals from overseas, like you, do our girls no favours! At least they know what to expect from us. Why the hell can't you stay in your miserable little island where you belong? You and your like don't belong here, make no error!" She stomped off next door. I sighed, wondering if I would be able to cope here, half wanting to catch the next boat home.

I did not drive, which meant using the buses and getting around, sometimes with the two small children, was not possible without taking Violet. Of course, things being as they were, blacks and whites had to use separate buses. An exception was made for black nannies travelling with white children, but they had to go on the upper deck. So, on our expeditions, Violet would bind Frankie on her back with a large shawl and mount the stairs, while I took Sarah inside. The logic behind this ruling was hard to figure out, but, of course, it was all too typical of the system. Neither could we eat together, even in the most humble cafés. More than once, Violet and I had tried this but were invariably turned away before we had even sat down. So we eventually resorted to taking sandwiches, eating them on a weedy patch outside the kangaroo enclosure in the zoo gardens. The irony of being just about acceptable as a unit in the zoo did not escape us!

There had been a problem from the start about where to house Violet. Servants were not allowed to live under the same roof as their employers; most houses had huts in the garden, blocks of flats had similar accommodation nearby. At first Violet stayed with her sister in a neighbouring suburb. Later she moved in with a friend called Dorothy, just down the road. Dorothy was a plain little woman with a disconcerting squint. They made an odd pair: large, handsome Violet and small, ill-favoured Dorothy. Nevertheless, after a few months Dorothy got herself a boyfriend, Johannes. This, understandably, put a strain on the women's friendship. Dorothy, waiting for Violet, brought him round. Though he was very polite and smiled a lot, I had bad feelings about this smarmy little guy in his shabby shiny black suit.

For many months Violet seemed happy with us. She hummed as she worked and sang old Sotho songs to the children, giving the impression that she felt she had fallen on her feet, working for this "bleddy liberal" family who treated her as a human being and paid her a reasonable wage. But after the first half-year she seemed to lose her previous joie-de-vivre, no longer humming as she worked or singing to the children; black shadows appeared under her eyes. I asked her if she was not feeling well, fearing that her work was too demanding, but she just shook her head, saying she found peace in our house. She began to stay late, finding odd tasks to do. I noticed too that she was constantly fingering the small leather bag she wore on a string round her neck. She had told me this was filled with good "muti" to ward off evil spirits; her mother had tied it on when she was a small child. One evening, just before leaving, she said: "Madam, I am frightened. Someone is working bad muti on me." I asked her to tell me more, but she shook her head, implying that I would not understand.

Suddenly, early on a Sunday morning, we were woken by a dreadful commotion in the yard below our window: shrieks of wild laughter, shouting and thumping. Hugo grabbed his pistol and charged through the kitchen door, fearing a "native" riot, the sort the government was always warning us about. On finding the commotion seemed to have a local domestic focus, he put the gun away and slunk back to bed, murmuring, "only women trouble". I dressed hurriedly and found that our Violet was at the centre of this business; scarcely recognizable, she was squatting on her haunches in a corner of the yard surrounded by a huge crowd of local servants all screaming with laughter. It was her face which threw me most. It had undergone a horrifying change: her large brown eyes bulged out of her head, her cheeks were grossly distended and her mouth seemed to stretch from ear to ear. I remember thinking she really looked like a huge, bewildered frog. Alas, there was not much sympathy shown her by the crowd. Resentment felt on account of her looks, intelligence, and of course her relatively good wages, was finding expression in the jeering shouts and the raucous laughter. A case of "how are the mighty fallen". Her feet were bare, but, thank God, they were not webbed! Poor Violet hopped clumsily towards me, tears running down her fat cheeks. She squatted down in the kitchen. I took her clammy hand and looked at her and, though she was still our Violet, her facial muscles had distorted her features; she was barely recognisable. Now, she started to sob, her distorted body shook as I put my arms around her. "Dear Violet, what has happened to you? Tell me, please?" She tried desperately to speak, but her words were drowned by a curious croaking noise which came deep from her throat, over which she appeared to have no control.

I left her briefly to phone our doctor who had been a medical missionary for many years and, I felt, might know something of the weird potencies of old Africa. He was sympathetic but acknowledged that this case was beyond the reach of western medicine. He suggested we talk to a certain Catholic priest, a Father O'Kelly who had apparently had some success with his church's Rites of Exorcism. I rang the good Father immediately and he agreed to come at once. He sounded full of boyish enthusiasm at the prospect of this challenge and arrived in no time in a bashed up Ford Popular. He looked about forty, tall and scrawny with grey-flecked, reddish hair and a sweet, shy smile. He wore a long, black habit with a tight, white dog collar which enhanced a very prominent Adam's apple. He exuded an air of eager innocence. After quickly downing a glass of Hugo's best whisky, he strode into the kitchen, shutting the door firmly behind him.

I didn't exactly eavesdrop, but under my intense anxiety for Violet was a marked curiosity to hear what was going on between the two of them; I only heard a continuous muffled buzzing, perhaps the intoning of the Rites. I suppose I was waiting for Violet to let out piercing screams as the devils leapt out of her, as in the New Testament miracle, but nothing dramatic appeared to be happening. After what seemed hours, a hang-dog and spent Father O'Kelly slumped out. He had aged ten years or more, and after a murmured goodbye slid into his car and drove off in a cloud of evil-smelling exhaust fumes.

I was so disappointed that I collapsed in tears. April, the gentle flat-boy who had found Violet for us, emerged from the shadows. He was a small, neat black man with a good face and a courteous manner. I had always found him helpful and considerate. He had only just returned from seeing his family on the reserve and so had missed the earlier dramas of the day. He shook his head after seeing poor Violet crouched in the corner and muttered, "Bad muti, bad muti." He was the first black person to show any sympathy for her. He bent over her, and I saw she responded by looking a little less troubled. He asked me about my children; I told him they were with a friend. "But what about tomorrow, Madam?" – I hadn't arranged anything as the present seemed to be all-consuming – I hadn't even thought about tomorrow. He disappeared for a few minutes and came back with two mugs of tea and some sandwiches. "Madam and Violet must eat," he said. I was touched by this small kindness and drank the tea down quickly, but poor Violet struggled. Her co-ordination seemed to be worse than mine, and though her mouth appeared huge she had trouble in drinking from the mug.

April sat on the floor at a respectful distance and said: "Poor Violet, I am sorry to see her in this bad state. But, Madam, I know a good woman. Anna lives in Soweto. She good woman; she work with good muti. If Madam like, I ask her to come to Violet." An offer of help from inside this alien world of what had become for me an alien continent, filled me with new hope. April asked to use the phone. He was told that this potential wonder woman, Anna, was visiting her sister nearby and could come immediately, and so he hopped on his bike to go and fetch her.

Again, I waited and kept running to the gate and peering down the road in the bright sunlight. Then I discovered April had brought Anna through the side entrance. She sat on our stoep, an ample woman of about forty-five. She looked pleasant and quite professional in a black smock dress with a red headscarf decorated with coloured beads. Her smile was warm and she carried herself well as she walked into our kitchen where Violet crouched miserably in the corner by the sink. April and I withdrew, but not before I saw Anna open her canvas bag and take from it an old-fashioned medicine bottle, some twigs and what looked like a bundle of chicken bones.

It was like a repeat performance as I once more waited on tenterhooks. Again there were no piercing screams; in fact, I couldn't hear anything at all. At last, Anna opened the door and I saw Violet, as we knew her, smiling tentatively. She spoke with her usual distinctive accent, thanked Anna and, turning to me, apologised for the trouble. I ran over to her and hugged her closely. She was grey-faced, haggard and quite exhausted, but she was herself; she was back.

We sat round the kitchen table. Anna sat easily with us but April hung back, standing until I patted the chair next to me and asked him to sit down. No-one said anything for a minute or two. Violet recovered some colour, holding herself determinedly erect, as though to distance herself from her recent horrible appearance. April broke the silence. It seemed he knew much, but said little, about things which went on among the locals. But now, it seemed, he felt the time had come to talk.

As the story unfolded he warmed to the role of narrator. He spoke slowly so we would miss nothing. He said, "Dorothy's new boyfriend, Johannes, he bad man. He thought he make much money so he make himself become a witch doctor, but he needed a room where he could make his wicked work. Then he met Dorothy, stupid girl, not beautiful like Violet, and see she live in big room with Violet. He move in with Dorothy, but he have to try to spell Violet to make her go away. Dorothy, always jealous about Violet, wanted room with Johannes, so she no mind what that bad man do to make Violet go. Good friend! And so, Madam, Johannes, that wicked man, set out to do a spell on Violet so that she could not do her work and would have to go home to Northern Transvaal. In this way he could have the room to do his evil. I am good Christian fellow and I had nothing to do with this man, but Dorothy, she great talker, so many people round here, they know about his accursed plan. Dorothy, that misguided woman, tell how he was going to put this spell on Violet. So, last night, I was told, because I just come back from holiday, Johannes sprinkled some white powder on poor Violet's head, telling it was good for headache and, as you know, Madam, this very morning she had been spelled into a frog. Johannes, he be mighty pleased. People say he make a good witch doctor, and Violet go from room, and he became rich man, he think." April held Violet's hand in brotherly fashion.

After another cup of tea, I paid Anna her modest fee of five rand. She left, perched side-saddle on the cross-bar of April's bike. While it had been all in a day's work for her, for Violet and me, a naïve European, she had produced a miracle. Hugo, on returning from work, was obviously relieved that it was all over, and on hearing the whole story showed a good deal more sympathy. He saw how essential it was that Violet should move from the shared room, understanding that neither she nor I could venture anywhere near it. He took his car and cleared out her belongings. We put her in our spare room, aware that this was breaking the law but having no option. Very soon after this happening, we moved away from that neighbourhood into a small house.

Violet had her regulation servant's hut in the garden. While these months spent in the flat produced a sharp learning curve into aspects of South African society, we felt more secure living in Parkhurst, a modest but respectable suburb further from the inner city but on a good bus route. This was most important as I intended to find an interesting job, knowing that Violet would take good care of Sarah and Frankie.

Day after day I scanned adverts in the local paper, the Johannesburg Star, for a job which would give me access to the locations as I was really keen to meet black people in their own milieu. What was the point of being here, just hobnobbing with whites, when there were, all around, places allocated rather than chosen, where one could experience the lives of those others. It was not easy finding suitable work, as access to the locations for whites, who were not part of the state apparatus, was limited, not that many would want to venture into them. After almost giving up and actually applying for a part-time teaching post in a local school, I found what I had been looking for: a request for someone to sell goods in the African market. Of course, I hadn't ever sold anything, except that stolen gold coin from my grandmother's desk, when I was eight, but when I looked at this advert I shrugged off this disadvantage. Here was the opportunity I had been waiting for all these weeks; nothing was going to stop me applying for it anyway. Hugo was abroad, working for a few weeks in Zambia, though I didn't suppose that would have made any difference. So off I went to Soweto with the conviction that this venture into the interior would lead to the great African Experience I was seeking.

CHAPTER 13

Pretty Caskets

I stood in the doorway of the warehouse, peering at these lozenge-shaped slabs; beautiful they were, jewel-coloured, ruby, emerald, amethyst and sapphire. On looking closer into that gloomy interior I saw they were three-dimensional, like large oblong boxes. Mike, the Irishman, a great burly fellow, put his hand on my shoulder, saying, "That's what I make, caskets. Good, aren't they? Aluminium, so the body doesn't rot, it just goes on like John Brown's," and he hummed the tune as we stepped into this cavernous space. "Well, lady, do you reckon you can flog 'em?" That's what job's about. I don't read much but I heard that a lot of 'em believe in ancestor worship. Sure, they don't want to think of Uncle Zeph coming back full of maggots." Mike seemed a reasonable bloke, and the job, though a touch unusual, promised to provide the opportunity I had been looking for, so I decided to take it. I told my rich old settler cousins, who lived in a suburb called Balmoral, and we were never invited again to those absurdly old-fashioned tea-parties, served by black Alice, dressed up in Edwardian cap and apron. The woman in the corner shop shook her head, saying, "I just hope you won't be eaten like that nun in the Karoo, last year," but my enthusiasm for the job was not diminished; if anything it was heightened by these negative reactions. Mike wanted me to start in three weeks.

He was originally from County Kildare. His soft Irish vowels clashed with the much harsher tones of white

South Africa, resulting in a fine hybrid accent. He was a welder by trade, with ambitions. He had just returned from Mozambique where he had made a pile from a perlite mine. Back in Jo'burg he was embarking upon this unique enterprise. His staff consisted of Johannes, the little Xhosa foreman, two boys from Basutoland (now Lesotho) and Joseph, a huge Zulu who had large holes in his ear lobes where heavy metal rings had been hung when he was a child. I liked his wide grin and was glad it was he who would be my chauffeur and bodyguard when I went on my rounds. He was proud of being able to drive the battered old Buick, though this was not the only skill Mike had hired him for; he was a heavy-weight boxer, the proud winner of countless contests. Nobody wanted to cross Joe and his skills quelled any fears I might have about the job. Johannes was honey-coloured, small but handsome. He'd been Mike's assistant for some time and the two men had more than a working relationship; they were good mates across the colour bar. Two boys from Lesotho had just been hired so were desperate to impress by their capacity for hard work. They were forever asking us if we wanted tea.

Work, particularly semi-skilled work, was hard to come by if you were black, so if you had it you strove to keep it. All skilled jobs were reserved for whites, though, as in Johannes' case, some blacks were just as good as their white bosses and some were better. So on the Monday morning I went into Mike's small, stuffy office prepared for this new adventure. He explained his plan of action while we sipped mugs of very strong tea. Whites could not sell goods or own shops in the native locations so we had to think in terms of being wholesale suppliers. This is where Mike's entrepreneurial skill in a difficult marketing situation showed up. Diverse varieties of Christianity were encouraged by the government as it was reasoned that it kept the blacks away from politics. Mike's idea was that I should contact as many church leaders as possible, weld them into small groups and persuade them to open small shops which would be stocked with our unique products. Mike had done his homework. He had listed thirty separate sects in small, shabby Nelspruit where we were to run our pilot project.

The following day I set out for Nelspruit, sitting beside the beautiful, hunky, bulky Joseph in the old war horse of a car. I was very excited as I kissed my children goodbye. I had managed to get the special permit necessary to enter a native area, but only just. The young Afrikaner in charge of the office had collapsed with laughter when I told him about the coffin business. It was only granted after I complimented him on his bright blue pullover, saying how well it matched his very blue eyes! The official at the main entrance to Nelspruit, an older and fiercer man, was very suspicious. He bent down, shoving his fat face with its piggy eyes into mine. "What the hell is a bleddy English woman doing here? I've had no big trouble in this place and I don't want any now! You shouldn't go poking your nose around, you bleddy liberal, or should I say commie?" I told him I had no political interest, just a job to do. After exclaiming about the nature of my job, telling me I must be "bleddy bananas", he slowly opened the gate. I knew those little blue eyes would miss very little.

Nelspruit was little better than a shanty town. Half-naked children milled round, playing in the mud, and after a couple of minutes the boldest of them was trailing us, asking, "Tikkie, missus, please?" A tikkie was a small coin worth about five pence. The street stank as there was fetid rubbish everywhere with flies buzzing in my face. Some futile attempts had been made to make a road but it had obviously been abandoned long since, although the left-over bits at least provided stepping stones. Joseph never left my side, taking my arm without hesitation when the going was rough, a gesture for which he could have been arrested in a white area, such was the insanity of South African law.

We turned a corner into something more resembling a street, lined with small houses made from breeze-blocks, perhaps the posh part of town. This was the address of our first church leader, the Reverend Patrice Fulani. His modest house, the vicarage, had a little front garden dominated by a huge bougainvillea, which softened the crudity of the cement blocks. Mr Fulani was at the gate ready to welcome me; he must have got my note as, of course, Nelspruit had no telephones. Though he was small and tubby he had quite a dignified presence. He bade us enter, showing us into his cramped parlour, dominated by a huge radiogram which took up the whole of one wall. It was covered with colourful plasterwork figures, mostly various saints, I presumed, evidently a High Church man or perhaps they were presents from grateful members of his congregation. But, on looking closer, I was taken aback to spy, right in the middle, an almost naked woman with enormous breasts. I recognized her. It was Mae West! A new saint? A large black artificial leather sofa took up much of the remaining space, with a couple of old office-type chairs and a small, scarred coffee table filling up the gaps.

I was bidden to sit on the sofa while my host rammed himself into a chair. He had an easy manner and seemed very enthusiastic about becoming a coffin salesman and he knew of a small empty shop. Before I left I knew I had made a staunch convert. Blue was his favourite colour, so he liked the idea of blue Anglican coffins. After he had given me a list of other ministers with whom he would like to share the coffin shop, I left with fulsome goodbyes. He had mentioned someone who called himself Bishop Sekekune of the New African Zionists, whom he regarded as his sworn enemy. He and his mother, the Prophetess, had founded this new sect: "a devil-inspired thing" as the Reverend Fulani described it.

All agog, I decided this wicked bishop must be our next port of call. Fortunately Joseph knew where he lived – in palatial squalor. It was almost round the corner: a sprawl of inter-linked mud rondavels housing five wives, twenty-nine children, four race horses and two Cadillacs. Joseph's brother had once been one of the flock so I was well informed on the way, as the old car heaved its way through piles of rubbish and mud. The bishop had been given a special permit to visit America, but I was welcomed most effusively by his secretary, Zed, a sinuous, youngish man, who was not slow to see great pecuniary possibilities in this new take on the death trade, always a brisk one in these poor ghettoes. He paused a few seconds when asked about what colour he thought the bishop would favour for his coffins, before asking if we could do them multi-coloured. I felt around in my bag for a rough colour guide Mike had made with its swathes of blue, red, magenta, purple, orange and brown. Zed confirmed that he thought rainbow colours would be most pleasing. He was keen to talk about England, having recently returned from taking part in a religious conference in Brighton. He had liked Brighton, particularly the nightlife, which, being a long way from home, he had allowed himself to visit. Before I left his exuberant company he assured me he knew of a small shop and had minister mates who would be eager to share in this new enterprise. He thought the retail chain we hoped to establish should be known as "Christian Caskets"! In meeting Mr Fulani and Zed, I seemed to have covered the extremes of Christian worship here in Nelspruit, ranging from the ultra-conformity of Mr Fulani's flock to a sect that was known as "devil worship" to other God-fearing folk.

Every day for the next few weeks Joseph took me round to interview prospective shop-keepers. They all seemed keen to join – hardly surprising, given that they were being offered fifty per cent of the profits for "church use", which was of course open to interpretation. It could mean a new concubine for Bishop Sekekune or a new altar cloth for the Reverend Fulani. Every day gave me fascinating new insights into the lives of those others, the great black majority in this extraordinary society.

During these weeks Mike was churning out coffins as if the Black Death was upon us. In an unguarded moment, or perhaps to get at my liberal sentiments, he exclaimed, with a short laugh, "Ach, man, what we need to get business really going is a bonzo riot, here, in Nelspruit – we would be coining it!" I did not laugh. It had not been long since the Sharpeville shootings which had shocked the world, hundreds of innocents shot in the back by riot police. This ill-judged remark might have been merely meant to be humorous but he was so keen to become Businessman of the Year that I suspected in part it came from the heart.

Just as the first shop was about to open, its mainspring, Mr Fulani, had a huge heart attack and fell down dead. I was quite sorry, having become used to this plump, pompous little man who had been such an enthusiastic protégé. Mike, ever the instant opportunist, promptly visited the widow, Naomi, and offered her not only a free coffin, but a free funeral as well. She naturally accepted; funerals were expensive, particularly those of church leaders. Good for business, Mike said; a bit of goodwill. The battered old Buick was tarted up with a lick of paint and transformed into a credible hearse. Joseph borrowed a smart black suit. I wore a dark brown tweed suit, hardly worn since it had long been labelled a mistake. It had come into its own, at last. Mike and I were driven to Nelspruit and dropped off at the small Anglican church, while Joseph went on to collect the widow, the child and the body. The curate, Mr Herate, was most polite to us, but we did get many strange glances during the course of the service from the numerous mourners. Whites were not known to attend black ceremonies in the locations. I was enjoying the beautiful sound of the unaccompanied singing while, I suspect, Mike was busy adding up figures in his head.

Suddenly, with a huge banging the doors were flung open and in crashed six huge white policemen. Blond, burly and red-faced, two of them came up to us, laid heavy hands on our shoulders and made plain the reasons they were there. The sergeant, a big brute, forcing us to turn and look at him, shouted loudly in our ears: "Your interference in native affairs in this location is a contravention of the laws of the state! You are therefore being arrested forthwith." And so we were marched but not handcuffed into another black Buick, a much newer model. We were in shock: I was precipitated into a very spastic state – arms lashing out all over and head shaking so vigorously that I felt my neck might break. Even big bold Mike was sweating with fear. Terrible visions of our possible fate swam before my eyes. The two of us sat huddled together in the back seat like frightened children. We were driven swiftly down the road from Nelspruit and pulled roughly out of the car at Kensington police station, the nearest white suburb to the Southern locations. After signing a form acknowledging our presence in Nelspruit, and emptying bags and pockets, we were shoved into two cells. Mine was a very small, smelly place with no natural light and a dirty floor, its only contents a couple of filthy grey blankets and a big stinking chamber pot. Even now, I can recall the horrible smell of shit and the despair which engulfed me as I sat on the floor and moaned.

After a long miserable while, the door opened and in slid a small, dapper man. He spoke quietly, with a strong Afrikaner accent: "I am detective Jan van de Merve of Special Branch. I want to know exactly what you were doing in Nelspruit. We have good reason to believe you are a journalist working undercover – that cover being a commercial racket involving some churches in that location. All foreign journalists who have no permits, nosing round our native peoples, are assumed to be spies, most especially when they are thought to have been members of the Communist Party." How had he known about my very brief flirtation with the party at university, many years before? But amazement only enhanced feelings of extreme terror and I began to shiver. I felt completely isolated and even longed for Mike.

After another lapse of time I was given some disgusting stew and then I begged to be allowed to phone my husband. Later, a large ugly woman officer ordered me to get up and I was escorted to a telephone. He came immediately; I had never been so pleased to see him. The fact that he worked for a subsidiary of South Africa's best known diamond company, De Beers, was most fortunate. After a couple of hours' intense talk, he managed to convince them that I was not a spy, not even a threatening foreign journalist. I was just a silly little English woman who must learn not to go where she was not supposed to. I couldn't afford to care about this patronising attitude, just as long as I could go home to my family, who had never seemed so dear to me, with my somewhat bemused husband. Later I met Mike, for the last time. He had been released as he knew the brother of the Minister for Sport. Ours had been a working relationship, and, while I did not dislike him, I deplored many of his attitudes.

Back inside the police station I had to hear Van de Merve's valediction. "Lady, any more of your bleddy liberal English games and you will be deported forthwith. You know what that means; you will be put on a plane to England. Go home, like a good woman, and look after your husband and children." I looked contrite, but having regained some spirit, rejoiced in knowing that I had just signed up to teach a group of dissident African students in a night school of dubious political reputation. So I had foiled Van de Merve and his merry men and had slipped through the net.

CHAPTER 14

Teaching across the Colour Bar

Assuming I wasn't going to make coffin-selling my lifetime career, I had already been in touch with a budding organization, the South African Committee for Higher Education, known as SACHED. A handful of liberal-minded university teachers, financed by money from abroad, were intent on building up a scheme which would provide higher education, free of the taint of racist philosophy, for Africans and other non-Europeans: a precarious experiment in the heart of nationalist South Africa.

It was proposed that carefully selected ethnic students should be offered one-to-one tuition in courses geared towards external London University degrees. This plan was devised with the aim of avoiding breaking the law of a land which held it illegal for any white person to teach a class of blacks, though it had nothing to say about the possibility of one white teacher tutoring one non-white student. Also it was realized that London University was well beyond the reach of the law, while any national institution offering degrees beyond the pathetically limited ethnic colleges would be sure to be prosecuted. This brave, far-minded endeavour might well have come to nothing had it not been for a man called Oscar Britzius whose Jewish family had been persecuted and almost extinguished by the Nazis. Mr Britzius had a very successful tutorial college in the centre of town which mostly crammed students (whites of course) for university entrance. When hearing of the plan he came forward and generously offered to make his college available to SACHED on Saturday mornings for a modest fee; unsurprisingly, many Jewish people were among the small white minority who were involved in anti-apartheid movements.

Now there was some money, a venue, a few dedicated souls with teaching skills; all was in place except some suitable students. *The Golden City Post*, the popular township paper, accepted a discreetly worded advertisement which produced over two hundred replies, such was the hunger for proper education. Many applicants were weeded out as they didn't have the minimum qualifications or good enough references. Family circumstances were taken into account and tests of general ability given, also some assessment about their capability to stay the course and their dedication to study under difficult circumstances.

Before I left, after a couple of years, I asked my students to write me brief life histories. These writings, which I still treasure, certainly produced a welter of fascinating material about the lives of young urban Africans during the high tide of apartheid. A few of these essays showed that, in spite of the limitations of township life, a few candidates lived relatively contented lives. Most had parents who struggled hard to give their children as good an education as they could. As one student wrote: "I am happy with my struggling education. I have loving parents, though Father's salary is very low and Mother works hard as a washer-woman to help us." Most were less lucky, especially those who had been rehoused after their land had been appropriated for white occupation: "Home is now a nasty hovel of mud and sacks in the filthiest location I ever saw. People are stabbed and killed each weekend." The most affecting and tender of these comments came from the youngest student, Peter Sekekune: "Mummy is an old lady who has struggled hard as she wants us to be the men and women of tomorrow." But one or two came from families who didn't understand the ambitions of their children. One student wrote: "I was very shocked when my father told me he had organized a job in the mine for me." Luckily, an uncle paid for him to continue his studies.

Though candidates were supposed to have basic qualifications, Peter was an exception, a shy streak of a boy who had had to leave school before taking his exams, as his grandfather had become a banished person as a political suspect. He became our star pupil, together with Thabo Mbeki. Of course, this was my dream work – I wanted to teach but not within the framework of Christian National Education, the established government school system, and was eager to have contact with Africans as equals, outside the master-servant role.

I had four students to begin with, to whom I taught an introductory course in History which would prepare them for A Level equivalent. Being incarcerated in a tutorial cell for an hour a week with each of them, it was inevitable that I should learn something of their home and family life. For them it must have been a strange experience too, most having never known a white person who was not their "baas". With a few of the older students I never managed to penetrate beneath the surface, but with most, I managed to dig out quite a lot about their home-lives. So, in addition to watching them blossom intellectually, I came to appreciate just how tough it was, living between cultures, the lot of urban Africans in an industrialized country which resented their presence while depending on their labour. The conflicting pressures felt in everyday life were summed up very elegantly by Peter, who really had a way with words. He wrote, "The mailed fist of the government bids us to return to the land of our ancestors and to the simple tribal life, but the claws of commerce demand our labour and our money and promise in return that we shall be rich and comfortable. What are we to do?"

I taught Peter for three years. This shy, ungainly youth with a disabling stammer had, initially, very little self-confidence.

He hated any form of violence and it was a wonder that he had survived life in the locations – rough by any standards. He retreated into his studies, ignoring the world around him. His dedication was soon recognized: he was given the first full-time bursary. He lived in our small library, and was reputed to sleep on an empty bookshelf. It was wonderful to see how he developed a capacity for real analytical thought which, allied to his intense love of learning, in most societies would have ensured him an academic career.

Pitso Mphiring, though clever and perceptive, was a very different character. He was small and very black, with deep tribal scars; he moved and spoke very quickly. He could have been described as cocky. His early years had been blighted by violence. He wrote about this. "Late one night my brother came running into the house with blood running out of him. He told us that Daddy had been attacked by four men. He had tried to save him but he was stabbed too. Our beloved Daddy passed away in hospital and my brother became a cripple. Mummy was valiant, and she got work as a washer-woman. We had little food and old clothes but Mummy saved money so that I could go to school. Later I was awarded the only 1st Class African Matric in the whole country. Mummy is glad she struggled to educate me." In spite of this accolade he was not a real scholar, though he was very keen to learn about revolutions, in particular the French Revolution – violent and bloody enough for him! He liked the Russian Revolution too, though he was no Marxist.

Pitso was desperate to become a lawyer, like his hero, Nelson Mandela, who was just becoming a real thorn in the side of the authorities as an astute and fearless advocate for the human rights of the African. Though Pitso in no way rose to the heights of his inspirer, he might very well have done well in his chosen profession, unless he became a victim of the police or location violence, like his father – the likely fate of many, particularly young blacks.

Andrew McIntosh was my only Coloured student. He was

a very good-looking coffee-coloured man, another assiduous student who allowed himself only four hours' sleep so that he was able to write his essays before running for the overloaded train to work at five o'clock. His home was made of brick and they had a radiogram and good rugs on the floor, he told me with great pride. His grandfather, Andrew, had been a Scottish miner from Aberdeen, and, unlike most white men, had supported his black mistress and their son.

Another talented student, who later managed to get to the UK where he graduated from Sussex University, was Thabo Mbeki, who later became Mandela's successor as leader of his country. He was a quiet, self-contained man who came from one of the very few African middle-class families. He carried himself with an easy dignity and seldom laughed. He wasn't my most likeable student, though one knew he had a sense of his own destiny from the first. He certainly had a future, becoming the first Prime Minister after Mandela.

Jo Mshongolo was a large, ungainly, shambling man, with those tribal scars and distorted ear lobes which marked many Zulu men; until he smiled he looked quite forbidding. He was probably the least gifted but showed such perseverance and enthusiasm that I found teaching him a really good experience. For three years before he came to us he had to work in the mines to keep his ill mother and went to the few available classes and read every book which came his way. We were so impressed by his determination that we gave him a place. We were all fond of Jo. If any of the younger ones had a problem Jo would listen. I saw a lot of him as I gave his extra English lessons which he valued. One Saturday morning when he did not turn up I was worried. That evening, glancing through the evening paper, my attention was grabbed by a small heading: "Ammunition found in location yard…native arrested." Not an unusual line in The Star but, on reading on, I saw the "native" was Joseph, accused on the evidence of a twelve-year-old boy and given a twenty year jail sentence. He had obviously been set up, perhaps by those who envied his further education opportunities. The loss of this good man made me understand more about Verwoerd's South Africa than anything I had ever read or heard before. I felt sick at heart; we all mourned him.

Ben Makau, a student I taught occasionally, saw revolution just round the corner. He was bright, likeable and so politically passionate that I feared for his future. He spoke with alarming intensity to me, regarding me as a sort of foreigner, about his plans for the whites, both Afrikaans and English. "We will push the white people into the sea. This is our country. They have no right here. They steal our land and treat us as slaves. They are the outsiders," – his eyes sparkled with rage. Even though I had been given personal exemption, this forthright language made me cower inwardly as I knew it echoed the everyday talk in the locations.

During my time we only managed to recruit one woman student which, of course, said a lot about their status and expectations. Grace Makeba was small, plump and funny. Her aim was to become a domestic science teacher. Although she was no great academic she was a born organiser. She was married with four children but she still managed to arrive on time and set up a soup kitchen which ensured that the neediest students had one decent meal a day. The money which came from well-wishers abroad was well used, not only for basic food but for travel bursaries, and, in one desperate case, a grant for a bed. In spite of these measures the drop-out rate during the first year was high. The juggling between work, family pressures and study was too difficult for some to manage; the discipline and dedication shown by those who managed to continue was remarkable.

After I had been teaching at Britzius for about a year, I heard, through the academic grape-vine, that Wits (University of the Witwatersrand) was looking for a part-time History tutor, so I went for it. A lurking part of me had always been conscious of that might-have-been academic career, so here was a possible opportunity to clamber into the outer portals of the ivory tower. I was offered an interview by return of post!

Professor Marais was an aged, genial Afrikaner, known for good work on early settlement history but also for his life-long absentmindedness. (He had recently left his latest manuscript in a string bag on a train luggage rack.) His department was quite chaotic, and it appeared that his retirement was eagerly awaited by his colleagues, though everyone I met seemed to love him. I stumbled over piles of ancient volumes and trays of old papers to greet the professor, a little old man sitting at his desk which was covered with yet more yellowing manuscripts in no apparent order. This made me feel at home as it reminded me of my own study space at home. "Find yourself a seat, if you can," he said, giving me a twinkly smile. He told me the job entailed not only giving tutorials but leading seminars, and marking numerous essays and end of year exams. Not very exciting but I felt I had put a foot in the door, particularly when he asked me if I had any thoughts about taking a higher degree. As the interview went on I felt the suppressed scholar in me re-emerging, taking me back to those fascinating hours spent in Bishop Cosin's Library in Durham. As I threaded my way through the stuff on the floor, I sort of knew the job was mine. And so it was; a charming hand-written note arrived a few days later offering me the job and apologising for the small money it paid.

Term did not start for two months, thus plenty of time to organise the household round this my new work. I was of course continuing teaching my black students. I found myself wondering how it would be getting involved with young whites, many of whom would probably be passive upholders of the terrible status quo, and what new insights this would give me. I would be teaching across the colour bar, a privilege given to few – though not wanted by many either.

★

The job was quite dull, at least compared to my existing one. I took seminars and tutorials with first year students and marked endless essays, mostly badly written, uninformed and utterly boring. I soon knew why the quality of most of this stuff was so poor. Wits accepted most students with basic qualifications, took their fees, and threw them out at the end of the year. I liked the odd mature student like Norman Levy, who was a political activist; he had had a searing experience with the police: a brave man, one of a pitifully small minority of protesters from among the student body. But the staff in our department were politically aware, many of them subsequently going overseas. They were very friendly and in no way was I made to feel inferior with my status as a sort of academic dogsbody. I made a few good friends, and Hugo and I were often invited to dinner and, notably, to the very Afrikaans wedding of the Prof's daughter, Elise. A mad extravaganza: everyone got wildly drunk and the dancing went on all night. We left at 3am. The work, though unexciting, brought with it a rewarding social life which we had lacked, after falling out over the coffins with our posh cousins in Sandringham. I remember writing a bragging letter to Coops about enjoying lunch with three professors. She responded with a terse postcard message: "What a pity you never learnt to spell 'Professor' correctly!

CHAPTER 15

It's a Boy

At about this time I found I was pregnant once again. Unplanned as usual, though we had made some attempts to stop this one. The Pill was starting to be available, but in a fairly crude form. I was prescribed it but found it had bizarre neurological side-effects, as did many different pills, with my words emerging back to front which of course affected my teaching. So I dropped them and immediately became an expectant mother for the third time in as many years. I continued to teach until the baby was almost due. Peter Sekekune gave me a woolly rabbit, knitted by his mum, which touched me greatly and the students watched my developing shape with interest; most had never seen a pregnant white woman close up!

During this time of course I attended pre-natal sessions at the monumental Queen Victoria Infirmary. There were no scans then, so nothing much was known about the developing child, except if it was alive or not; no foreknowledge about its sex. I have heard so many mums declare that they did not care as long as it was "all right", but I did care: I desperately wished for a boy, after having two daughters. Hugo did not mind, I think. A few obstetricians were engaged in an experiment, which had its origins in the Afrikaans ideal of producing a Super Race. Most of the mothers taking part were the wives of Afrikaans academics and some from their business fraternity. I volunteered to take part, as always up for the new! I don't remember being overly ambitious for my child; curious perhaps.

A very simple procedure was involved. A Hoover-like device was attached to the mother's body which lifted the pressure of the womb from the foetus every few weeks. It was known as "compression". (There was one bed in Guy's Hospital in London where this was practised on request, so it had a small international following, I suppose.) When the birth was imminent the apparatus would be strapped on and, hey presto! The baby would have a much easier ride than usual and the mother less pain.

Every few weeks I wore this machine for an hour. I felt nothing untoward; I don't know about the baby. It was due just before Christmas but that came and went and nothing happened. I was huge, sweaty and uncomfortable; the baby was a big kicker, like my rugby-playing father. After a couple of weeks I was threatened with an "induction", which involved a drug being given to hasten the birth. The next day it happened; after an hour or so of almost painless labour, the baby slid out, a bit blue as the cord had been round the neck, but, at over 9lb, a fine specimen. The Afrikaans doctor, who knew I wanted a boy, kept on repeating, wickedly, "It's a girl, it's a girl!" and then, he shouted, "Ach, man! No, lady, it's a boy!" Hugo, who had been waiting outside, the custom in those days, looked suitably impressed.

We called him Matthew, though had Hugo been on speaking terms with his parents, he would have been known by his other name, Edward. I liked the image the name Matthew conjured up: big, bluff and hearty, with a touch of the soil perhaps. Violet took to him immediately though the reaction of his sisters was somewhat mixed. After we had been back a couple of hours, Sarah, who was just three, in an unguarded moment, lifted him out of his crib and carried him over the polished sitting-room floor before being stopped by me. We wondered where she was intending to take him! Like the others he was a good baby, sleeping from midnight to six o'clock, he fed well, grew rapidly and soon greeted everyone with an irresistible smile.

As a product of the Super Race experiment, every few weeks we were visited by a Super Development Visitor who took various measurements including length and head-girth, tested reflexes and examined physical and mental progress. We were told he was well-advanced in all respects, and was on the path to being a member of the sought-after Super Race. Mrs van de Beer was pleased, but sorry that this Super Specimen belonged to the wrong community. "Ach, man, let's hope Matthew becomes a true South African, a Volk boy." Very unrealistic but we took it as a compliment. How valid the results of this strange experiment were, it's hard to say; Matthew was a very bright child but not given to over-exerting himself, so this temperamental shortfall may well have affected the results.

I stayed at home most of the time, for two or three months, which luckily coincided with the long vacation, while feeding Matthew myself as I had the others. But I continued to teach my beloved black students on Saturdays, only deserting them for about three weeks.

After Matthew's birth I left most of the household organisation to Violet, upgrading her status to house-keeper though, of course paying her extra responsibility money. Her life changed in a more personal way too; her three-year-old daughter, Valerie, came from the Reserves to live with us. As already mentioned, we were breaking the law by allowing this, but the sheer delight shown by Violet, when we told her we would be willing to have Valerie with us, was worth the risk. A broad smile, tears and laughter greeted this news and she immediately asked Jacob, her brother, to fetch her child from the Bantustan in the northern Transvaal. "Madam, I have never been so happy in my whole life. I dream every night about my baby being with me, but I never thought she would come. Thank you." She danced round the kitchen singing, very tunefully, a song from her childhood, a lullaby she told us that her mother used to sing to her. We were all touched by her happiness. Sarah said, "Mummy, I think Valerie and I will be like sisters. It will be nice to have a black sister to play with; Frankie is too little and stupid." Hugo said it was worth the risk to see the joy on Violet's face.

Valerie arrived a week later, looking like a miniature version of Violet, down to the patched shoes tied up with string, though her hair was glorious tangled fuzz, flying free like a ragged black halo. At first she was very shy, she hadn't seen white children before, but after a day or two she and Sarah were rushing round the small garden together, chattering away in their different lingos but nevertheless communicating in ways small children do. All was well for a few months though we were constantly aware of the sharp eyes of the Afrikaner neighbours, and so wishing the hedge between the gardens was a bit higher and the children's voices not so shrill. One Sunday, we were enjoying a brandy and ginger, a favoured South African drink, in the garden, when Violet appeared, grey-faced and trembling, with a weeping Valerie in tow. She had just heard that they were searching our street for native children of female servants. Luckily it was quite a long street and they were working from the top and we were near the bottom, so we had time. Violet was useless for once and Hugo was all important. I was trying to stop the children crying – they were all howling now, sensing our acute anxiety.

Hugo reckoned she must be stowed in our large wardrobe but not of course before he had made air-holes in the back. He got his drill out and made six large holes and, of course, pulled the vast cupboard a few inches away from the wall. I found a huge box of Smarties for the girls which instantly stilled the racket, but there remained the problem of getting poor Valerie to stay in the dark wardrobe until we got the all-clear that the inspector was gone. Violet had mercifully recovered and was able to tell Valerie, in her own way, that this was a funny new game and that part of it was that she should make no noise at all. A new doll with lots of exotic clothes was miraculously found and so, with a small torch, the child was induced to go into the wardrobe while I hovered nervously outside. Violet had to return to her hut as it was her day off – all servants had Sunday off so they could attend church, an example of the government's thoughtfulness about the welfare of native servants!

Sure enough, a short time later, two Afrikaans auxiliary policemen showed up at the front door and politely asked to see the servants' quarters where Violet was quietly sitting knitting. They stayed a few minutes before issuing a statutory warning: "As you are from overseas, we want you to know you will be liable to a fine of £1,000 rand should you have your maid's child or children on your premises. It is our duty, lady, to look round." I held my breath as they wandered through the house and poked their heads into Violet's room. If Valerie had given the ghost of a cry we would have all been done for. But she didn't, and they left. After a few minutes, in case they returned, we opened the wardrobe and Valerie stumbled out clasping her new doll. In the kitchen Violet and I burst into hysterical laughter while Hugo looked on benevolently. When she had recovered, Violet said, "The Lord must have been watching over us, madam, and you, sir, he must have sent you a message about how you could make Valerie safe." Valerie was safe for another few months and Violet, her laughter spent, could not stop thanking us. It was true that we were risking this huge fine by having Valerie around, and of course Violet knew this. A side effect of this unwelcome happening was that we came to regard our Afrikaans neighbours with less suspicion and even began to exchange occasional visits, it being obvious that they had not informed on us, though we reckoned that they must have known about Valerie.

I was very much aware of the privileged life we were leading in this country. But as the months rolled on we were having to ask ourselves, and the few other liberal Brits we knew, the burning question: how could we continue to make this place our permanent home, while being very much aware of the evil treatment meted out to the black majority? I had endless talks with my Irish friend, another teacher, Ruth, about it. Ruth said: "It's almost a case of God versus Mammon. Either we stay, and enjoy having blacks to do the dirty work, lots of sun, and more disposable cash, or we go back to an existence of domestic drudgery, lots of rain, and less dosh, but with our principles more or less intact." What a conundrum, I thought. Could I use my almost complete domestic ineptitude, my wangly arms, as a get-out clause?

As the political scene worsened, with terrible cruelties inflicted on those suspected of treason, which here included any kind of protest, and more and more laws being passed further restricting the rights of "the natives", we began to consider seriously our option: going home. I was very nervous about how I would manage the three young children and a difficult, undomesticated husband. And then, bingo, I was once again pregnant. This helped us make up our minds as, if we were to let this baby see the light of day, we would have to stay, so I had a medical termination, and we set about leaving, with many regrets – the loss of the unborn child, the relative hardships about to be faced, and of course our work and friendships.

Sarah and Frankie in South Africa 1962

Matthew with Violet 1962

CHAPTER 16

Home Again

So our African years came to an end. For Hugo, who had never worked elsewhere, I know the prospect of leaving Africa meant great sadness. As weeks passed and terrible abuses of power became ever more blatant, and yet more cruel and idiotic laws were passed, we thought we had made the right choice, but it took two events to confirm our decision.

Sarah, who had just started nursery school, came home one day and told us that her friend Natalie had said, "All black people smell bad. That's why they have to live outside." Sarah said, "Violet and Valerie don't smell, so there." Natalie didn't want to play with her any more – a real shot against the bows. How could we let our children be exposed to such views day in day out?

And then there was the phone call early on a Sunday morning. An odd time, I thought, as I stumbled out of bed to answer it. I almost fell over on hearing the heavily accented tones of a certain Lieutenant Van De Merve asking, or really ordering, me to attend his office in Marshall Square (Police Headquarters) on Monday at 4pm. That this policeman made the call himself rather than using his secretary made it all the more frightening. Hugo said: "I expect it's just to wish us bon voyage," but I was scared; my body, as always when I was upset, went into manic mode, which was particularly difficult as I had to work on Monday morning. With flailing limbs and in desperate heart I took a cab to Marshall Square. It was all over in a few minutes. The policeman, another blond Boer, said, "It has come to my notice, Mrs Antonia Peake – and we have been observing you for some time, as we know you hold certain views – that you are engaged in an activity which we consider inappropriate and possibly illegal. It is understood that you are teaching non-whites in a school which is under surveillance. We do not need people like you, immigrants, to interfere in any way with our system of education. If you continue to abuse this country's hospitality, I am warning you, lady, there may be consequences, which would not be good for you or your family."

After a few more political platitudes, he got up and leant over me, so closely that I could smell his over-sweet aftershave, saying, "There's no place for people like you here. Make no error, we will continue to keep our eye on you. Lady, take it from me, go home."

Although I had expected much worse, the message was clear, and of course the decision we had already made was sharply reinforced. It didn't have the éclat of a definite deportation but was enough for us to put our house on the market the very next day and hurry our departure plans.

★

We arrived after an unremarkable voyage at Southampton in mid-November. The children had all caught a bug just before we landed so were unusually subdued. We were met by my old school friend Dilla with her new husband Michael. We stayed with them in their lovely old manor house for two weeks: a great boon, as we were all very shattered by the transition, the greyness and gloom of the English winter and, of course, the loss of Violet. I struggled with the old-fashioned cloth nappies we used then, sometimes pricking tender little tummies with large cruel safety-pins, but at least while we were here my unpractised domestic skills did not have to extend to actual cooking or, Heaven forbid, cleaning anything except children – this was hard enough. Matthew was particularly upset by the lack of sun. He would ask, plaintively, a dozen times a day: "Mum, why is it raining?" It wasn't, but he took the cloud-laden skies to mean it was.

The honeymoon fortnight we spent being looked after by Dilla and Michael in their well-ordered household was followed by a seemingly endless period with Dad at The Dorretts while Hugo looked for work. The contrast could not have been starker. Only the weather remained the same. The old farm was even more derelict than I had remembered. The shabby, unhinged gates of the barn leant against the wall; the veranda which had been blown down in a gale, two years before, had never been replaced; all that remained were the cracked wooden supports, with the glass all gone. The poor old hill-top house was now completely unshielded from the elements. As we drove into the yard memories of my "gap year", spent in this horrible place, overwhelmed me, though of course I managed to greet Dad with genuine warmth. I think the old man was not entirely enthusiastic about this great family invasion, but he put a good face on it. He really liked Hugo; that shared bottle of whisky, with which the two men had sealed the marriage deal, not so long ago, had been a good investment.

Hugo and I were given the guest room with its twin army surplus iron beds and horse-hair mattresses, torn cotton yellow curtains, scarred old chest and small built-in cupboard, and of course, no heating. The kids shared the huge back room, like ours but with bare floor and no curtains and badly cracked window panes. But there were plenty of those coarse grey army blankets and some new slippery nylon sheets – a concession to cheap modernity.

Very soon the bad memories were joined by the horrors

of present realities: the cold (no heating except in the squalid kitchen); three mewling children, two still in nappies – Frankie was a late developer in this respect; no fridge, still only the bashed up meat safe in the leaking larder; no washing machine, only a back-breaking old sink in the scullery; no means of drying clothes or nappies; but above all, an overwhelming consciousness of my own hopeless domestic incompetence. As for Hugo, to begin with it was beyond him, but he soon rallied, seeing that something must be done if we were to survive. He went to the local town, Chepstow, and returned with an electric clothes drier which would also heat the children's bedroom, a small heater for our room, packets of disposable nappies, a large bottle for Dad and a bunch of chrysanthemums for me. A pleasant girl from the village, called Rita, was hired to do the washing, and Dad lit a fire in the large drawing room with its tattered wallpaper, lighting surrounded with grandiloquent rings of stags' antlers, a huge Welsh dresser with its blue Swansea plates, the high Cromwellian chest, covered with silver cups won by Dad in his athletic past, a Deuddam (an old Welsh oak food cupboard), and a huge, squashy sofa which he had bought for Mum when she returned from the sanatorium, which, of course, she never did; a sad reminder. I noticed a small recent leak in one corner was gradually eroding plaster and paper even more; the smell of damp was always around. Although things became a little more manageable, with Sarah going to the village school and Rita taking Frankie and Matthew for walks in the afternoon, while I threw myself down on the lumpy bed for an hour, life was still fraught. Dad showed me, with great glee, the huge sack of swedes he had stowed in the larder, which he served up nearly every day with the mutton stews which were his speciality – about his only one. In the middle of the table there was a huge bottle of some noxious commercial mixture labelled "Dad's Sauce", a jokey name we thought, but the only concession to variety of flavour!

After a few days the ancient drains got blocked up with the new paper nappies and Dad, who had shown remarkable restraint till now, started shouting at me, just as he used to. "God, woman, you've blocked the bloody lav! Putting those nappies down it like that. Malpas will have to unblock the damn thing, and these days he costs a fortune. You bloody bluestocking, even now you haven't grown an ounce of common sense! You always were stupid...should have stayed put, where you didn't have to do anything practical." I was beginning to think perhaps he was right, and even to yearn for the place we had left. But I said, "If you hadn't let the house go to wrack and ruin and got some decent domestic appliances, about which you know nothing, life might have been a lot easier... The place is absolutely freezing." Hugo was out job hunting, or it might have been more muted. I agreed of course to pay the plumber, but, as it turned out, the lawn had to be dug up as the ancient pipes had burst over its whole length. Of course we were responsible for this damage too, in Dad's eyes, and found ourselves paying for the renewal of almost the entire sewage system. When he added to this the cost of extra electricity, Calor gas, hot water and all the mess made by the kids, which meant Polly, his cleaner, had to work an extra hour, the bill was astronomical. Hugo, who had a laid-back attitude to money, particularly in this instance, as I had said I would finance the family until he got work, told Dad we would settle up. (Those pre-marital ill-gotten gains came in useful in times like these.)

As time went on, the kids seemed to be adjusting well enough; Matthew had stopped moaning about the rain and they all enjoyed playing with the remaining animals, chasing the hens, and peering at the new kittens in the barn, while Hugo was getting good feedback from his job applications, but I was still feeling very adrift. Firstly, there were the physical hardships, and though I tried to look after the children I found it all so hard. True, I managed to do most of the basics, though essentials, like helping them clean their teeth, I found most difficult. True, I could read them fairytales and tell them stories, but I found them all just so physically exhausting even though I had the afternoon rest. When I hear about how very demanding children can be, night and day, I realise how good ours were, bless them, but I had never had to care for them full time, even in normal civilized conditions. Dad, though he had been so good with me as a baby, all those years ago, had forgotten how to communicate with the very young, and, although he did not quite subscribe to the old "should be seen but not heard" school of thought, his patience was tried with Matthew crooning endless little ditties to the kittens. He loved those little tabbies and would spend hours with them, but his persistent droning got on the old man's nerves so much that he took the animals back to the barn, which meant that the poor boy spent too much time in this freezing place; it had lost its main doors and their remains swung uselessly from their broken hinges.

Dad obviously preferred the girls and they both got away with things that brought his wrath down on their small brother. The old man had lived alone for so many years, it was not surprising that this family invasion bothered him. On looking back, I think he could have been much more difficult. Mind you, the money he charged for sheltering us must have gone some way towards reconciling him. As already shown, money meant a lot to Dad. I think his insecurity about it, which led to his meanness, probably stemmed from childhood. His widowed mother had to manage her large family on very little, her praiseworthy priority being "Education, education, education" even for the girls meant there was not much dosh left over for lollipops.

A couple of months crawled by, and winter turned to spring elsewhere, but it took its time to reach our Welsh hilltop; no buds, still the odd flurry of snow, and although we piled on the army surplus blankets (Dad's supply seemed inexhaustible), the children still complained about the cold nights. By today's standards we would surely have ranked as a deprived family, and even then, when many people had fridges, twin tub washing machines and cheerful gas fires, life at The Dorretts was far from that experienced by the average British household in the middle sixties.

Though the kids were surviving, after a few weeks I started to feel desperate, barely coping, haunted by past experiences of existence here. One night I had a blackout and fell downstairs. Dr Miller said he thought it was a sort of seizure and an appointment was made to see a neurologist in Bristol. In the meantime this good-looking, charming doctor called round most days, ostensibly to see how I was although we also had much good talk about many things quite unconnected with my health, like life in South Africa and particularly my brush with authority there.

Ruby, the friendly owner of the village pub, said I should watch it as he had "a reputation"! These visits cheered me up but I was continuing to wonder how we could have ever thought of leaving South Africa, longing for this dreadfully difficult interlude to end.

Hugo had a few job offers, and decided to accept the one made by a large steel company near Cardiff. This caused Dad to make an extraordinary offer. He asked us if we would like to buy The Dorretts for a knock-down price; he would move into the barn cottage, a tiny, two-roomed place with no proper bathroom or kitchen. "No, thank you," I said firmly. What a diabolical idea! I could see where Dad was coming from, all too clearly. A dear daughter on his doorstep to help with whatever old age would throw at him, a son-in-law for masculine company, and grandchildren to make him feel like a patriarch, and of course to do little jobs like collecting the eggs, shutting the hens up and feeding the cats! Hugo quite liked the idea until I stamped my foot and said I would rather die. Dad was surprised and very disappointed; he had never understood how much I hated the place.

The report from the very understanding neurologist I saw in Bristol said that any major stress, such as moving house, might cause a kind of spastic breakdown, meaning the usual dysfunctional muscle pattern would be exacerbated for a time and this might result in another seizure; the fact that we had not only moved house but country as well and in doing this I had had to cope with a much more arduous life, perfectly explained the blackout or seizure, as he called it. He advised Hugo that we should not move again for at least fifteen years. (We were to up sticks again in six months!) Later on in life when I experienced a few more extreme situations like deaths and divorces, as well as many house-moves, I was glad of this explanation.

Hugo settled into his new job and we decided to live in Cardiff. Delighted to be returning to the city of my birth, I set about finding a house, which I did in double-quick time, desperate to leave The Dorretts with all its harsh memories. By this time I think Dad was almost as keen to see us off and return to peaceful solitude as we were to go.

I found much to like about this new life in Cardiff: friendly people, a lovely little school down the road for the girls, and some interesting out-of-house opportunities, as I intended to get back to work or further study just as soon as possible. I thought about some further training in social work or, of course, teaching. I did some volunteer work for the Spastic Society, talking to parents of children with cerebral palsy, trying to encourage and explain. This was interesting work but not enough. I wanted a proper job. If I was serious about getting a post in a school, I was told about the Welsh way to go about it by Adam Parry, the nice gardener who cut our lawn.

His uncle, Edwin, was on the city council; Uncle Ed's sister, Auntie Gladys, was Head of St Fagans School for Girls. He said as he put the mower away, "If you like I could arrange for you to meet Uncle Edwin, a very nice helpful guy... I'm sure he would be pleased to help you." And so he set up a meeting between me and his uncle on the City Hall steps at eleven o'clock on a certain morning. I went, though I hadn't really made up my mind about what I wanted. I was just so curious about the way things were arranged, at this time, in my native land. I approached the steps with care and, lo and behold, there was this small tubby grey man, with a bulging briefcase, standing at the top, obviously waiting for someone. "Good morning, Mrs Peake," he said, smiling. "I hear your father is Colonel Price who commanded the Fifth Welch Regiment in the barracks here, a few years back. Is that really so?" I nodded; he smiled broadly before going on to tell me what a wonderful influence Dad had been as commander of the training centre just up the road. "Your dad turned so many of our Valley boyos into men. I know a few of them, and one, I have to tell you, is actually serving with me on this very council – now, if that isn't something! I would be only too pleased to help Colonel Price's daughter in any way I could – a good man, your father, and a brave soldier, highly decorated in the First World War, and I heard he got an OBE for the way he ran our barracks. As I said, he was a good man, your father, and a good Welshman." Jesus, Dad's ears must have been burning! After enjoying a good cup of coffee with the councillor in the posh Town Hall café, I thanked him for his interest and said I would be in touch. A classic example of Town Hall nepotism! But I was secretly proud to have old Dad acknowledged as having been a force for good.

Though this had been a kite-flying operation – I was not quite ready to decide on which way to go – I now knew why the backs of many application forms for Welsh public service posts were stamped in heavy lettering "Canvassers will be disqualified"! This exercise turned out to be completely theoretical, as after a mere six months Hugo decided the Welsh steel industry wasn't for a Home Counties boy like him, and accepted a job in West London in the wine trade. I was sad to leave the city of my birth, where I had been prepared to settle and had already made some interesting friends.

I took a day return ticket to London in order to spend a few hours finding a suitable house. I had an idea that Richmond might be an interesting place to kick off from, though houses here were far too expensive, so I concentrated on the neighbourhood. I looked at three properties and bought the last one. This was near Twickenham, in a small triangular place called Hampton Hill, though the hill was never located. It was a large detached late-Victorian pile, attractive, but not without some basic faults as we were to discover, though considering my limited buying time it was a good bargain.

But as that good neurologist had predicted not so long ago, the immense stress of moving, actually moving twice within a single year, was to affect my spasticity badly. Within a few weeks of the house-buying expedition, my back pain became much more intense and I could hardly walk. The hospital in Cardiff trussed me up in a plaster cast which lessened the pain, but caused me to lose so much muscle tone that even stumbling along became more difficult, even with a stick. Our kind Welsh neighbour helped with the move.

★

When we first moved I spent a lot of time lying on the floor, surrounded by children and toys, reaching for the brandy bottle by the late afternoon; thankfully, I never learned to like the taste – it might have added alcoholism to my other problems.

The kindly old doctor round the corner told me about the nursery round another corner for Frankie and Matthew and a small school down the road for Sarah. I came to regard Dr Hogbin as a friend; he was so helpful and sensible.

We were not so lucky in the local woman we found to take the children out in the afternoons. Mrs Hawkins was a fervent Jehovah's Witness though we did not hold this against her, though after a while it was clear the kids did not like her. Years later, Frankie told me she used to smack their bare bottoms in the park, and that her son, Paul, exposed himself to her. Such things were still too difficult to tell parents. I never knew about this.

Before long we decided to find an au pair. The agency sent us Monika, a plump Austrian girl from a small village, who loved children; she also made delicious Apfelstrudel. She rescued us, staying for four years. Monika really looked after us, and rode the family rows in robust fashion. Hugo's temper did not improve with the years; he once called her "a fat cow". She stood her ground, saying, "You are not so thin yourself, Mr Peake!"

So, while Hugo flitted from job to job, his innovative skills in the early computer age enabling him to do this, I wondered, once again, about the best route back to work. My walking remained bad and the back pain, which I have never really entirely lost, persisted, so I continued to drag my weary old carcase around.

Again, dear Dr Hogbin rescued me by nagging me to register as a disabled person, telling me there would be substantial advantages, particularly when I got a job. I hated the idea of being labelled, but was persuaded to pocket my pride when the good doctor said he would back an application for an invalid car which, if successful, would make going to work much easier, and life in general, as the house was a good step from both station and shops. Yet, in my inner self, my desperation to pass for "normal" was so ingrained that despite the lure of that car I might not have gone for disabled registration if I had not had such respect for that doctor.

And then, enter Charlotte Gaffron, without whose help I might have led a much more limited life, possibly becoming really crippled all too soon. I learned about her and her remarkable skills on the local grapevine, after I had made various forays into the world of private medicine – having given up on the NHS with their horrible plaster casts and Victorian corsets, I had suffered sessions of traction, a kind of mediaeval stretching torture, and been offered fairly radical back operations by a maverick Cypriot surgeon. Charlotte was a medical gymnast from Berlin who had settled in London in the early thirties as the partner of the well-connected Ursula Scott-Monteith who lived on the fringes of the Bloomsbury set. During the next ten years Charlotte had seen to the aches and pains of these august intellectuals, and, as she was multi-lingual, well-read and into intelligent talk, she became a welcome guest at the dinner tables of many of her clientele.

Then came war; as a German national she was interned in a camp on the Isle of Man. Being Charlotte, though this was devastating, she made the best of it, but she must have greatly missed her lover, Jean, and all her Bloomsbury contacts.

After the war she and Jean set up home in Notting Hill Gate, then a much more mixed area. Though she was now in her seventies she continued to work, giving exercise classes as well as seeing patients. I hobbled into her room on my stick. She sat on the wide window sill, smoking, a tall spare woman, slightly hunched, observing my every move. To me, she looked incredibly ancient, wrinkled deep in time, but instinct told me she was kind and clever, though not quite the miracle worker I was convinced was necessary. When she had examined me, she retired to her window seat, took out another cigarette, and said, "Come to see me twice a week for six months, do the exercises twice every day, and you will be able to throw that stick away." I almost believed her, her slight German accent adding an authenticity to her words.

And so we worked together, treating it as a joint project. Of course I knew the cerebral palsy was lifelong but, as the weeks went on, my muscles grew stronger, the pain lessened, and one triumphant Sunday afternoon I threw that bloody walking stick into a deep pond in the local park. After a few months I was able to walk as well as before, the pain only came sometimes and I knew that dear Charlotte, though not a miracle worker, had kept her word; I was much better and well equipped to face the world outside. I went on seeing her at intervals for several years.

Some time after we moved in, the Tukituyus came to live with us. As we had spare space upstairs – a small in-house flatlet – knowing how desperately difficult it was for black people to find accommodation, we decided to ask the British Council for a couple of African students. On interviewing us and seeing the rooms they asked us if we would perhaps consider a Fijian family with two small children instead. What a great idea, we both said.

They arrived on a wet Sunday afternoon, somewhat bedraggled as they had walked from the station, smiling tentatively, while they put down their heavy suitcases in the hall. Marcus was an engineering student at Brunel University, a small wiry man with amazing hair. Hannah was much taller, with a long grave face and a lovely gentle smile – a missionary's daughter, we learned. The children, Rachel and Sarah, five and seven, looked shyly around, their fingers in their mouths, hiding behind their hair, at what was to become their new home. Sarah, the elder one, had huge serious eyes and long fuzzy plaits, while Rachel, with her wide grin, seemed very soon to feel at home; she turned out to be the "wicked little demon" she was dubbed by her parents, but we all came to love her and her big sister.

They settled in quickly. Hannah, who had a natural grace and an intuitive intelligence, was as much an asset to me as their Sarah and Rachel were to our children. We were very sorry to say goodbye to them when they went home after two years. We continued to house British Council students, mostly Africans, for many years – this being one of the few issues on which Hugo and I were at one!

★

Soon after, I heard the Government was allotting me an invalid car: the name rankled, but the reality of the mobility it would give me gave me great hope. In a few weeks it arrived on the forecourt, complete with a nice-looking young man who showed me how to drive it. The turquoise-coloured vehicle, which was like a three-wheeler motor-bike, made of fibreglass with tiller steerage, was very noisy and had a top speed of seventeen miles per hour...but for me it was as good as a Ferrari!

After Graham Hill, the racing driver, tried one, he pronounced it lethal, as it turned over so easily. A few years later they were taken off the road, but I loved the thing as it gave me the independence I yearned for at that time. As well as being crucial to my quality of life, it was fun. When going into London, I was able to nip in and out of the traffic, squeezing through narrow gaps, causing mayhem, hardly by speed but through excessive vulnerability! Once, I became caught up in the inner lane on the roundabout at Admiralty Arch in the middle of London where there were five streams of rushing traffic. I went round and round for what seemed like hours, terrified to do a left turn into what looked like certain death... At last, taking a huge breath, I made a break for it, shattered but alive. I parked in a side street and, crying, shouted out loud, "Oh, my God, you did not forsake me in my hour of need!" –

me, a much vaunted atheist, but remembering a key verse from my school days. I didn't do central London roundabouts again.

*

Monika was in charge of the domestic front, the children were all settled in various schools, I was as fit as I would ever be, with only intermittent pain and, with my new little car, knew it was obviously time to get back to work.

CHAPTER 17

Getting Back into Gear

My first workplace was somewhat off course, but not altogether, on looking back at my African adventures in the coffin trade. I took a share in a small stall in the antiques market in the Portobello Road with Shirley, a South African friend. I had successfully applied to Garnett College to do a teacher training course in further education, so this detour into "bygones" was a temporary activity. I made intensive use of my trike; two days a week I rushed round buying "collectibles" as they were known in the trade then, penetrating dingy warehouses along the lower reaches of the Thames, which had a very Dickensian air about them: ill-lit and sinister with smells of damp, decay and of something less tangible, ancient ill-doings perhaps. I would peer through the gloom, imagining I might encounter Fagin round the next corner. But of course, while being a bit scared, I really relished the novelty of it all; it felt like a trip on a fairground ghost-train. In any case it was a wonderful release from the dull domestic round where my clumsiness frustrated and angered me, making me manhandle or drop things, although I did sometimes produce, with great effort, an edible cake on Sundays which the children called "Mum's guilt cake". Of course by this time we had Monika, so it was perhaps more the sheer joy of getting out, meeting people, and embracing new situations in the wider world.

The Portobello market was a kind of mutual Mecca; tourists loved it, thinking they were getting amazing bargains, and sellers loved it too, knowing they were making big profits, fleecing poor ignorant buyers. I dealt in a range of small metal objects, from pretty antique silver spoons to old-fashioned tourist tat. Sometimes I found a piece I liked, a Victorian cruet set or a bracelet. I spent time studying silver hallmarks and knew something about most of my wares. Many dealers appeared to be sort of upmarket rag and bone men, knowing and caring little about what they were selling. This was disappointing as I had hoped to learn about all sorts of bygones in between talking up my goods and selling them.

Apart from doing over those dreadful warehouses, I had to get up to Notting Hill by 7am on Saturdays, to catch the vans coming down from far flung places like Lincolnshire and East Anglia, with their loads of old stuff, and to make sure no one else had moved into our small pitch, always a possibility in this decidedly rough trade. There was the noise – raucous voices ramming your eardrums, often raised in angry argument, the roar of incessant traffic crawling down Portobello Road and the fragmented English of foreigners trying to beat you down – all part of the game, but wearing. Cash would run through my fumbling fingers; I would be forced to scrabble frantically around in the gutter for dropped coins, chivalry being in short supply here. Once I had a real run-in with a bearded old beatnik whose knick-knack stall was next to ours. I had noticed him giving us odd, quite venomous glances from time to time, but thought little of it. One Saturday, I tripped over the kerb and knocked over one of his ramshackle shelves. After easing myself up I apologised, but this was the moment he had been waiting for. He went off into a real rant, his small eyes glinting with anger. "You fucking ugly posh bitch, what the 'ell you doing 'ere? Serve you right if you'd broke your leg instead of upsetting me stuff!"

Six months was enough of the huckster's life and in any case it was time to go to college, a retreat into the familiar.

The children were all at school now and Hugo had found a steadier job. The household continued to be run with Teutonic precision by the fabulous Monika; it was time to start serious work. We had sent four-year-old Matt to a small private school down the road. At the end of his first term he came home, threw his cap on the floor, and said, "Mum, I am not going back to that horrid school. I'm too young to do homework. Mum, I want to go to Carlisle. I know they don't have to do homework there and they play proper games like football." (Carlisle was the local primary.) We conceded. Matt always seemed to know exactly how he wanted to run his own life. Perhaps this was an effect of the strange Afrikaner birth experiment I had been part of, at the Queen Victoria Hospital in Johannesburg, or maybe genetic.

This was to be my lotus year. Garnett College was a strange institution, attached to London University at the time, which gave it a kudos it didn't perhaps altogether deserve. It trained people from varied backgrounds to teach in Further Education: cooks, retired sailors, hairdressers, secretaries and engineers, with a sprinkling of graduates. The academic standard was not exacting, the work hardly arduous, the hours short; plenty of time for enjoyment between lectures and occasional seminars. The college was set in the grounds of the Alton council estate, which had been the cause of much controversy as it had been created by chopping off a huge swathe of Richmond Park. It was all very spacious and green and there was even a Henry Moore sculpture to gladden the eye just outside the college grounds.

The staff were mostly ex-teachers; some, it was said, had been "retired" to Garnett rather than selected on merit. I made a lifelong friend of my tutor, Justin, an English tutor, a bright but troubled man, whose wit and learning were perpetually undercut by self-deprecating comments. Later, I learned that he was nine when his mother, married to a Methodist minister, had been sent to prison for going through the coat pockets in the church cloakroom while her husband was preaching. This explained much about him: a kind, intelligent but damaged man.

We students spent many hours in the local pub or sitting outside it in the sun. I wish I could say we were mulling over the contents of our lectures; most unlikely. We learnt most through teaching practice, the most valuable part of the course. I was assigned to the engineering department of a local college where I was faced with rows of bored-looking plumbing apprentices whom I was supposed to enthuse with a love of "Cultural Studies". On my first day a big bluff lad shouted out: "Miss, you goin' to show us a boring old film then tell us what it's about?" After that I only showed them a couple of films which I chose carefully for their relevance.

I remember playing a lot of word games, getting them to write on the board for me, keeping their attention most of the time, though the odd one would sometimes fall asleep. They were day-release students who spent the rest of the week engaged in more hands-on activities, like unblocking drains or replacing toilets. I was very glad they seemed to take my difficulties for granted – but then teachers were regarded as an odd lot anyway. Are they nowadays? I don't know... Sometimes we had a good laugh together, me and my boys; even this was quite gratifying, given that the course was mostly regarded, by those on it, as a waste of time. But I found the experience quite valuable, being chucked in at the deep end.

Apart from the qualification gained, Garnett for me was like a year off: fun-time, between the horrors of full time domesticity and the world of work. I revelled in the company, men and women; for some it was definitely a time on the spree! Most students lived in as they came from all over the country. Long-term staff would take bets on the divorce rate for the current year; dodgy marriages were put under threat and even

solid ones sometimes came unstuck. Mine didn't, though I
didn't say no to a bit of a flirt in the pub! There was Steve who
used to give me lifts, christened by my rude kids, Jelly Belly
Whiskers. No temptation there, he looked like a plump walrus,
with his pot belly and droopy moustache. He did, however,
over the course of the year make hopeful suggestions, like
"What about it? Why don't we stop off in Bushy Park for a bit?"
I quite liked being told I was a handsome woman but, though
I really enjoyed his company, and of course the lifts, the idea of
a roll in the grass with him was very unappealing. His wife was
pretty and bright so I found this invitation mystifying. Had it
been the stunningly attractive ex-marine, the story just might
have been different!

I had never felt less of an oddity; not being made to feel
"the other" I found very liberating. For the first time ever I
was starting to be able, occasionally, to talk about my spasticity,
in response to the occasional sympathetic question. But
there was one bad incident, which lingers in my mind. A
lecturer, Miss Amelia Jones, an acid woman, whose seminars
I had found useless, and therefore skipped, turned up as my
exam invigilator. (Separate invigilation because I typed.) She
remarked, as she walked in: "It is not as though you are blind
or deaf, you are really abnormal, aren't you?" The surge of
energy produced by my diverted anger may have helped me to
write some good stuff; as my tutor, dear Justin, told me later,
my papers were among the most focused. My time at Garnett
had given me much more than a diploma – it had given me
back my self-confidence by playing to my strengths, after time
spent struggling in the domestic ditch. Also I had found a
new and very special friend, Valerie. Valerie was a generously
built woman, about my age, not a bobby-dazzler, but kind and
straightforward with a perceptive mind, who was a fellow Real
Reader. We became very good buddies almost at once; she
lived with a charming lackadaisical artist called Tom in West

Hampstead. The first time I really mourned anyone in my life was when she died a few years later: a terrible death from lung cancer. Visiting her most days in the Royal Marsden, after work, I watched her die, struggling in unbearable pain as the morphine stopped working long before her next dose was due. As she frantically tore off her wig and clothing, her agony was unforgettable. "Tell that bloody nurse to give me my injection, please, please, Antonia!" Her pleading words are unforgettable. Of course the bloody nurse had her orders – only one dose every four hours – and so I would have to leave her, her voice ringing in my ears, driving my trike home, getting stuck in traffic over Putney Bridge, seeing through a mist of tears. Poor, dear, brave Valerie. She was only forty-four. I have never stopped thinking about her: the cruelty of Fate.

★

My first job was in Bermondsey, a long way from our West London suburb. The small college was housed on the top floor of a Victorian primary school, sited between a tannery and Sarson's vinegar factory, and so a rich mix of smells hit me as I got off the bus on my way to the interview. Ninety stone steps had to be climbed before I finally arrived. In spite of the stinks, the steps and the shabby, almost derelict building, or perhaps because of them, I sort of felt at home here. The work was varied but not arduous, teaching mostly mature students O Level History, Sociology, and Religious Knowledge. The other teachers were a very odd assortment; for many of the men, teaching seems to have been a last resort, as at that time a teaching qualification was not required by Further Education colleges. At the last moment I was asked to take a class in British Constitution, considered an easy option at O level. I was faced by six Greek Cypriots, six Turkish Cypriots, five Pakistanis, three Indians, two Nigerians, and one lone Briton. These days this mix would be the norm but, back then, immigrants were fewer; it was just beginning to become a political hot potato, and Enoch Powell was about to make his landmark "Rivers of Blood" speech. This rich racial diversity gave me something to meddle with. I arranged small group discussions between Greeks and Turks, Pakistanis and Indians, and the Cockney lad with the Nigerians. At least they had to talk together; though I doubt there was any long-term change in their social attitudes. And then I tried to lighten this dreary subject, also giving it more meaning, by taking my students on outings to Parliament, County Hall, the Public Records Office, and best of all, the Old Bailey. I hadn't checked the cases and we ended up in a courtroom where a woman brothel-keeper was in the dock; she was questioned about every detail of her activities. This was by far the most popular expedition, particularly as my students were mostly male. One cheeky Cypriot said, "Antonia, why we not going there every week instead of sitting here? ..Quite boring, we learn more there than here... More interesting!"

The college was fairly chaotic, run by an elderly woman, Miss Hudson, reputedly an advanced alcoholic. She decided the library should be shut for repairs a month before the O level exams. Great timing! My sociology class, mostly mature and home-grown, whose political awareness had risen throughout the year, got up a petition, made posters, wrote letters to County Hall, and even arranged a meeting of the college governors on a Sunday. The result: the library doors swung open, repairs were postponed and they were taken down the pub and treated as heroes.

My very favourite student was a Turkish Cypriot called Kassim Ali. His English was so bad at the start that I thought him a doubtful exam candidate, particularly as he worked night shifts in a toy factory supporting his divorced sister and her child, giving him little studying time. But Kassim, the seventh son of a landless peasant, was bright and persistent, apart from being beautiful, which I suppose cannot really be left out of the equation! His written English showed amazing improvement with every essay but nevertheless his self-confidence lagged behind his attainment.

By the end of the year I had to take him out to lunch to the local greasy spoon to drum into him how important it was that he continue his studies by taking A levels at a neighbouring college. It was worth raising a few sniggers in the staff room. He listened to me over baked beans on toast. Seven years later I got a letter from him, which I still have, saying, "I think you will be pleased to hear that I have just been awarded a doctorate from the LSE. I thank you with all my heart for all the encouragement you gave me to continue with my education." I was very excited by this extraordinary achievement, particularly as it was followed up by an invitation to a celebratory feast in Whitechapel where he shared a flat with his sister and nephew. It was in one of those gloomy old tenement buildings, long gone, another trip into Dickensian territory. But the sitting space was draped with vast multi-coloured curtains, hanging from the centre of the ceiling, making it feel as if it was an exotic Arabic tent. And what a feast was laid out on the ground. Of course we ate sitting on floor cushions, not easy for me, but I managed. The wonderful flavours of this succulent, colourful middle-eastern meal were like nothing I had ever tasted. Besides which, I felt very honoured to have been invited. During the next few months we met and went out to the theatre several times; at the end of the evening he would kiss me gently on the forehead. I think I was a little in love with my beautiful Turk, but he was Muslim, and had, on account of his advanced education and resulting social poise, become virtual head of the Turkish Cypriot community in London. So, 'twas but a fantasy. But I was so very proud of him. My trophy student.

At first I was frustrated by the low level of teaching, but I soon realized that there were compensations as I had more time and energy to help these students, on an individual basis; as indicated, many were very recent immigrants, while others had left school some years before, previously labelled as slow or reluctant learners. The challenge and interest lay here, in exploring, hopefully in a non-intrusive way, their very diverse backgrounds. I had my own last-ditch battle to fight, an unexpected one. After being appointed a full-time lecturer and starting work, I got a nasty letter from County Hall telling me they had turned me down on medical grounds. I was furious. I was better qualified than almost all the staff at this small college, and I had been working full time for three months. After appealing to my union, doing some astute networking and managing to make the Chief Medical Officer giggle, I got County Hall to reverse their decision, but I had to have annual health checks, a small price to pay, though the whole business did nothing to quell my lifelong issues with authority and officialdom in general. But I was part of the world again! I left this small college to seek higher level work, continuing to teach for the next ten years, in various institutions, but I never forgot the joy of working in that small crumbling place in Bermondsey.

Enjoying end of term party

CHAPTER 18

Break Up

Things on the home-front were becoming difficult. Hugo had been head-hunted by Rolls Royce in Derby and wanted to move up to this dreary little Midland city. Knowing his propensity for changing jobs, I set my face against it. He agreed to stay up there during the week for the time being. Actually, I think I was greatly relieved at the thought of a part-time husband as the marriage was now in terminal decline. Age had done nothing to improve Hugo's temper, and with my renewed self-confidence I had begun to answer back, instead of rushing into the loo in floods of tears, which for the last few years had happened much too often. Hugo could not stand his own coinage being thrown back at him, and so he upped his game: attacking me physically – punching, pulling, pushing; mostly just bruising me. But once, after a fierce row, he very nearly killed me, putting a pillow over my face and pushing it down hard; this violent act frightened him as well as me, as when the swathe of anger had passed, red, sweating and shaking, he said: "I am sorry, Toots. You didn't deserve that; I might have lost you." That was a big deal. That night he slept on the sofa, for the first time ever. The day after, he went to see the company doctor who sent him to a psychiatrist, though this didn't really change anything, as the vast quantity of Valium tablets he was given just lay unopened in the medicine cabinet. His abusive behaviour was not always the result of him losing his temper. He had a favourite game which was to flick his tie at my legs when I was getting dressed; sometimes I fell over which was perhaps his idea of scoring a goal. Fun?

After another bad bout, some months after the attempted smothering, I visited the good Dr Hogbin who said, on seeing my bruises, "A good divorce lawyer is what you need, Antonia, not me." And that is eventually what I got.

Small wonder I found life outside the house more attractive. Apart from the verbal and physical abuse there was the question of space. Not long after we moved to Wimbledon in about 1970, he announced that the main living-room would make him a good study where he could house his huge library. After a few months he left Rolls Royce, having been once again head-hunted, this time by IBM. The children had the garden room, while I had a desk in the corner of our bedroom. It was a really Victorian set-up in that the children had to knock before they were permitted to enter his study.

★

These years of marital decay were among the darkest of my adult life. Of course I could not just walk away: I might not have been a great mother but, even following a particularly bad bash-up, I never saw leaving my children as an option. There had to be a plan. Thank goodness for that element of calculation in my make-up which countered the impulsive "anything goes" bit. In the meantime my life outside, my work and a gaggle of woman friends made life possible. But I shall never forget those endless Sundays: "Sunday, Bloody Sunday" rang true, when Hugo's presence was all-encompassing, sitting behind the enormous Victorian desk like an angry giant toad. One Sunday after yet another vitriolic row, I felt such despair that I took a great handful of Hugo's unopened bottle of Valium tablets. I told him, blearily, what I had done; he just told Sarah to sit by me and to call him if my lips turned blue! No comment. I don't remember what happened next.

★

The house was quite large, an Edwardian villa, so Hugo and the children did not have to fall over each other, which meant they were insulated from much of what went on between us, except of course at meal times. These were sometimes enlivened by him throwing his food at the ceiling; for months a mucky mess of dried muesli hung over us as we ate! My plan, ironically, was put into motion by Hugo. He liked spending money on anything that caught his eye; from out-of-date trilby hats to the latest models of car, he had to buy it instantly, but most of all it was the latest electronic gadget which he simply could not do without and this gadget had to be the best one on the market. After a few blessed days away, I returned to find two brown square pillars, like coffins up-ended, dominating the study, which were loud-speakers as adjuncts to his new precision hi-fi system. He had placed a large vase of flowers on each. Horrified, as I knew he had little spare cash, I asked, "Hugo, where did you get the money?" Looking a bit sheepish, he admitted to borrowing the money from the children's savings accounts! I had never thought he would descend to this level, though he did pay the money back eventually.

Hugo's need for ready money led to his suggestion that we should pay off the mortgage on the house. "Toots, how about you buying me out? Why not sell those ridiculous shares of yours, so we have more ready money?" As this was my nest egg, I had to give it thought. Not for long though; ten minutes later I agreed. "OK, Hugo. Yes, I suppose it would give you more dosh to buy new toys for you to play with. I can't see you spending it on anything we really need, like a new boiler. But

I will not do it unless you agree to put the house in my name. Re-register it, I mean. That's only fair." He accepted this condition immediately, not taking one moment to consider the implications it might have for him in the future, unlike me. Later, he was to call me a calculating bitch, but, as I said, he just saw this as a way to lay his hands on lots of extra cash, meaning he would be able to buy more and more sophisticated electronic paraphernalia, keeping up with the ever-developing market. After a couple of months there was a brand new red Rover saloon in our driveway. No mention was made of this purchase but, normally not very observant, I did notice that, though the colour was the same, the registration number had changed and inside the seats smelled new... Those cars were really for him; he rarely took the family out anywhere.

Though I did not go round the house and garden, telling myself, "All this is now mine", I knew I had the means to escape from Hugo when everything became too much to bear, or when the time felt right. He was, after all, the children's father, and though he did not put much time or energy into his role, except as a disciplinarian, I know he was fond of them in his own way. I don't think he ever bashed them. When they were young he made a really imaginative climbing frame; later he would buy Airfix kits for Matthew but then assemble them himself, Matthew's role being to watch his clever dad.

About this time I met another man, Alistair, on a day when there had been yet another bad row and I was feeling particularly sore and angry. I was looking in the poetry section in Wimbledon Library when I noticed this chap holding a book of poems by Ezra Pound. His physical appearance was not instantly appealing: tall, angular and lop-sided, though his bright blue eyes, with their incisive gaze, made me give him a second quick glance and I had a sudden flash-back – this man who I was covertly observing, who was covertly observing me, reminded me of that old man in York Library, thirty odd years before, with whom I had enjoyed much good talk. Perhaps this tenuous connection emboldened me to meet that enquiring look, which led him to ask, raising his eyebrows, "Do you understand much of this modern stuff?" This opening led to brief talk about our favourite poets before moving on to our wider reading habits. He suggested I try David Lodge and Malcolm Bradbury for a good laugh, and I told him to read Germaine Greer for a feminist education. The joy of our literary discourse was not shared by the scowling woman at the next table so we moved on. "How do you fancy a drink?" he asked me. I said, "What a good idea. What about The Alexandra, next door?" This was a pick-up, I realized, delightedly, or if it wasn't one now I was going to do my best to make it one! I liked this odd-looking man who shared my taste in books. Him indoors counted for nothing in this interesting possibility. Even if it was just a glass of plonk in a local, that would be a cheering episode. We shambled round to The Alexandra, an unspoilt Edwardian pub, and only then did I see he had a marked limp. He could get along: I reckoned his gait was not quite as strange as mine, though it was noticeable. I had never had a remotely disabled friend, having purposely avoided disabled people when young, not being able to bear the idea of being part of a double act. Now this sounds horribly incorrect, but that is as maybe; I was young in the middle of the last century. But with my brand new pick-up, his problem did not faze me at all; in fact perhaps I welcomed it: maturity or desperation?

We continued to talk of books and jobs and last of all we touched on our families. I heard about the childhood polio which had left him with a withered left leg, and felt I had to return this disclosure. I skated quickly over it, as I wondered what role it had played in his approach to me. Had it all been about shared intellectual taste? I never knew. Alistair drank red wine – a drink he was, I later found out, a bit too fond of –

while I stuck to one glass of shandy, knowing that I would have to steer my little fibreglass monster up the hill, home. He was decidedly posh, being a Deputy Secretary, a mandarin; the snob in me was quite gratified by this. He lived in a large Victorian house down by the tennis courts – better and better, both rich and powerful, but I am glad to say that, really, our shared literary interests mattered much more. He was older than me, fifty-four to my forty-two, which meant I would come to think of him as a kind of father figure, though not necessarily a sugar-daddy! In a way this was what, at some level, I felt I needed at the time. Before we parted, when the pub closed at 3pm we had found out that we also shared a liking for swimming, so a follow-up date was arranged for Saturday. Seeing each other almost naked would be a real test of mind over matter!

Over the next few months, he and I became close friends – friends more than lovers, since he wasn't really up to it, years of abstinence and perhaps excessive volumes of wine having left him with "balls the size of walnuts" to quote his friendly doctor. Poor man, he cared a deal more than I did, but he was almost exactly what I needed: an affectionate, perceptive, generous and grown-up companion who took my physical short-comings in his stride, or rather in his hoppity-hop step. His job was particularly challenging at the time, as he had to travel the country, shutting down many small teacher-training colleges, a cost-cutting exercise. Brick-bats came at him from every direction. The Guardian ran a long article about him, labelling him, "Haddon the Hatchet Man", with a hideous photo. I went with him on a couple of his northern forays, to Manchester and Lincoln, inventing suitable courses to cover absence from the domestic hearth. I hoped my support on these missions was valuable to him, as he really hated this aspect of his work. "When I see the look in the eyes of those poor college principals who have worked so hard to build up these small places, I feel ashamed of this ghastly mission I have to carry out," he said, wiping the odd tear from his eye.

The long car journeys in his surprisingly battered old Audi were an opportunity for us to tell each other about our families and backgrounds. I knew about his South African wife, whom he married in wartime, after going out with her for a couple of weeks in Cape Town. He had shown me a family photograph where I could see she had been a beauty and was still handsome, though for years she had not shared her bed with him or anyone else for all he knew. But they had remained married though their two children were long grown. They appeared to have little in common. Sheila had never worked and was a good housewife; not my kind of person, nor his either it seemed, after she had put a good dinner on the table! I had told him about my clever cruel husband and of course my three very different children, but only in outline. We had been too busy talking books, going to art exhibitions and lunchtime concerts, enjoying each other's presence, getting to know one another without trailing too much baggage.

We took a detour on the way back from Manchester, through the Potteries in Staffordshire so that he could show me the place where he was born and grew up in the 1920s. His father had been a Master Potter in a small pottery village near Stoke. This meant he was the factory boss who not only had charge of the works but had to overlook his workers' lives, literally, as his big house was right in the middle of the village, next door to the factory. This was social death for the family, as it meant they fell in between the rungs of the class system; no hobnobbing with villagers or their children, while the local gentry and prosperous farmers wanted nothing to do with the Master Potter and his family, living where they did, contaminated by industrial process and its labour. The children of such class crossbreds had very few playmates, and often none at all. We stopped in this place, Milton. "That's it," he said. "That's where we lived." We stared at the grim old stone house set amidst blocks of post-war council property; although it had been renovated it still looked incongruous in its updated setting. We walked round the fence wondering who lived there now. He was visibly moved by the gloomy memories brought back to him. He said, "I do remember being a rather solitary child; I suppose that's why I did well at school – no distractions." His mother had in a way mirrored the circumstances. She cloaked herself in religion, so, as God presumably doesn't do class, she bore the isolation with pious fortitude expecting her child to do likewise. Father was out at the works day and night and, though he was more approachable than his stiff-backed mother, he remembered him as a decent man but one who was hardly ever there. I shuddered at the thought of that poor solitary boy in that forbidding old house.

As we drove off he told me how he had been sent away at eight to a prep school, as was de rigueur in those days for boys whose parents were what are now known as aspirational. He was badly bullied, having little idea how to relate to other children, but he was clever, though this did nothing to increase his popularity. After a scholarship to Rugby where he was still bullied, though less as he learnt to stand up for himself and made a couple of friends, he got a Maths scholarship to Cambridge and ended up as top mathematician of his year. He spent the war years in the Intelligence Service, ferreting out information in safe havens like South Africa. And so, almost seamlessly, he joined the Civil Service, through the ranks, working in various departments as a shrewd advisor until he had almost reached the top. The fact that he hadn't quite made it, he put down to his impatient work style, but I think his irreverent humour might have had something to do with it, perhaps touching the odd bureaucratic nerve.

From the very beginning we had a tacit agreement that, as his marriage worked on a certain level, our liaison should not disturb it. This suited me. I wanted freedom. No more marital shackles, even velvet-lined ones. Over the months I developed great affection for him as he was such good company. He wrote me letters and poems which I kept for many years. He said he loved me and I believed him. Did I love him? I quickly became fond of him, dependent on him being there. With Hugo at home rampaging around, becoming worse as the days passed, having Alistair as part of my life kept me from wanting to jump over Putney Bridge. Though I spent time in his posh mansion when Sheila was away, cuddling up on a sofa looking at family photos or reading poetry to each other, I never went upstairs nor even into the kitchen. He only came to our front door once, to give me a book. As our house was almost always full of Hugo, the children and their friends, or the lodger, it wasn't the place to conduct even the most respectable liaison. He was generous too, in a way Hugo had never been, giving me a sweet silver sovereign case on a double chain for my birthday, which I regard as my favourite and probably most valuable piece of jewellery, and loading me with copies of his favourite books. Even though most of our togetherness happened on neutral ground, I believe he gave me a sort of supportive love I had rarely experienced from either my original family or from anyone else, including Hugo.

Of course, it had to happen. I left one of his billets-doux on my desk in the bedroom, under a book which Hugo picked up. He obviously seized the letter, read it, and then I heard him rushing down the stairs, roaring like the bull of Bashan. This discovery was all the more painful for him as I don't think he had any idea about my alternative attachment, being always so utterly engrossed in his work. I hopped out as fast as I could, almost leaping into my little vehicle, and drove like the devil to Wimbledon Common where I sat on a bench, all of a judder, trying to pull myself together, so that I could phone him; he was heading a conference in the Midlands. At home I was met by an angry but triumphant husband who shouted: "I've done you, Toots, done you both! I've phoned her, your lover-boy's wife. I can tell you she wasn't pleased when I told her to keep her old man on a shorter leash." He was so pleased with himself that I escaped the bash-up I was expecting, for the time being anyway. I was furious with myself for leaving the evidence around and wondering why Alistair had used headed notepaper. My husband and I avoided each other for the next few days. And then a much unexpected letter arrived, from him to Hugo on the same blue paper. Of course this clever man spent his life writing diplomatic letters on challenging subjects. The nub of this letter was that because I was worried and upset I had chosen to confide in him, an older man, and that he had no designs on our marriage, but I had looked to him for support and he had given it. This was not untrue but I found it rather patronising and, of course, limited. But it worked in that Hugo was able to continue to help IBM make its millions without being deflected by the torment of sexual jealousy.

But I knew Hugo's time with me was limited. I had made up my mind that I was not going to continue to lead this compromised life. Of course he must have been aware at some level that the marriage was in peril, or perhaps he thought doing nothing was the only option. Naturally the children were affected and the girls anyway showed signs of distress. Sarah was a day-girl at Claremont, and though this meant long and difficult travel, she worked hard, and made a few good friends, ending by taking ten O Levels which in those days was regarded as an incredible amount. She went on to get a scholarship to a highly academic school in Ealing. Sadly, she found it difficult to adjust to very different teaching methods as well as coping with domestic stress, so failed to get the university place she wanted. Frankie had opted to go to the local girls' comprehensive, Ricards Lodge, where she began an inglorious back-row career, mostly, it turned out, because at some stage she had lost some of her hearing – not that this could really be blamed on home circumstances, rather on our new GP, a stupid fellow, Dr Miles. Frankie's real naughtiness showed up after her father left, but I think the seeds were sown before. Hugo was, of course, the controller, a Victorian paterfamilias, and, when he was no longer there to reign over us, everything was to change. Matthew showed little apparent reaction, though he had become a very private child, going his own way, at least within the house.

Hugo seemed even more preoccupied with work for a time after the letter episode, but I sensed it was the calm before the storm. On a Friday evening, we had just sat down to dinner, when the explosion came – the ultimate one. Hugo demanded the crust from the new loaf; Sarah for once questioned his right to it – she wanted it. He took it, making an offensive remark to Sarah which angered me. I said, "I suppose you are giving the kids a good example?" His instant fury was terrifying, though of course this was not the first meal he had ruined. He grabbed a heavy mug and clouted me on the back of my head with it until I was dripping with blood, then hauled me out of the chair and threw me into the corner of the room. "Clean your bloody mother up!" he yelled at Frankie, who in a bemused state had stuck around – the other two had scarpered. He disappeared into his sanctum, not to be seen until the following morning, after sleeping on the sofa.

Apart from my dented scalp, being chucked across the room had resulted in a sprained wrist and a mosaic of purple bruises. Much worse was the fact that this assault had happened in front of our children. Shouting, swearing and throwing things around had been habitual but his beating up of me at a family meal was something else. After a painful night, I knew this was the moment. When he appeared in his study doorway, before he opened his mouth, I said quite quietly, "Hugo, you must go, now." To my surprise, he agreed. Before he could say anything else, I went out, round the corner to the post office, and scanning the advertisement board found a couple of suitable flats some distance away; the one in Balham looked just right for him, near the Tube, and not too expensive. I asked the post-master to write down the details and back I went. I thrust the paper into his hand and told him to go and look at it. I was in complete control, for the moment. The emotional backlash was to come later. He took the flat and moved within the next three days. By the end of the month I had seen a lawyer who wanted me to plead cruelty but I didn't, going instead for a two-year separation, as I thought this would result in less bitterness. However, it seems that Hugo never really forgave me for holding on to the house, though perhaps our children were another matter. When asked by the judge during the divorce court proceedings about how much access he was applying for, he said, "None, your worship." The judge shook his head, mumbling that this was most unusual. And so Hugo was gone.

★

Although his departure was timely and necessary, looking back over forty years I realise that, in spite of his awfulness, and defying analysis, I had really loved him and I know some feeling for him will never really die.

Antonia, free at last!

Kids' night out

Welsh Peter and me

CHAPTER 19

Chaos of Freedom

Joy, relief, fear, sadness: just some of the tangled emotions which engulfed me during those first few days of separation. I tried to concentrate on the practical. The success of this diversion was soon put to the test as just a week afterwards we woke to find water pouring through the kitchen ceiling. How to turn the water off? Was this possible? I, who had felt so much in control a few days before, was now completely at a loss. I slumped into a tearful lump but suddenly I remembered our plumber from Hampton Hill, old George Hill. I phoned and he told me where to look for a thing called a stopcock. Wriggling around in the lavatory cistern I found it. The dear man came, taken aback to find me on my own. Sobbing on his shoulder, much to his embarrassment, I said, "Oh George, I'm all on my own now, and I don't know how anything works at all. It's all so terrible. The house will probably fall down. I'm so hopeless – no idea what a stopcock was; sounds like something rude." He patted me gently on my back and murmured some vaguely comforting words, before turning to mending the broken pipework, with some relief. He hadn't reckoned on doing any other kind of patching up.

Where was Alistair whose shoulder I should have been crying on? In South Africa, visiting his wife's family on a month-long trip: bad timing. Of course there were phone calls and air letters, but I yearned for my dear old Daddy figure to hold me tight and tell me I was his darling girl. He would be back, but I needed him now.

Those first few months found a household in chaos: the kids testing for non-existent boundaries, while I sought salvation in work, taking on an extra class but also having to find time to see a counsellor in St George's psychiatric clinic. At a time when decent domestic help would seem to be most vital, we had a succession of the worst au pairs imaginable. First, poor Susan who really was ten pence in the shilling. Her English was non-existent and naughty Frankie and Matt spent mealtimes telling her to say "bugger" for butter and other suchlike vulgar substitutions. Hugo came round to collect books from time to time and, as these visits were always accompanied by roaring and shouting, poor Susan would run upstairs to hide under her bed. Our house was no place for the fragile. She didn't really cook either. She soon went. The next was very different but equally unsuitable. An Iranian doctor, capable, but an opportunistic lesbian who tried to seduce Sarah over the kitchen sink. I told the agency she would be suitable for a family with all boys. Leah was a much older Italian woman, really old and wrinkled, good with the Hoover, but her cooking was limited to a single dish: spaghetti doused with tinned tomatoes. She left after a vociferous anti-pasta rising! No more au pairs – rent-paying students plus a local cleaning lady made better economic sense, as no money funnelled through from Hugo for weeks. Betty kept the dirt down but cooking was minimal and we ate mostly peanut butter sandwiches, though this was supplemented by lots of fruit. Somewhat basic, but as no one showed signs of scurvy or rickets it was presumably nutritionally adequate.

Over the months a very different kind of family found itself; today's social workers might well class it as borderline dysfunctional. Frankie began to bring numerous friends round after school, so our kitchen became a sort of ad hoc drop-in centre where her class-mates enjoyed, guess what, endless peanut butter sandwiches! Many seemed to come from large rowdy families with very loud voices; I would come staggering home from work in search of peace and quiet and find the house rocketing with raucous laughter. But most were intelligent and basically decent teenagers who I came to know and like.

It was as well that Matthew's school was further away! But his trouble was he was neglecting his homework, his inherent laziness under-cutting his intelligence more than ever. I only realised how much this was affecting his chances after being told, at a parents' evening, that he was expected to take just three subjects at GCSE. This from a hypothetical member of the Afrikaner super race, guaranteed to have automatic membership of Mensa! What a horror story, our boy genius ending up as a lorry driver was enough to pull me out of the lethargy I had sunk into: phase two of the post-marital reaction. My godmother had just left me a legacy, not huge, but enough to pay for Matthew to go to a school where he would have to do his homework, a boarding school. I rang round a few schools which an agency told me would consider taking a bright but lazy boy of thirteen. Most of the Heads I spoke to sounded like Dickensian clergymen who, for the grace of God, were perhaps prepared to help out a hapless divorced mother, provided she had a big enough lump sum, but then I had a real conversation with a human Head, who not only showed genuine understanding when I told him about my paradoxical son, but cracked the odd joke! On seeing Bloxham I just knew this was the place for Matthew. As well as the Head, I liked all I saw: the shabby Cotswold stone buildings, the sheer space available, the few teachers I met, and the boys who looked involved and happy. The legacy was enough to cover the basic fees so I signed Matthew up without much ado, knowing, for once, I had made a good practical decision. Good old

Godmother who had made this possible. Not only had I made it more likely my son would make better use of his brain, but it would remove him from Petticoat Pandemonium. Sarah had developed a taste for travel, so, after a bit, she set off for Israel, to a kibbutz, happily imagining she would be picking peaches, only to find she had to work in a factory, making paper bags. She didn't hang around but packed her rucksack and went off to explore the desert and live a nomadic life with Bedouin Arabs.

After those years of domestic suppression, sudden freedom made me feel rather like a newly independent African state: a country unprepared for its new status though not quite the Congo! I'm not proud of the way I muddled through. Hugo had had a more positive role in the family than I was able, at the time, to credit him with. His efficiency, though erratic, often excessive, and undermined by his terrible temper, kept the show on the road.

I know on my own I was not a good enough mum. I had not had much of a mum myself but never seriously took refuge in using this as an excuse, as I knew of women brought up in orphanages who grew up to be marvellous mothers. As the weeks went by I seemed, at times, to regress, almost morphing into a fourth adolescent, though I was always grown-up around money, paying bills on time, insisting lodgers paid rent when due and, as the kids still remind me, refusing to buy them biscuits because they were a waste of money. But then the photo of me languishing on Frankie's bed, smoking a large joint, tells another story! It is just as well that I have never really liked the taste of liquor, perhaps imbued with a memory of my headmistress warning me about the perils of drink, years ago, saying I was quite bad enough without it!

Old Alistair and I still met often for delicious little lunches in Soho or the odd exhibition, but there was, of course, that missing dimension which began to irk me as the weeks went by. The physical side of marriage had always been important to Hugo and me, the best part by far, and I began to feel really deprived, and I also wanted to play, to get taken out to dinner, to enjoy evening entertainments, to meet new people – always gregarious, I wanted more of a life. I suppose I have always wanted more! I think it was in response to the assumptions made in childhood that I was likely to have a very limited existence – sort of cocking a snook. I was tired, sometimes exhausted, had bad insomnia, but still I yearned for more. I wasn't lonely, and certainly was not looking for a new partner. That Good Time Girl wanted an outing, that was it. So I began to look at the back pages of my old friend *The New Statesman* and then *Time Out*. My first date was with a pathetic Jewish violinist who said he'd been bashed up by his six foot wife! I felt instant pity for him, but after downing a glass of sherry I fled from the pub, pleading a sudden migraine. This debacle was followed by other more classy encounters, involving good dinners, plays and even an opera or two. Although there were a few follow-up meetings, most were just too ordinary, thus boring. I did feel an affinity with a bright barrister called Adrian, a *Time Out* pick-out, who was very likeable, witty and stylish, but perhaps here I was the one who was lacking an essential ingredient as he only lasted for two dinners. The dinners and various amusements I got taken to were mostly quite good fun and of course meeting such a variety of men, even the dreary ones, was an education in itself. The biggest putdown came from a sloppy-looking history teacher who I met in a pub near Waterloo station. Having fixed me up with the usual glass, he went to the gents and that was the last I saw of him! The violinist avenged.

I decided to take the initiative so I put an advert in *Time Out*: "Pretty, witty woman, 43, seeks bright, bookish man." I had over a hundred replies. Most were chucked; only about ten were worth a second reading. I phoned half a dozen, arranging to meet a couple. Peter was Welsh, very Welsh, with a beguiling Under-Milk-Wood accent, a quick turn of phrase, a floral waistcoat, and a trim goatee. He was short but very compact. Later, after meeting the children, he became known as "the Welsh gnome". Being Welsh, of course, gave him a head start, but he was also very much into music, proper music, and knew a lot about it. His admiration for Wagner probably accounted for his beard and the beret! He was a volunteer usher at the Festival Hall which meant free tickets for most concerts. Though a devoted listener to Radio Three, with a "know what I like" attitude, I had always found music as such elusive and tantalizing, as if I lacked the key to unlock any real understanding of it. I liked Peter's joie de vivre and of course his musical know-how, so we arranged to meet at the Festival Hall for an evening of Schubert. After the cultural overtures had gone so well, came the other possible part of this mating game. It was all a bit of a let-down – not a walnut problem but more about attitude. Anyway, we settled for friendship, one that lasted many years, and took us to countless concerts. I don't think I could ever have trusted him in a closer role anyway (Welsh, you see) but, as it was, it worked out well. Peter never made me feel self-conscious about my awkward movements, though he felt free to ask the odd question which was reassuring and releasing for me.

Over the years, though I had come to accept that my spasticity was an intrinsic part of me, I still felt resentful about it, cursed by it. Now, it was not so much the staring of strangers, though this still niggled me, as the encroaching pain of my disordered muscles which were pulling my spine into a kind of S shape. This merciless process was starting to limit my physical capacity and gradually to impinge upon the enjoyment of everyday life. By opting out of most manual stuff that I found laborious and time-wasting, like housework and all but basic cooking, I saved myself much frustration and fury, but as arms are crucial to activity I was continually irritated when I dropped things, or yanked them apart; even buttons often defeated me. My ineptness was variable. On bad days I had to ask strangers to help me put on and sometimes do up my coat – no problem except hurt pride if there was a woman around, but there was the hopeful doorman who took it for a come-on and I found myself clasped to his uniformed chest! But it was much worse when my red knickers fell down at South Kensington tube station. My arms went into spastic overdrive and my legs colluded with them as I toddled to the nearest bench before being able to remove these ridiculous shackles, and shove them in my pocket!

Of course I knew I could only aim to lessen the pain, which was not bad but unremitting. It seemed there was no help to be had; how I longed for the Old Gaffer (Charlotte) to be reincarnated. I consulted so many healers, everyone between highly orthodox doctors in Harley Street, and exotic shamans in Brixton. Osteopaths, chiropractors, homeopaths, naturopaths, physios, acupuncturists, masseurs, rebirthers... All deliverers of false promises. I saw them all. Every time I approached a new curer with hugely unrealistic expectations, I was left with the same old pain, sometimes a worse one and of course a hole in my purse. Sadly, I still suffer from this stupid syndrome: someone only has to mention a healer and I am there, the next day or week, waiting full of hope that this time relief will be found. Pathetic, but hope does spring eternal with some of us. It took some years of gradual decline for the aches and pains to really start to undermine me much, but I did find I got tired much sooner than most people; tiresome, as my nature abhors a vacuum! I managed work by taking evening classes so that I could go home and rest in the afternoon.

One day, a brown envelope arrived with a letter announcing mass withdrawal of all invalid cars. Oh, God! I thought, but reading on, it informed me that, if I passed a medical, I might be eligible to apply for a REAL car. I knew that I was going to have to pass this, the latest trial to be undergone. Armed with a pill, a muscle relaxant, I passed. Weeks later, after a lot of bureaucratic doings, a magnificent yellow Ford Fiesta appeared in our driveway. Now I had to pass the driving test. I contacted a small downtown driving school with a fearless funny young instructor called Mike. I nearly killed us many times, and he just straightened the car up and we had a good laugh. As it was obvious I was going to need interminable lessons, we colluded in a slightly dubious scheme. He borrowed the car from the school at seven o'clock in the morning, before the owner arrived, and brought it round and I had my lesson half price. I liked Mike; we chatted between bouts on the road. Once, we had stopped for him to have a smoke when he really began to open up about himself. "Antonia, you're a posh type, so you might want to sack me when I tell yer I've got a record. Been to Feltham Young Offenders, didn't do me no good, went to Wandsworth for a couple of years…got beat up most days by nasty old buggers. I was a pretty boy, see. Mum nearly died… she was so done in by having me, always in trouble. She's a good 'un, Mum, so I'm going straight now, proper job, steady girlfriend, Stella. Bet you can't guess…she's a store detective in Harrods. Now yer know, OK?" I said, "That's fine by me. Glad you have a caring mum and a tough girlfriend. You're a wonderful instructor and I have a lot to thank you for." So it was very sad that he wasn't there when I eventually passed my test. Sadly, he had gone back to jail, in spite of his steady law-enforcement girlfriend, though not for borrowing the boss's car out of hours! I haven't ever forgotten this cheeky young man who showed such bravery and patience overseeing my frightening efforts to become road-worthy.

I passed my driving test at the third attempt, but only because the kind examiner helped me steer the car backwards round a corner! The extraordinary freedom given me by this new skill went to my head. I spent hours in my bright yellow car, driving nowhere, just for the joy of it. But early on Sunday mornings I did the serious stuff: motorway trips and down to the South Coast, mostly to Eastbourne. These were no joy-rides, but an attempt to get over my fear of those terrifying motorways you could not avoid if you wanted to go any distance. I'd start about six o'clock, arrive about two hours later, have a coffee and bun at some sort of Happy Eater, look at the sea and drive back. Eventually my aim was not simply motorway driving without fear, but to revel in the excitement of the wicked fast lane, whizzing past lorries, buses and more circumspect drivers; this filled me with the kind of euphoria which my mother must have felt when steeple-chasing or my dad in the boxing ring. In the genes, perhaps. Whatever, it would not take a psychologist to figure out why I gloried in this risky "sport".

Returning to the dating scene after I had acquired Peter the Welsh gnome as a friend, I met Alex who, it turned out, had been at Cambridge with Freddy, my first long-term boyfriend. Alex had known Freddy well, which seemed to be a promising and unexpected starting point. He was pleasant to look at, with dark wavy longish hair, tall, and well-proportioned though not muscular, and sported a lovely brown velvet jacket. He lived a bachelor life in West Hampstead. Though what was really intriguing about Alex was his career as a spy! After Cambridge he had been recruited for MI6 from which he had recently retired. Alex was very clever, and of course the long dark hair, this exotic past, and the fact he was into high culture made him instantly attractive. After our first meeting, at the bar of the British Film Theatre, which was much more fun than most first dates, he rang to ask me to accompany him to a series of concerts at the Wigmore Hall. "Lovely. I don't know much about music, but I know what I like." Of course, through being educated by Welsh Peter, I did know my Schoenberg from my Shostakovich, but never reckoned on having any in-depth knowledge. The music to be played all seemed to be by composers of whom I had barely heard. No Classic FM favourites here! Of course I was pleased and flattered – seemed to be punching above my weight for a change! After the second concert, mostly works by Tavener, he asked me back and, as I had come to like him, I went. No attitude problem here, at least not yet. After a month or so he came down to Wimbledon. We had an amble on the Common with our old dog before going back to the house for a meal. He seemed progressively more ill at ease, even though he didn't have to meet any of the family, apart from the dog. It wasn't my cooking; he was starting to appear uneasy before we ate. He kept glancing at his watch, and his talk became stilted and hesitant. Where was the suave cosmopolitan Alex I knew? I gave him a small glass of some sickly liqueur I had been saving for an occasion but this had no effect. Making some feeble excuse, he bolted off at an indecently early hour, leaving me, saying, "I am sorry, Antonia, I forgot I am expecting a long distance call." I was puzzled but not distraught. I liked him very much and, had I been looking for a long-term partner, could have gone over the brink. I suppose it was just as well I wasn't. He was a great conversationalist, but over those few months he hardly ever mentioned his family, previous relationships or, more understandably, his work. He turned any questions very shrewdly, not surprisingly, and I would end up telling him about myself. I had resigned myself to his strange departure after a couple of weeks, when I got a letter. Alex did not exactly explain why he had done a runner; really just an apology, though I picked up some indications that he was scared of any kind of intimacy. Of course he had chosen a career in which secrecy was central; he had never married. Poor Alex. I heard from Freddy, who I met again socially a few years later, that he had died from cancer aged fifty-six.

★

In the gloriously hot summer of '76 I went to Ireland, to the Yeats Summer School. I have always loved Yeats' poems and had always intended to revisit Ireland, the place where I had experienced something like happiness with my family, all those years ago. True, Sligo was in the Republic while we had been in Northern Ireland of course, but we had actually gone on holiday there. There were about a hundred students on this course: eighty Americans, three Brits and two Aussies, with the rest from Europe. All the lectures were given by American academics. We had dormitory accommodation in Sligo Boys' Grammar School which was of course quite basic. On the first evening after arrival, we were given a grand welcome by the Irish Tourist Board. I went, expecting to have a glass of wine and, with luck, some good talk. It was a hot evening so I was thinking I might have a cold beer instead, though I didn't really like the taste. Just then, someone, as if reading my mind, thrust a large glass into my hand. I turned round and saw this big smiling bloke. "You looked as if you could use this!" he said, sitting down beside me. Bob was an associate professor from Boston. He was good-looking, about my age and obviously sociable. I felt flattered as there were many attractive young women around, though perhaps it was my pristine English accent which caught his ear. Accepting the drink I remarked on the number of Americans around. "Yes, but of course a lot of us Yanks relate to Yeats' work because of our strong feelings about our Irish roots, especially us Bostonians. You must be English with that pristine accent." I replied, "No, actually I am Welsh, which is almost as different as being Irish, except we were conquered by bloody old Edward III." Not a statement of fact: an expression of emotion. We chatted for hours, mostly about books of course, but later more personal things. He told me how, as a young reporter, he had been detailed, with others, to escort a very drunk Dylan Thomas round Boston, part of that last fatal journey which is thought to have done for the famously alcoholic poet. Bob was a good talker, full of American affability, and was, it seemed, seeking more than just companionship, for the duration of the course. He was, he said, unhappily married, contemplating separation from his apparently bossy wife, Delia – a familiar line!

The next day, I left Sligo Grammar School dormitory with its hard narrow bed and straight-backed chairs for a lush bedroom with silky sheets and a soft mauve carpet in a modern bungalow, and Bob of course. Here I was, living in luxury with a handsome attentive swain in this delightful small seaside town, enjoying the fruits of American academia on a subject dear to my heart. In addition, there was the wider company. The pair of us seemed to become the focus of a small group of students, including the two Australian women who obviously adored Bob. Our red-headed landlady, probably a good Catholic, kept her suspicions to herself, though our breakfast talk too often revealed the fact that we hardly knew each other. "I am surprised you play golf," I said – an unlikely comment between a married couple!

I think I supposed myself to be in love, love at first sight, and perhaps I was. I must not allow my cynical older self to disparage this feeling experienced in middle age, believing it to be the stuff of women's magazines and slushy novels. Of course, had I met him on the Clapham omnibus it would probably not have been the same. Whatever the intensity of emotion, it was a truly idyllic holiday. When we were not studying, we were going round graveyards, looking for Bob's Irish ancestors – this, of course being a favourite pursuit of Americans, particularly those from Boston, as Bob had already told me. We walked on the lower slopes of the Bricklieve Mountains, Bob being most concerned I should not get too tired. He took my difficulties in his stride; he had a sister who had polio. He was a very good people's person, chatting easily with the Good and the Great professors heading the course, and then sitting down on the craggy pavement to enjoy a Guinness with some road-menders!

After the course we decided to spend a week in Dublin, in those days quite a small unsophisticated city. As well as the timeless elegance of the eighteenth-century buildings and the magnificent theatres, there were intriguing byways and curious small shops, furriers, theatrical costumiers and numerous old sweet shops. We were aware of a bitter campaign called "Hands off Dublin" being waged against the new arterial motorways which would slice through the middle of the city, wiping out many of the old terraces and ruining the canal walks, not to mention the destruction of many popular old pubs. Bob knew the American-Irish producer of "The Playboy of the Western World" playing at the Abbey Theatre, so we enjoyed a few drinks in thespian company as well as seeing the play twice.

The time came to say goodbye; though Bob seemed as sorry as I was, and asked me to cross the Pond to go with him to a conference on Irish literature after Christmas, how could I be sure if this encounter had just been a joyful episode and nothing more? He promised to write. He did write – marvellous letters in great loopy handwriting, at least once a fortnight – and of course I wrote back. But sadly he fell and had a heart attack, shovelling snow, just before Christmas, so we never got to meet at that conference, though the letter-writing continued for a year or more.

I suppose I knew really that this love affair was just that, before we even parted, long before it became just an interesting pen-friendship, and the bossy Delia was still around. After a few weeks of regret, but no bitterness, I chose to remember Bob as part of the Irish idyll: a wonderful interlude, and his letters were a continuing source of pleasure. I still have them!

Frankie and Mum, 1976

CHAPTER 20

Death of Dad

As Dad grew frailer in body he became gentler in spirit. My sister and I made more frequent visits, though the journey was long and complicated, the nearest station being 25 miles away, fearing each time might be the last. Dad had let go of a lot of his old animosities, just sitting in his scuffed leather chair, talking and joking about flirting with the girls in Woolworths on his local shopping sprees, and how delighted he was that his barber kept on telling him he had never known such a head of hair; he actually bought a new tweed jacket, his first new garment for 20 years, I reckoned. He still enjoyed a drink in The George in Chepstow, though he had fallen out of the doorway at least once. After he had stopped driving the ancient Alvis, he took the bus; and after that he got a lift with his old widow friend down the road...

Some months before the end, he insisted my sister, Veronica, and I go to see him together, in order to choose items of furniture we wanted, by turn in order to avoid future upsets, he said, though of course, given our history, he probably knew these were inevitable. He seemed entirely focused on his possessions; if he had deeper feelings they weren't for sharing. When we tried hard to talk about his funeral wishes, he would start on about the way Mum and he had paid half a crown for that old Welsh oak chest and two shillings for a Regency chair at the village auction sales in the thirties. Burial or cremation? Builth or Monmouth? He finally lost it, shouting, "When I'm

gone, I'm gone! That's it...I don't care. Put me in the orchard."
In the event he was cremated and his grandchildren sprinkled
daffodil bulbs in his beloved orchard.

He died a few months after that visit as the result of
an accident in the house. No one knew exactly what had
happened. The evidence suggested he had fallen, hit his head
somewhere and then managed to stagger up to his bedroom
where he was found partially undressed on the floor. As his
bedroom faced the village green, the drawn curtains were
noticed the next morning, and the local builder, Mr Malpas,
came and put his ladder up to the window. The ambulance was
called and an unconscious Dad was whisked off to the Royal
Gwent Hospital, the place to which he had always dreaded
going.

When I saw him in the ward, he had woken up, but he
had entered a distant world, that of the First World War. As
I approached the bed where he was sitting up, he shouted,
"All present and correct, sir!" He looked me up and down and
then said: "You are a nice girl, you are. I like your jumper."
In his world I suppose I was a voluntary worker or a strolling
tart. I stroked his arm; his face did not look old, the skin
had smoothed and his hair shone. This time warp was an
extraordinary thing to behold, unbearably poignant, especially
when linked to his nightmares of recent years which I knew
about as, when staying, I had too often heard him bellowing,
sometimes even screaming, in his sleep, those terrible long-
repressed memories of life in the trenches surfacing in old
age. I stepped away to wipe my eyes and as I went he roared,
"Over the top! Over the top!" Of course this delusion meant
nothing to the young medical staff, just an old man with a
brain injury, who was probably on his way out. The revisiting
of this most traumatic and intense experience when many
of his friends had been killed, he had been badly wounded
and then awarded the Military Cross for something he never

spoke about, showed how the rest of his life had been lived in its shadow.

I came every day for a week, staying in the house, but had to return home as term had started, with the assurance that contact would be made if there was any change. In spite of ringing the hospital social worker every day, who kept assuring us he was doing well, neither my sister nor I heard the truth about his deteriorating condition until it was too late. Then we learnt that he had come out of his special world, or delusional state, to die of pneumonia after a few days. We were just told he was dead and asked to pick up his few belongings. Apparently, his ancient widow friend who visited him had been asked by a nurse to ring us but she had lost our phone numbers.

Sadness at his death was made much worse by the manner of his going: nobody there to hold his hand or tell him of our love for him during his final hours... I cried more about this than the actual death, particularly as he had apparently returned to a more normal state and probably been conscious of dying very much alone. Oh, poor dear Dad.

Who was this man, my father? Through these pages a curiously mixed picture must have emerged. In childhood he was my hero, but also my comforter and source of fun. Later, in adolescence and beyond, I had often hated him, slated him, ignored him and lied to him. He shouted at us like a sergeant-major, denied us small luxuries, like bananas and biscuits. After we had left home, when we lived in the wicked big city, he was terrified we would come to moral harm: at the least, fall into an unfortunate relationship or, at worst, present him with a bastard grandchild. When I played upon these fears, by telling him I was going to marry a black man, he would say: "Bring him down here and I'll run him through." (With the ancient sword kept by his bedside!)

I suppose he did his best as a single father of two daughters, but he was not well equipped for this role. He had been a man among men for most of his life, seeing women as subsidiary in the business of living, almost as frilly accessories. He chose a wife almost half his age who had little knowledge of the world. True, he had several sisters who, I was later told, he tended to patronize and often run in competition with each other, which is what he was inclined to do with his children, Veronica and me – one reason why we never really got on. Once, as one of our few joint outings, later, when we were trying to come together more, she and I had booked to see a production of King Lear, but at the last moment I felt I could not bear to go: too close to home.

And yet, on a social level, women of all ages adored him, certainly judging by the regimental tea-parties, though I only went to one. When it was time to leave, I couldn't get near him, as he was knee-deep in widows! He was a tease and a joker, more than a flirt; women felt safe with him and they loved him because he made them laugh. A man for the moment, not for life, shown by the brevity of his second and third marriages: neither lasted more than a year.

That said, during his last couple of years, he and Frankie, my most delightful but troublesome child, became great buddies. This friendship apparently involved drinking quantities of Dad's favourite old-age tipple, barley wine, and smoking endless Woodbine cigarettes. On being asked what she did at Grandad's, she said, "Oh Mum, we mostly just sit round drinking and smoking and laughing at awful jokes, but I did paint the kitchen in between times." Frankie's deep attachment lit up his closing years. There were many good laughs together, but she also showed him great tenderness by binding up his horribly ulcerated legs, surely a labour of love. I believe she missed him more than anyone.

When I think about Dad, I dwell on those first few years in Wales, when he was my hero – not so much on later times when the relationship became difficult and confrontational. I always wish we had managed to display more affection to each other which would have countered the negative aspects, also that I had made more effort to go and see him more often in his old age. But I am glad he was my dad.

*

Frankie and Matthew had left school: Frankie went on to train as an electronic technician and Matthew got into Portsmouth Poly to read Business Studies, while Sarah was still wandering round the Middle East, being a real traveller and managing to acquire some beautiful bejewelled Bedouin dresses. She finally came to rest in Germany where she was to spend the rest of her life. After a year or two living as an au pair she met Reiner in a Munich pub. They moved in together, and later married. After thirty years they are still together. What Frankie was going to do was a problem, as a single O level in Art didn't offer many options career-wise, but she had always had a way with mending vacuum cleaners, a talent for understanding the intricacies of machinery which she certainly did not inherit from my family. I heard about a new course in Electronic Technology especially for girls down the road at Kingston College; she seemed keen so she signed up for it. As all the lecturers were men with loud voices, her deafness was less of a problem; in any case I think she actually enjoyed most of the course and must have done well as she went on to get a job with the international firm Philips, repairing hospital equipment, where she created mayhem among her male colleagues. She was very attractive with her long blonde hair, miniskirts and outgoing nature, but after a while the attention she was given became a pressure she could have done without, leading to abusive behaviour; sad, as she was meant to be a trail-blazer in a man's world. But she survived, leaving after several years to marry; not one of her team-mates though!

After his academically undistinguished but sociable time at Portsmouth Poly – he discovered the whereabouts of the library two weeks before his finals – Matthew went off to the States, ostensibly to sell ice-cream as part of a student scheme for a few weeks, but ended up staying for two years, travelling round in a bashed-up old van picking up work where he could, as he didn't have that essential Green Card, while getting to know the country better than most and at a level few foreigner travellers had penetrated. He was adopted by a family of Mexican café owners who taught him how to cook, wait and manage the shop. One Christmas I visited him in Texas, an extraordinary place where the men flaunted those big boots and wide hats, and the women were very much women. Matt, at that time, slept in the boiler house of a home shared by five salesmen. I asked, "Matt, where can we find a B and B for me? I can't share this beastly little boiler place with you!" He said, "Of course not. Look, I have a clean sleeping bag here – you can commute between rooms, as there's always one free. I know you're not fussy, Mum, so it should suit you fine, and save money!" How well he knew me! I slept in all five of these blokes' beds, at least one always being on the road. They all had water-beds which were very comforting for my difficult back. We hired a car and saw enough of Texas, and I crossed the Rio Grande to spend an hour or so in Mexico. Colourful, lively, but sad, so sad: all those little street kids begging for a dime or two.

*

So my family had flown and were basically self-sufficient. True, Frankie needed some persuasion to go, particularly as Wimbledon was the pivot of her extensive social life, but finally she went to live in Streatham with her boyfriend Chris, with a small financial incentive.

I had always thought of Richmond as a kind of local Mecca, so I moved there, to a large Victorian semi-detached house, suitably shabby, but with five bedrooms. I had compromised on the immediate location though; it was almost sitting on the Chertsey Bypass behind a small petrol station. On the other hand it was a few steps away from Richmond station and the Tube, which was a great advantage. There were of course those accursed planes, roaring pitilessly overhead every two minutes, from Heathrow just down the road. Though it was considered to be a good address, or perhaps because it was, I found, with too many of the Good and the Great living there, it to be the least friendly place I had ever lived. It was as well that I managed to create a kind of alternative family, which was why I had bought a five bedroom house even though the children had gone. So I set up a lodging house, intending to fill it with three interesting male self-cookers.

I put an advertisement in the local paper and, moments after, the phone began to ring, but I wasn't going to take anyone. The selection process was almost as stringent as a Civil Service entry test! The first successful candidate was Darwin. He was thirty-seven with a ponytail and a wide attractive grin. He came from Norfolk, where he had been striving to attain a self-sufficient life on a couple of acres. It hadn't worked so, as he had an engineering background, he was taking up a new job at the Twickenham Tech. He arrived with a hand loom tucked under his arm. Throughout the first year the clothes line was festooned with sheep fleeces which he wove into wool, then knitted into very distinctive pullovers: the relics from his last life. It was a new beginning for him as he had just been divorced by his wife who had not really shared his ideals. We liked each other on sight and I thought him a good first choice.

But before he had been in the house a couple of hours, he asked me if I would consider a younger man, not just as a lodger. Amazed and amused, I just glared at him through an imaginary monocle and said, "Call me Auntie." (Later, I took him with me to a party where he met a far more suitable squeeze.) But he was a great lodger and stayed with me for the whole fourteen years I lived in Richmond. Once a week he would cook us both a fine meal while I contributed a bottle of wine. Over the years I ignored the sequence of women who I would hear pattering up to his bedroom in the evenings.

The second man was Yaski, a delightful Japanese gentleman who provided the exotic element. He worked as a trader in wool and took flying visits to the North to find fine cloth. He and I went to Japanese films, a posh Embassy party and, once, to a famous gambling club in Piccadilly to play blackjack: a great experience as a one-off.

The third man was Paul, a security guard at Kew Gardens, a real Cockney who played the drums in the top room. Against the background sounds of traffic and planes, the throb of his music was almost a welcome diversion. Apart from this he was a very quiet man, a bit of a loner. One candidate failed the test because I thought he was gorgeous, just my type. No mixing business with pleasure though; as already shown, I was wary of those chaps who might become "cock-lodgers", in the vernacular. When he rang to ask if he had passed the test, I told him he hadn't and why! He said: "That's the nicest reason I have ever had for being turned down." But he didn't ask me out! The fourth room was given over to casuals, paying guests, who wanted somewhere for a few nights, mostly friends of friends, but it was primarily for family and friends.

So the house paid for itself, and gave me that extra income I needed for the new expensive training courses I was later to embark on, the travelling I went on over the years, and the more utilitarian expenses: the new roof, double glazing and an upgraded gas boiler.

After creating my new "family" I decided to write a novel,

based on my childhood. I have always enjoyed writing, though for years focused on poetry before realizing I did not have that certain something which transforms a versifier into a poet. I had written a few short stories for the BBC which had all come back with nice polite comments, a few protest letters to the local papers; these had all appeared, but that was all... This magnum opus was eventually called "Camilla – Bloody Little Imbecile" – a most unappealing title but one from which I would not be moved. I suppose it was quite funny in parts, but bitter too, in a covert kind of way. It was, in itself, a very therapeutic experience. On leafing through it recently, I realise how much my perspectives have changed during the last thirty years, due partly, I suppose, to the gentling of nature which ageing sometimes brings.

Sarah's wedding

CHAPTER 21

Autumn Love

After moving I had given up man-hunting as a hobby, but then I met Graham, a much younger man, at a poetry group in Balham. This small group met once a fortnight in a room over a pub just off the high street. We were mostly women of a certain age with a sprinkling of younger men. Graham was quite ordinary looking, tall and skinny, a typical ectomorph, with a fresh complexion, green eyes, black curly hair, and a real feeling for poetry. He was working as an unqualified social worker with autistic teenagers; he seemed to have a real feeling for this too. I really didn't notice him much at first, though I liked the stuff he wrote – about his work and Brixton where he lived. After the group had been going for a few months, as I read a poem I had written, I was conscious of being eyed intently. On looking up I met Graham's gaze which quickly became a shy smile. He was a diffident man which was perhaps why I hadn't been especially aware of him sooner. The group broke up at ten o'clock as usual but, as I was turning to go, he said, "I don't suppose you'd like to have a drink with me downstairs, Antonia?" I thought for a moment and replied, "Yes, why not?" We sat at a small table, him with a beer and me with a gin and tonic. It was high summer, very warm, and I was wearing a Laura Ashley dress with a fairly low neckline; in those days I had a generous bosom and a narrow waist, though I rarely thought these supposedly enviable measurements were any recompense for my difficulties. We talked about how hard it was to write a half-decent poem, various modern poets we both liked, and our work. I was wary and, when we moved on, pecked him on his cheek and said: "Well, that was a good talk. I enjoyed that. Thank you, Graham." He smiled broadly, nodded, bid me goodnight and went to catch his bus.

Driving home, I wondered. I was wary because, being a woman of some experience, I sensed that he fancied me; it was not all about our common cultural interests. And not from words spoken or touch felt. I was both frightened and flattered. Did I need the possibility of another involvement at this stage of my life when I was thinking about leaving teaching and finding an alternative occupation? A branch line? I thought not, but everyone knows that thought too often succumbs to emotional need, and physical longing. No exchange of phone numbers, so it was a question of waiting for a couple of weeks, fighting that inevitable internal battle. And then, after all that nervous waiting, he wasn't there. ..Apologies sent to the poetry group, but no reason given. I sighed, feeling an immediate stab of relief, but beneath was a degree of stubborn and unbidden regret. Had he felt unable to come, frightened too, like I was, only more so? Grace, an ill-named woman, asked me loudly, as we were sitting down, about to start, "Antonia, where is your toy-boy?" I stared her down.

The next few days passed, and then there was a phone call. It was him. In those days most people's names were listed in the phone book; he had obviously looked me up. He asked me if I would like to see "The Tempest" with him, as someone had given him tickets. We met the following Saturday at The Lyric, Hammersmith, to watch John Gielgud play Prospero. Afterwards, he kissed me on the cheek before we went our different ways. No one-night stand, this! I asked him if he would like to visit Richmond in a couple of weeks. I knew he'd like the park as he was keen on birds and beasts, and walking. He came, we went to the park with my dog, Cindy-Lou, and then ate a good dinner at The Orange Tree pub which was across the road from the station. After the play, we kissed briefly in the shadows; after a moment's hesitation, he turned quickly towards the station and was gone. I don't know what I had expected but I knew as the woman old enough to be his mum I wasn't up to making any definitive move. Stalemate: he was too young and scared; I was too old and scared.

At the end of the next poetry meeting, he read a poem, a love poem, centuries old. He blushed and stammered once or twice but read it well. I blushed too, as he sat down shuffling his long legs, crossing and recrossing his ankles. I have a note of the poem's opening lines:

"Go, lovely rose –
Tell her what wastes her time and me,
That now she knows,
When I resemble her to thee,
How sweet and fair she seems to be."

We left before we had to endure the raised eyebrow, smirched comment, or suppressed giggle and drove home without a word.

I wish I could say we enjoyed a feast, but all I had on offer was a tin of tomato soup and the inevitable peanut butter sandwich. The bread was good anyway. Had he been a gourmet he might have fled, but he wasn't much interested in food, at that juncture anyway. We spent a good night.

It was a glorious autumn. We walked in Richmond Park or by the Thames; the tints of the turning leaves had never been so vivid, or the waters of the Thames so glittering; I don't remember being so at ease with myself, both in mind and body, as we strolled hand in hand through a kind of Never Never Land. During this state of euphoria we didn't care what people thought, though, in retrospect, we may have attracted the odd backward glance, as we probably appeared a little strange, the lanky youngish man trying to slow his pace to that of his older lame companion. We often paused to sit on nearby benches, sometimes to read new-found poems to each other or just to rest and appreciate the beauties of the surroundings. Graham often said, "Antonia, I am just such a lucky guy." And I would reply, "And I am the luckiest lass I know." Oh, the banalities of love.

After a few months of toing and froing from Brixton, Graham moved in, carrying all his belongings in two shabby suitcases on the Underground. As we sorted out my bedroom, making space for his few clothes, and put his files in a bookcase in the study, I asked myself, for the first time, if this was really going to work. We had a slightly cynical observer, Darwin the lead lodger, who stood foursquare in the kitchen doorway, saying, "Antonia, I am surprised, very surprised. I never thought this would happen... Good luck." Was he a little jealous? I don't know, but I think he had enjoyed being the Special Lodger and saw his position threatened. Household politics or personal feeling? I guess the two were intertwined.

I had never told Graham exactly how old I was, though I had guessed he was about 35. Soon after he moved in he came across my passport; he then learned I was 51. Not being very aware of age, he had assumed I was in my mid-forties. He was visibly quite perturbed by his mistake, though I suppose I might have been quite flattered by it. "Antonia, you are almost the same age as my mother, did you realize that?" he asked, and I replied, crassly, "So you appeared when your mum was still a teenager and I suppose she had to marry your dad." This was a hit below the belt – stupid, as Graham was fond of his mum, though he had no time for his father... I left the room as this might have been our first real tiff, and I didn't want it to develop into a row.

We were married a few months after he moved in. He was very keen on the idea, never having been married. Looking back, I must have slept walked into it, but I was very involved at the time in finding a new vocation after leaving teaching, so perhaps my thought processes were not sufficiently engaged in the matter, and I did so love him! The deed was done at Richmond Registry Office, where Graham fell on his knees while he put the ring on my finger and I saw his cheeks were wet with tears. We held a small party at home which was all right, though I was very aware of the conflicting views of some of the guests, but the funniest one was expressed by the old lady from next door who said, "Antonia, I don't mind the age difference, but, my dear, I hope there is not going to be any of that sex stuff!"

We spent Christmas with his family in Norwich. This was, to all appearances, a success. I liked Maureen, his mother, and his feisty old Cockney granny, cherished by him. Nobody seemed to care about the age gap, and it meant that Maureen and I, being the same generation, had quite a lot in common. But I realised as soon as I met Alf, his father, we would never have anything to say to each other. I was to him, I instinctively knew, "that posh old bitch" who Graham, his least appreciated son, had got hitched to, though the thought that I was relatively well-off may have been a slight consolation or, more likely, envy. He was a small, paunchy man, whose smarmy manner hid any real thought or feeling; though if you could bear to watch his face long enough, the cynicism and falsity showed up in the down-turned mouth, the often raised eyebrows and an inability to look anyone in the eye: he reminded me of an evil old elf. I knew from Graham that he hit his wife sometimes. His welcoming words: "What a great pleasure it is to meet you, Antonia. So kind of you to come. How good of you to drive all this way; unfortunately, my lazy son, Graham, has never bothered himself to learn. Expects others to do all the hard work, always has," showed up the rift between him and his elder son, and was certainly a small window into his unpleasant nature.

It was a nice enough Christmas though. Maureen, a large, kindly woman, had made a tremendous effort to make us feel welcome; the meal was splendid. Afterwards Alf was persuaded to drive us round Norwich. But though I did not feel my love of Graham was diminished by meeting his family, it was the start of noticing how much class and culture matter in our society, the significance of odd differences in modes of living and being.

Never before had I allowed myself to be bothered by this, perpetually managing to defy my own family attitudes and prejudice on social status, but after leaving that small ex-council house in Norwich, with its shoddy furniture and trashy ornaments, I found this same inherited but long-denied mindset unwontedly surfacing, for the first time since I had spent joyful hours in that other small council house in York, as a child, with Olive and her "different" family. I didn't want to be aware of these disparities; I was really ashamed of the surfacing of these prejudices, though for the time being I was able to separate them from my love for Graham. In some ways we felt closer after that Christmas. One night, after a drink or two, Graham, bit by bit, told me about his father's sexual abuse which he had endured as a small child; he had never felt able to talk about it before to anyone: how Alf had crept into his narrow bed, all too often, to "mess about with him", with his wife asleep in the next room. It seemed to go on for years and years. He remembered that, when he got older and tried to yell, a small sponge was stuffed into his mouth. He remembered also the beating and verbal bullying which had only stopped after he left home to work in London. At one time Alf had managed a small news agency and Graham had often been kicked out of bed to sort out papers at 5am, before school. Of course this revelation was terribly sad and did a lot to explain Graham's oddities, but together with the compassion I felt for him gradually grew fears about living with someone who had experienced such damage in childhood.

During that next summer I began to have more reasoned doubts, but they were never really raised between us. It seemed Graham's reticence was infectious. Also he could not make any real contact with my friends... When we went out with them, to the theatre, dinner or a concert, he turned into a timid rabbit, social events being a real ordeal for him. He preferred to "go down the pub" across the road, The Crown, with just me or alone. As a very occasional drinker I found this boring. He just sat in a corner staring broodingly into his glass of beer and I doubt he spoke to anyone when he was by himself. So I took to going out with my close women friends without him; I liked going out but not to the pub. Though the social cracks deepened as the year wore on, the more intimate part of our relationship continued to be fond and fulfilling. And there were still evenings when we read poetry to each other. He became a good rough cook, out of necessity perhaps, as he did not share my penchant for peanut butter sandwiches. In the summer holidays we did go on a couple of memorable holidays driving to the North, visiting my old stamping grounds, York and Durham, and ending up in Berwick-upon-Tweed. I was proud of being the driver, and got a real buzz from exceeding speed limits in the fast lanes. But when we got back nothing much had changed.

By this time I had embarked on my new vocation, and Graham was into the second and final year in his training. We were both involved in study, though he often took his books to the pub, and I spent more time with various work groups. When we were together we rarely had rows; Graham didn't do rows, but he sulked sometimes.

We were bound together, practically, for another year as he was financially dependent on me while he studied. Still, certain tenderness lingered between us, and I would say to him, from time to time, "Do you love me, Graham?" needing him to say "yes"; but he wouldn't reply, just smiling vaguely. Darwin, the lodger, watched what was, I suppose, the unravelling of our marriage, from the wings, saying little, but being a man with a heavy expressive presence, I was aware he was monitoring the situation. He did stop me one morning, after Graham had gone out, to say, "Antonia, I am sorry to see how things are with you and Graham." I gave him a silencing look. This love of ours, begun with such hope, though against some odds, was, it seemed, dwindling: incredibly sad, but I was so taken up by my new work that the gathering misery of what was happening, the fading of feeling, failed to really get to me, until one Saturday morning in July, when I returned from my weekly swim, I found an envelope on the kitchen table. I opened it, knowing it was from Graham, wondering what on earth it could be about as I had just had breakfast with him before going out. I read, "Dear Antonia, I have been offered a job in the London Hospital as a trainee Hospital Social Worker. I will be going to live near the hospital in the East End. I have a room with a Chinese family in Whitechapel; I have taken all the things I need. I don't suppose I will be coming back. I am sorry about this but things were not working. It was all my fault. I couldn't cope. I don't suppose I ever will. Thanks for everything. I hope you will forgive me sometime. Graham."

My reaction was extreme; I screamed with shock and fury and then was overcome by a spastic seizure, a prelude to the most awful back pain. My anger and sorrow at the way he had done this meant I was unable to think at all. But Graham must have done plenty of thinking. Darwin, who didn't do tact, pointed out that "the scheming bastard" must have planned this move well in advance, getting this job the other side of London, and then the room too.

I can't remember the next few days but later I know it was Darwin who cared for me, making me endless cups of tea, taking me to the park with the dog and driving me to the doctor. He was very angry but of course had foreseen it, living under the same roof. Many of my friends' reactions were tainted by an "I told you so" attitude. Apart from Frankie, who had liked and got on with Graham, the family had little to say on the subject. My doctor just gave me pain killers which didn't work, though she wanted me to have a week's rest in hospital, which I refused. After a few weeks, when I struggled to come to terms with Graham's leaving, Darwin suggested making a big bonfire in the garden where we could burn all Graham's relics – clothes, books, presents I had given him over the few years. This, I enjoyed. It was a good exorcism but much too soon for closure.

Looking back, I think this late romance was a last-ditch attempt to experience what it was like to have that Significant Other. It was sad, so sad that I have had a deep reluctance to face it or talk about it, outside therapy, after all these years, and then there was the terrible coda. After one suicide attempt, when he was rescued from drowning in the Thames by a couple of drunks, he later succeeded. I don't know how – his mother, who I used to ring at Christmas, told me the tragic news, but no details, though I think it was probably the lure of the river again. When I think how we used to walk beside it, our close ardent talk in the first thrall of love, I still feel grief.

Graham

Second wedding, a modest affair

CHAPTER 22

Late Vocation

In 1981, a year before I met Graham, after moving to Richmond, I left teaching, my decision being hastened by the appointment of a brash new head of department, a tiresome little rule-book man, and also my encroaching deafness, an unlooked-for add-on. I was tired of the travelling, new nit-picking regulations, and of course the work – all made me know I could no longer give of my best. After leaving, I missed the students but few of my colleagues. Odd to begin with, to be without routine or commitments. I didn't lie abed till noon but as my back ached less I began to enjoy having more energy and being able to go for short walks in the park with my delightful new collie-cross dog, Cindy-Lou. But after a short time I knew relentless leisure bored me so I began the search for some interesting voluntary work.

I thought visiting long-term prisoners' wives might be eye-opening, as going to flats in tower blocks in Peckham and slum estates in Brixton certainly was, but after being failed by too many broken lifts which meant having to stagger up many flights of stairs, I began to have doubts. The final straw was upsetting a cup of tea down the back of an elderly client's television set which resulted in her yelling: "Fucking hell, look what yer've done! Yer've ruined my telly, brand new it is! I knew as soon as I set eyes on yer, yer were what I calls a no-good do-gooder, one of those posh bitches with more money than sense. It better work or I'll be suing your rotten stupid charity!" She pursued me out of the door, standing at the top of the stairs, shouting and swearing, brandishing a fly-swatter. Terrified, I stumbled down that first flight, shaking with fright. Once safely in my car I took a few deep breaths and knew instantly that this work wasn't for me.

Miraculously, a few weeks later I found this small alcohol-addiction clinic five minutes' walk away where, after an interview and a barrage of personality tests, I was taken on to train as a counsellor. Apparently my score was unusually high on the psychopathic scale whereupon the supervisor raised her eyebrows, saying, "It's a wonder you went to university; these results suggest a female borstal as a more likely background!" She smiled and told me I would come in handy dealing with the ex-cons and social deviants. My physical difficulties did not seem to matter; they might even be viewed as something of an asset. The centre was a small local organization, not exactly in competition with AA, but for those who were looking for something else. It had been the brainchild of a rich eccentric American ex-alcoholic, who had a deep need to help others overcome the torments he had been through. I liked the set-up; the management was quite eccentric, though we had good supervision with Molly Evans who later became a close friend. The clients were given intensive group and personal therapy, advice sessions and Lorazepam pills which, ironically, later became known as the most addictive benzodiazepine around, a controlled drug and a street favourite. I just hope none of our clients exchanged one addiction for another.

My first client, Eileen, had been found "drunk in charge of a bicycle" in Richmond Park. She was an elegant lady in her sixties with a cut-glass accent. She'd developed a taste for cooking sherry over the years; it didn't take long to find the probable cause of her habit. It was her husband, Wenceslas, a dictatorial Pole who frightened her, though his battering was emotional, not physical. He sought to control her every move, even telling her what pattern she should embroider, and, together with dogs, smoking and Jews, he banned alcohol from the house. "Ah, she said, "but Wenceslas didn't know that I decanted the cooking sherry into old sauce bottles as he never went into the kitchen, lazy old blighter." After working together for some months, she was able to tell him she was leaving. She went to live with her sister, Agatha, who had always loathed her brother-in-law. So, job done, and as this was my first case I was quite pleased, though I don't know how much credit I could take for the result.

Over the next few years I trained as a psychotherapist at various institutions and underwent the necessary twice weekly personal therapy. Though intellectually not demanding, emotionally the course was draining and occasionally traumatic. At my first supervision session, James Hunter, for all he was a godly American, spent time making offensive remarks about the possible effect of my disability on clients, while his wandering gaze was slithering up and down my neighbour Virginia's endless legs. She always got the best clients! I was shocked when he tried to persuade her to take on a young gay man hoping her beauty might heal him, as he phrased it. Offensive, even in those days.

I hated him, and resented her, but realised that he had his own physical shortcomings when he heaved his overweight body out of the chair and grasped a walking stick. A case of projection, I said to myself with all the wisdom of a first term student. The theory went alongside the practical; we were given clients from the first day. At the alcohol clinic I had been singled out to work with psychos, this time I was to be allotted "the angries". Later, in my own practice, of course I worked with a huge variety of people from noisy aggrieved men to silent desperate housewives.

The initial heavy core training was followed by excursions into other modes of working: Gestalt, CBT (long used by the

NHS), Transactional Analysis and, later, Couples Therapy at the Maudsley Hospital. In the holidays I often went to Skyros, a small Greek island where an enterprising American woman, Dinah, ran courses in alternative therapies, some useful, others quite way-out. These were fun holidays too where I was able to indulge my passion for treading the boards. I remember writing and acting a skit about a dotty old duchess who had been washed up on this island of crazies, all shouting and screaming in the agonies of primal therapy, who after initial shock soon transforms herself into the community goddess!

An essential part of the training was, of course, personal therapy. How could you possibly hope to understand others unless you understood yourself? My therapy started some time before I even thought of training. As I already said, when I first left teaching I wrote a novel based on my childhood. On leafing through it sometime later, I realised what a bitter and vitriolic version of my background it hinted at. I knew my feelings were no longer so relentlessly negative; I had moved on after writing the book, entitled, tellingly, from my mother's calling me a *Bloody Little Imbecile!* It had been an essential part of my therapy, a sort of precursor to the formal therapy.

Before starting the main course, having been selected from a preliminary one, I was presented with a short list of suitable therapists. I tried four of them before I settled for Jenny who was about twenty years younger than me. I think I chose her because she was about the same age as my mother was when she died. At the start, many sessions centred on my issues with authority, unsurprisingly, given my rebellious past and present difficulties with my supervisor, and several other male members of the faculty. Later, we worked through my challenging childhood and in particular the ways I had taken to manage to steer between becoming "a poor brave thing" and a borderline psychopath. At this stage I never wept but sometimes shouted and screamed during the sessions, releasing anger rather than sorrow. More than once Jenny had to ask me to quieten down for fear of disturbing the neighbours. My therapy was useful but not mind-blowing, perhaps because I had partially dealt with stuff from my childhood in writing that book. Finally I had to face and work through the ending of my brief second marriage. I broke down and wept buckets as my grief over Graham lasted for many years, so the understanding therapy gave me failed to assuage my feelings; it was all too near.

Setting up my own practice room was not difficult; I simply partitioned off the long sitting room, positioned two comfortable armchairs at slight angles to one another and bought a suitable couch, placed a box of tissues and a glass of water on the table and waited. Well, it wasn't quite as straightforward as that – I had cheated by asking the clients I was working with at the Foundation if they would prefer to continue with me in leafy Richmond, or stay and see someone new. Five came and two stayed. This formed the nucleus of my new practice. Joining a local supervision group with five others in the same trade proved fruitful and fun. I loved this job, feeling I had at last found my real later life vocation. Being answerable to no one while knowing that I had behind me a good training, a mass of life experience and a "feeling for the work" as I had been told early on, gave me great satisfaction and real happiness.

After the first year I had enough clients; in those days there were far fewer therapists around than now. I know my twisted neck and awkward movements may have put a few people off, perhaps those that phoned after the first session to say they had changed their minds, but I continued to feel that my difficulties made me more acceptable to some. I saw many more women than men, though now there are apparently more men than women in the frame. I often saw my first clients at 7am, mostly city folk on the way to work, and later in the day there were the housewives, the self-employed, students and the unemployed, and later still, those on their way back from work. Twice a week I had evening sessions, but I always had an extended siesta. I charged the early morning city slickers a lot, but my fees slid down to a few pounds for those on benefits and students. As I opened the door to a new face, my heart would leap with expectation; I never knew quite what new journey might be undertaken. Of course I had a fair share of the bizarre, the refuseniks, and a few who I felt disliked me, though sometimes there were surprising about-turns; those who hated me at the start sometimes went the furthest. I later learned that I was known by trainee therapists as "that woman who eats nails for breakfast". The clients I really liked working with were certainly not the most exciting: middle-aged women, either full-time housewives or those with boring part-time jobs, who, having raised the family, sometimes crushed by dominating or step-out husbands, no longer had much sense of their own identities or the point of existence. To help these women extract something of substance from their inner beings was a real privilege, almost like a birthing process, which never ceased to excite me.

Eloise, a Swiss woman, rising fifty with a rich but flighty husband and four grown children, one of my first referred clients, came because of feeling no longer necessary to her family, which had for so many years defined her. As she said, "When I was young, I wanted to change the world; now I don't know why I am even in it any more!" She knew Charles, her husband, found his pleasures outside the marriage bed, and her kids hurt her by their apparent disregard. She hadn't let herself go, though – attractively got-up in a smart matching blue dress and jacket, which set off her red hair, she wore a stiff, determined smile. I felt her depression, though real, was hopefully not endogenous, or built-in, but more circumstantial: she seemed to have lost her way; her role had gone.

She wept for most of the first session, telling me, between sobs, how nobody needed her any more; her relatives in Switzerland had died or drifted away, and she had lost the knack of making new friends. Later, I learnt about her early passion for swimming: how she had represented her canton in national sporting events, and had even won a diving contest in Geneva when only sixteen. These had been her glory days. A few years after, she had come to London to be an au pair with a well off family and had very soon fallen for the younger brother of her hostess, who was, of course, Charles, a smart young man about town, with an eye for pretty girls. After that, the inevitable years of comfortable domesticity in Richmond, living in a house rather further up the hill than mine! She knew Charles was unfaithful from early on, but he had always assured her that the other women were mere "flibbertigibbets", so she had put up with his wandering ways, concentrating on raising the children and shopping. Now they were gone, and Charles was spending more time away than ever, on what he termed "private business".

A few weeks later Eloise said she had started going to the local baths, remembering how much swimming had once meant to her. Being in her element, as she expressed it, had brought back so many good memories that she had decided to go every week. She really seemed much less stressed. As I opened the door to her before the next session, she positively bounced in, her usual polite smile replaced by a big grin; she said, before she had even sat down, "Antonia, when I went for my swim last week, a group of very disabled teenagers were being hoisted in at the shallow end. I watched them and was so moved by their difficulties, and the way they screamed with delight at being in the water, that I couldn't think about much else for days. So yesterday, at the pool, I screwed up my courage and asked their teacher if she needed any help. Anita, she was called, said that that would be just wonderful and we could give it a go. I asked her if I could start by helping Shaun, the boy with no legs. After hesitating, Anita agreed I could. She said he was a great lad, so brave, and they always had a good giggle together. So, after being shown how, I worked with him, on his strong arms and his breathing. Anita was watching me to see how I did, but I knew I was sort of instinctively doing the right thing." This was an amazing early breakthrough which we built on.

A few weeks later, Eloise burst in the room almost shouting, "Antonia, Shaun can swim! Breast stroke – I taught him! Oh, I am so thrilled! And Anita suggested I should take the special instructors' course and make a regular job of it. What do you think of that?!" Of course I was pleased, but knew that, though it was a significant milestone, there was still work to do. After the next few months she felt strong enough to ask Charles where he had spent the previous night. They had a real row which ended by her telling him that unless he stopped indulging himself in younger flesh she was going to divorce him. Though I was not in the business of marriage breaking, I was pleased she had at last got the guts to challenge him. To cut it short, as he continued in his ways, she did divorce him, though this was sometime after the therapy ended. But she had found her way and now, I hoped, had the strength to navigate the rest of her life. I was pleased with us both for this outcome.

At that time most clients were women, men were almost rarities, but when they did sign up for therapy they were usually more damaged, often desperate as Ethan clearly was. This young American came shambling in, a sad stooped man, already balding though only thirty-three. He wore torn stained jeans and a faded grey T-shirt, and brought with him the unpleasant smell of old sweat. His bad stammer and drawling accent made him quite difficult for me to hear, though he was basically very articulate. His family background was horrendous: an alcoholic father, a mother with early dementia, and a brother who had multiple sclerosis. He had come to England to get away but hadn't managed to build much of a new life. His immediate problems concerned his job in a college library where he was being badly bullied by his women colleagues who he described as "the witch-bitches". I saw only too clearly how this could happen, but found it disconcerting. A few months later, after working with the library issues and delving into his troubled childhood, he hurled a thunderbolt into the middle of the calm session. He shifted uneasily in his chair, his face darkened and his voice became a hoarse whisper, which I barely heard when he said: "Antonia, I have been avoiding telling you of my dreadful fear. It is haunting me. I think I may like children too much. A long time ago, when I was about sixteen, I touched my cousin where I shouldn't. I am very scared of myself; it is one of the main reasons I left the States, but I haven't left the mega anxiety behind. I don't know if it really is a part of me, or if it's because I can't find a woman who will go out with me."

His anxiety immediately became mine. I took a deep breath and said, "Perhaps you would like to tell me more," hopefully appearing calm, but inwardly quailing. So, between heaving sobs, he did. He talked about how he didn't feel frightened of kids the way he was of grown women, and just had a temptation to touch them, not to harm. He then said he had suffered so many rejections from women his own age that he now visited prostitutes. This relieved me, and I felt this was one up for the oldest profession! Could it be that not being an instantly appealing guy, very shy, these inappropriate feelings were a kind of displacement, a substitute for what he really wanted, but couldn't get – a suitable grown woman?

During the week before our next session, I thought hard about what course to take. In those days there were no specialist clinics dealing with such cases, even borderline ones, so, to whom could I refer him? Never averse to risk, I decided to continue with him, within a structured game plan, seeing him twice a week, and giving him open phone access. Ethan and I worked together for a year, and he never had recourse to the open phone, which, I trusted, meant he had kept back from forbidden verges. Yes, I trusted him and I think this was mutual, without which, of course, no progress could have been made. A growing sense of self-worth resulted in him giving himself a gradual makeover; after losing some weight he appeared in a new pair of jeans, next a really fetching turquoise T-shirt and clean white trainers. We never worked directly on making these changes but I always told him how good he looked in his new clothes. The day came when he told me he had bought a washing machine! He changed his job, and the bullying didn't reoccur. At last he met a grown woman, Sylvia, a checkout girl, who was twenty-four, uneducated but apparently bright and kind. With pride, he showed me her photo. He said, "She's really gorgeous, isn't she, and, Antonia, she really loves me. I want to take her back to the States." She was nice-looking, though I felt like saying, "It's early days yet", as a mother might, but he had got his prize at last. There was no stopping him; he married her and whirled her off to the States a few months later. I often wondered about him.

Devlin, an Irish ex-alcoholic, was one of my most delightful clients, and, as he was diminutive and bright, I called him privately "my little leprechaun"! He was forty-five, balding, and had small neat features. His was a sad story. He had a degree from Cambridge, where, together with Economics, he had learnt to drink to excess. After this, he had just sozzled his life away, quickly becoming an extreme alcoholic. Never able to hold down a job or make a relationship, he had spent years living in a centre for people like him. Though now a dry drunk, he was still unable to cope with women or work. He had kept his Irish sense of humour and the twice weekly sessions, apart from being insightful for both of us, often produced as much laughter as tears. Over time he was able to cope with a part-time clerical job, quite a breakthrough, but as well as suitable work he really yearned for a woman to call his own. One sunny evening, when I was wearing a fairly low-cut summer dress, he even tried his luck with me, saying, "Antonia, I often wonder what goes on in the bedrooms upstairs." I was astonished at where his imagination had led him, but shamefully, instead of mining it, just ignored it. A measure of his desperation or a cheeky try-on? After a couple of years he did get a proper job and later he met an intelligent and attractive American woman. He had done three years' hard work with me; I felt more than usually happy about him leaving therapy in a better place than when he arrived, but certainty of outcome is impossible, sadly.

Lydia too was a very interesting client. She was a forty-year-old Indian woman, a handsome woman, dressed very soberly in black. She had successfully broken through a couple of glass ceilings by becoming the Head of Pathology at a major London hospital. She had come, ostensibly, because she was being badly bullied by her fellow consultants, white middle-aged doctors who deeply resented both her colour and her gender. This was an eye opener for me: the idea that these senior doctors, esteemed figures, would stoop to make the life of a colleague almost unbearable, because she didn't belong to their tribe, I found despicable.

Later, I learned that she was married to a man who didn't work and lived off her salary, spending a sizable amount of it on his gambling habit. He browbeat her into compliance as she allowed him to have complete control of the family, not only of its finances. They had both been brought up in India. She was a Tamil from the south while Gawin came from the north, and she told me that Tamils are still looked down upon by people from the north, so it seemed that she felt victimised by another more basic type of tribalism.

In spite of her very successful career, Lydia obviously had very low self-esteem, expressed in both home and work. There were many tears, unshed for years, first, on account of those bullies at work, later, about the family scenario. One session, a month in, she not only wept, as usual, but found her temper, shouting, "That bastard Gawin has gambled his car away, so this morning he takes mine, telling me to take the bus! He thinks it's his right! Oh, God, why did I ever come to marry such a man?!" It took such a situation to raise her anger; this was progress and the beginning of the end of Gawin, I silently anticipated. Within a few weeks she saw a lawyer who arranged a quick divorce. Meanwhile, her white male colleagues were having a field day: they were always bragging about their Mercedes and Audis, so the idea that Lydia was seen using a bus became the joke of the month. Gawin was livid. He could not believe that his hitherto docile wife was capable of such an action. Not surprisingly, he found out she had been seeing a therapist; I soon got a barrage of vitriolic phone calls which were left unanswered. He went, but not before he had poured poison into the ears of their two children about their mother; after this he could only see them under supervision.

Lydia was free at last and Gawin had lost wife, children and his income. It took time for her to appreciate her new status; she seemed dazed, and very dependent on me, asking if she could come twice a week, seeking to replace one long-time dependency with another. We agreed to continue once a week and after some months she began to take her place in the world. She came to love her time at home, with her children; and at work she began to blossom. She bought a new car, new clothes, got an attractive hairstyle, and even developed a new walk; gone were the slightly hunched shoulders and the plodding feet. Those doctors, sensing a change, began to stop their bullying, even sometimes asking her opinion on clinical matters. There was the session when she came in smiling, saying, "Mr Macintosh, the heart surgeon, came over to me yesterday at lunch to ask me if I would join them at their table. What do you think of that?" I was so pleased at this acknowledgment of her by these elitist "boys". She had arrived. We rejoiced together and, very unprofessionally, I fetched two glasses of wine after the session, and we drank to her future! She came for another few months at intervals and after she left she referred several of her Indian women colleagues to me, all of whom had had similar troubles in the workplace.

Of course, over the years there were the ones I failed: those who walked out after the first session never to return, a few who I never connected with, some whose problems were beyond me, and the ones I had allowed to lapse into a fruitless dependency.

CHAPTER 23

Once More unto the Breach

Perhaps the most meaningful brush I had with authority, in this country, happened when I was about 65, in the mid 90s.

Running parallel with my armchair work, it came about through a haphazard discovery; but one that could have helped many afflicted people, had it been allowed to succeed. That it did not and still hasn't is a sad commentary on the small-minded stupidity of the Powers that Be. I was delighted to be part of such a campaign, just when I thought I might be calming down into a compliant old age.

*

One summer evening, some years earlier, just before the family left Wimbledon, my wild daughter Frankie, home for a change, was sitting in her tumbled bed, smoking a weird looking cigarette with an odd smell. I asked her, "Pot?" She nodded, edging closer, asking if I'd like to have a puff, and, though never a smoker, I took her up on this, saying, "So, you're after corrupting your mum?" She laughed as she handed me the cigarette; I took a deep breath and coughed but, after a few more false starts, managed to inhale. I felt odd; spaced out, detached and dizzy, but what was extraordinary, totally unexpected, was that the horrid old familiar pain in my upper back had almost disappeared, as if it had flown out of the window with the smoke. "It's gone, Frankie! The pain... I can't understand it!" I shouted.

We were both amazed. After a few more puffs I said, "It's a bloody miracle. Why can't that old doctor give me some of this on the NHS, instead of those useless pills?"

In those days, in the seventies, although there were prosecutions, including those who took cannabis to help with the pain of cancer, MS and spasticity, I fancy the law was a bit more relaxed than now. I set about finding other pain-racked people who also might be experiencing relief from this illegal drug, though connecting with strangers was not so easy in those pre-Google days.

Later, after my move to Richmond in the early eighties, to a house with a garden, as well as continuing to dig around for fellow travellers, I thought I might do a little physical digging: try to grow my own pot, though I didn't think I would succeed. So I found a smart fishing shop, and asked for some seeds, enquiring with a laugh if they would grow. The man gave me a quizzical glance and said, with lifted eyebrows, "Oh, no, madam, they have been treated." I planted these unremarkable small seeds in pots and, as they grew, Darwin transplanted them into a long stone trough, and they grew and they grew and they grew. They became the most beautiful exotic-looking plants; it was almost as if they had been lifted out of an Amazon rain forest.

Then came another breakthrough. Frankie helped me again, by finding an article in The Guardian about the medical benefits of this stuff, for those with MS and chronic pain. Thrilled, I wrote to the author and had a quick and warm response from Liz Brice, who lived in Leeds.

Two days later, I was on the train to the North. We took to each other immediately. She clutched my hand, saying, "Oh, that's brilliant, we needed someone from the posh South-East, and here you are!" Liz was a bright brave woman: she had been diagnosed with MS at 24, an Oxford graduate in classics, just after she had been recruited by Yorkshire TV. But that disastrous blow meant her media career had been scrapped almost before it started. She quickly married her adoring boss and had two children, contrary to medical advice. Liz was a handsome dark-haired woman, with remarkable glinting brown eyes and a bearing which almost denied the severity of her condition. Her family was very welcoming, particularly her husband, Adam, whose support of her was exemplary: he encouraged her to do all she could but was there when she needed him to be.

She and I resolved to start a high-level campaign to free the use of this valuable natural drug from the shackles of the law for people like us.

Staying up late that first night, smoking while we plotted and planned, Liz used her media contacts to arrange for us both to respond to unfair prosecutions of medical users on no less than Radio 4's "Today" programme. She was to comment on the North and I, the South. I was absolutely thrilled to be on the campaign trail again and returned home full of hope and glee, to be once again bumping up against the Powers that Be for such a brilliant cause.

At first it was quite scary, sitting by the radio at 7am, waiting for John Humphrys to ask me to respond to the latest case of some sick person being arrested for possessing cannabis. My knees would be shaking underneath the table, though the voice remained steady while I expressed my viewpoint in a tone of suitably suppressed anger. Soon our small group gathered recruits among those victimised by inhumane legislation; Liz already had a network among people with MS, so we soon had a self-selected nucleus who were prepared to storm the barricades – to Westminster we would go!

Liz was a fantastic organizer. She got in touch with a sympathetic MP, Paul Flynn, who represented a Labour constituency in South Wales. He agreed to meet our delegation and to raise our matter in the House, as a Private Member's Bill, and treat us to lunch. So, on the day, our small group, some in wheelchairs, others with frames, met in the Great Hall of the Commons. I was conscious of the effort and pain this had cost some of us. Although there was an air of quiet excitement, we were realistic enough to know our mission might not be accomplished. We started off in great form with a huge delicious meal in the MPs' dining room; "Our reps don't half do themselves well," John, the guy with a twisted spine, remarked, while we all gobbled down smoked salmon, roasted venison and exotic meringues. After the feast we met Paul Flynn again, a lovely man with very real feeling for our cause who told us he himself suffered from bad arthritis, though we didn't ask if his backing of us was entirely disinterested! At 2pm we were ushered into the Commons gallery to listen to our matter being debated. Only seven MPs turned up and, though a strong argument was put, five voted against, including a retired doctor, so that was that. We felt belittled and angry that our issue had attracted so few members, and, of course, by the ignominious defeat. The press came to meet us, not much of a consolation though we did some very defiant sound bites on TV and radio. I said in a threatening tone: "We will be back, so they'd better do some rethinking in there!" The next day the Indie gave us a few lines calling me "a game old bird"!

It was a sunny day so, just after our debacle, we sat on The Terrace, ostentatiously stirring a mysterious green substance into our tea, laughing like a bunch of naughty kids, as there was this big bobby standing benevolently by. "Just wouldn't the press love this," Liz said, chortling. Even though it was a failed foray it had been a good experience of joint action.

I visited Liz several times over the next few months – we had become close friends – while we waited for something to turn up. It did.

A few months later I had a surprise call: it was Channel 4 asking me if I would be interested in appearing in a documentary about the medical use of cannabis. Would I just! Grabbing my astonished collie's front paws, I clumped round the room with her, knocking over a basket of papers, shrieking, "Cindy, we're going to be on telly! We're getting out there… Hurrah, hurrah, hurrah!" She seemed to enjoy dancing and sharing my delight.

Some time after, one evening, two glamorous women appeared – Lindsay, a film producer, with Aisha, a photographer. Lindsay asked the questions while Aisha took the shots. Our film was to be part of a Channel 4 event all about cannabis, a debate extending over two evenings.

Our half hour programme wasn't just a few static interviews; a few of us "users" were filmed in various situations. Cindy, as I'd promised her, was to take part, so we were filmed walking round the corner outside by the house, both wearing our bright red coats!

Just before the end of the programme I took a little silver-lidded box off the mantelpiece which was sitting next to a miniature bust of Queen Victoria. I opened it and, taking out a spliff, said, "Queen Victoria, here, used this stuff for her period pains so why can't we follow her royal example?"

Liz, the other leading lady, stayed with me on that momentous night when "our" film was shown. I think during this heady weekend we felt bound to win the next time we took off to Westminster. After the party which followed we sat up until the small hours, chatting excitedly about how this exposure might push our cause forward.

The following evening we all crowded into a small hall down the road in Twickenham for a TV debate on the pros and cons of cannabis, both as a medicine and as a relatively safe recreational drug. Our very own Professor Nutt, a strong supporter of the cause, presented the case for and a sour-faced psychiatrist from St George's Hospital spoke against; seeming to imply that society would come crashing down, if this drug was legalised. With lots of noisy enthusiasts in the audience, mainly young people, and some middle-aged folk including anxious parents, the discussion became heated. We had moved on from a special case scenario for medical release of the drug to a general one. Although Professor Nutt and another American scientist gave an impressive defence, we narrowly lost this debate. We were surprised and sad, of course.

During the following weeks, I was approached, often by young men, who congratulated me on my elderly stand: on Waterloo Station, in various restaurants, in bus queues and, more poignantly, in my doctor's surgery – not by the doctor, sadly, but a poor doubled-up patient. This really ancient lady, in obvious pain, said: "I think I recognize you; weren't you on that telly programme about cannabis for pain?" I nodded. "You tried your best, love, but it's not going to happen, is it?" "Maybe some time," I said. "I shall be pushing up daisies by then. I suppose I have to keep on getting that stuff off my grandson... Risky business, but better than those useless pills we get given here," she said, scowling as she pointed her cane at the doctor's door.

We did have another trip to Westminster with an equally depressing outcome. Although, after all these years, a medicine called Sativex, extracted from cannabis and approved by NICE (The National Institute for Health and Care Excellence) for certain conditions, is supposedly available, doctors rarely prescribe it. When I asked my recent GP for some, she almost fell off her chair and, raising her voice, said, "I am not going to give you cannabis!"

★

So was it worth it? Of course it was, as a personal endeavour.

It felt so good to be fighting the corner of a neglected minority – those suffering from the heedless attitude of the politicians and the ignorance and prejudice of doctors – the negative views of both being fuelled by the commercial interests of Big Pharma. Do we have to continue to buy stuff off the street or count on the kindness of friends visiting Amsterdam? Has anything changed during the intervening years? Probably not very much, though with the ageing of the Baby Boomer generation and an increasingly questioning attitude to medical authority, who knows? If society catches up with Liz and me, it may happen, one day.

At Westminster with MP Paul Flynn

CHAPTER 24

Epilogue

I stayed in Richmond, in that shabby Victorian house behind the petrol station, for fifteen years with my long-term lodgers, but when I decided to retire I knew I must move; a new phase needed new pastures. Richmond, though of course beautiful, seemed a socially sterile place, unless you belonged to one of the famous families living in gracious mansions around Richmond Green.

I thought about returning to Cardiff, to rediscover my Welsh roots, or to Hampstead, Mecca of psychotherapists, practising and retired, but I settled on Brighton, where Frankie lived and which I knew well.

Before the start of the new century Brighton was still a middle-sized town, quite poor, reliant on the tourist industry to make most of its money. It had always, of course, been known as an easy-going place, and, as such, acted as a magnet for those who sought freedom to leave alternative lives, as it still does. It was here where Graham Greene and other writers set their novels; artists, too, are drawn to this place as much by its life-style as the quality of light. It is now a city, expanded in size but diluted in character, its uniqueness changed by the inflow of big money.

But, on looking back over the twenty years I have lived here in Brighton, I reckon I chose well. I have made close friends of different ages and backgrounds, gone to Quaker meetings, done voluntary work, seen more of Frankie and my grandchildren, and altogether had a great deal of fun.

During my later years I have lived with my friend and housekeeper, Milena, from Slovakia, met through an advertisement put in the local Post Office window. What a stroke of luck! Milena and I are a first class team and have learnt a lot from each other; she now speaks fluent English, and I am fascinated by her tales of life in Slovakia, both as it is now and when she was growing up under Communism. The quality of my life since she has lived here with me couldn't have been better. She cooks good, simple meals, sees I eat a lot of wholesome, boring greens as well as tastier stuff, keeps me and the house clean and tidy and is a welcoming presence when I have guests.

Recently my nice new doctor asked me, "How have you managed to live to such a good age with your cerebral palsy?" I replied off the top of my head and without any thought, "Broccoli and bloody-mindedness." He laughed, and I wondered where this curious turn of phrase had come from.

★

Why this memoir? At one level an egotistical extravaganza, a wish to entertain. At another, a story for my family – a good project for retirement. But one work I didn't wish to produce was a sympathy-seeking tale about "a poor brave thing" going for it. I suppose these are the reasons the book has taken the shape that it has.

How the body is built, the way its components work together, often seem to determine the life that is lived. Impressions based on physical image play such a part in the perception of the person in everyday life; of course it has been so throughout history, not just today. Richard III wasn't such a cripple; Shakespeare made him a much worse one in the play for obvious reasons. Diana would not have been a princess unless she had been perfectly formed as well as a virgin! Disabled actors rarely get to play the lead, or any part at all. In legend and fairy stories villains and the pathetic are too often depicted as hideous or malformed: Medusa, Satan, Dracula, the Hunchback of Notre Dame, Cyclops, satyrs and of course Frankenstein.

At times life has seemed like a long war – a series of battles of will over body; a few of the apparent successes have later turned out to be pyrrhic victories and the defeats sometimes most humiliating. Physical strategies or shortcuts have sometimes had unfortunate consequences; because cleaning my teeth involves difficult arm positioning, once resulting in a dislocated shoulder, this chore has occasionally been given short shrift, and now I have a mouth full of dentures. Compromise, concession and a degree of deviancy have, until recently, been part of my survival technique as a more or less fully paid up human being. On the other hand the campaigns have often meant meeting challenges, and sometimes trekking over rough ground into strange places, meeting and appreciating people off the expected social radar.

Had I been an "Anyone for tennis?" girl born 80 years ago, life would have taken a very different course, perhaps equally fulfilling. But most likely I would not have felt compelled to risk my neck climbing over roofs at school, been about the only white girl on a black dance floor in Edinburgh, and at 23 had an affair with an ageing stockbroker who taught me about classy gambling, admittedly an interest sitting badly with my lifelong commitment to leftist politics. (Never mind, I am not the only "Prosecco" socialist around!) Later, in Africa, I might not have tried to get to know closeted Muslim women in Nigeria, sold aluminium coffins in native locations in South Africa, and, after that, taught black students there, a questionable activity under the Apartheid regime. Back home, I might not have become involved in student protests, and much later, between marriages, enjoyed a rampant and varied love-life, not fully documented here!

Now my problems are mostly about the constraints of age; the limits and pain imposed by my disability have sadly worsened. But, despite this, the years have brought a kind of peace; though not "God's peace that passeth all understanding". As a young child in York I gazed in wonder at the Minster, at its age, beauty and immensity. I explored the city's other mediaeval churches and, later, I remember weeping over a bombed out church in the city centre the day after the only air raid we had on York. As a student in Durham there was another vast cathedral to revere, a huge edifice rising from the banks of the River Wear. The heavy ecclesiastical presence at the university at that time meant that members of the Student Christian Union, aware of my possible "convertibility", would corner me and look ardently into my eyes while pressing bits of biblical literature into my hand. But being subjected to this missionary zeal finally put me off turning to God and so my early veneration of church architecture remained aesthetic.

So though I have never developed any hard-core spiritual faith, much later I enjoyed going to those Quaker meetings, especially if they were held in old eighteenth-century meeting houses, liking the emphasis on care, the acceptance of the human condition in all its complexities.

My different body image no longer matters; other oldies have odd shapes too. I feel acceptable now, though when a 95-year-old recently referred to my "deformities" I felt momentarily offended, but then I let her off; she is really old.

Of course I still have some regrets but they don't torment me now. I try to spend more time remembering the good times, the adventures, companionship and loves I have enjoyed, though these are not all in the past. When the dear friends I have made in Brighton come round, I prefer to entertain them with tales of my current "inappropriate" behaviour: exchanging angel kisses with the lonely old carpenter while drinking tea at the kitchen table, telling the handsome postman he has a lovely smile, or

– worse, much worse – in the bank, when asked an intrusive question by the cashier, "What do you want the money for?", replying in a hoarse stage whisper, "Sex"! And how all the bank staff burst out laughing, though an elderly customer, looking gratifyingly shocked, said, "What on earth is the world coming to?" Yes, I like playing the flirty old lady and occasionally raising a few eyebrows, so perhaps I haven't changed much.

I continue to smoke a spliff or two, for the enjoyment as well as pain relief, and on occasion eat cookies made with "weed". Recently, one Sunday morning, I got completely spaced out, unable to rise from my chair, while having kaleidoscopic visions, reminding me of those wonderfully coloured paintings by Matisse or the stained glass windows of Chagall. At the same time, I was not unaware that if anyone found me I might get dragged off to hospital with a suspected stroke. Oh dear, what then?

As to death, my troublesome body at times would welcome it, but the rest of me will, I hope, be happy to be around for some time yet. So many books to be read, so much stuff to be googled, and lots of good talk and laughter to be had. I am still most curious about what makes people tick and, of course, about the wider ways of the world now and debates about what may happen to it in the future.

In a corner of my small garden, amid the recently planted shrubs, there is a very old rose which has orange flowers streaked with scarlet. The outer petals are tattered and time-worn, the stance somewhat sagging, but the scent is still pungent, its essence still there. I like to think mine is too.

*

That neurologist who spoke so disparagingly about my future, when I was a young girl, could not have known how essential would be that deeply rooted bloody-mindedness.

ACKNOWLEDGEMENTS

Many thanks to my friends Liz, Paula, Janet, Hannah and Sue for being my critical readers.

Special thanks to Sally and most particular thanks to Jane for being such a precise and patient proof-reader.

Antonia Lister-Kaye
Hove, Sussex